# BAD BOY FOR LIFE

# BAD BOY FOR LIFE

## THE RISE AND FALL OF SEAN COMBS

CHEYENNE ROUNDTREE

GALLERY BOOKS UK

London · New York · Amsterdam/Antwerp · Sydney/Melbourne · Toronto · New Delhi

First published in the United States by Henry Holt and Company,
an imprint of Macmillan Publishing Group, LLC, 2026
First published in Great Britain by Gallery Books,
an imprint of Simon & Schuster UK Ltd, 2026



Portions of this book were published in *Rolling Stone* in the article "Bad Boy for Life: Sean Combs' History of Violence", https://www.rollingstone.com/music/music-features/diddy-friends-bad-boy-artists-abuse-violence-1235028178/

1 3 5 7 9 10 8 6 4 2

Simon & Schuster UK Ltd, 7th Floor,
199 Bishopsgate, London EC2M 3TY



www.simonandschuster.co.uk
www.simonandschuster.com.au
www.simonandschuster.co.in

Simon & Schuster Australia, Sydney
Simon & Schuster India, New Delhi

The authorised representative in the EEA is Simon & Schuster Netherlands BV, Herculesplein 96, 3584 AA Utrecht, Netherlands. info@simonandschuster.nl



A CIP catalogue record for this book is available from the British Library

Hardback ISBN: 978-1-3985-5521-1
eBook ISBN: 978-1-3985-5523-5

Designed by Omar Chapa
Printed and Bound in the UK using 100% Renewable Electricity at CPI Group (UK) Ltd

FSC www.fsc.org MIX Paper | Supporting responsible forestry FSC® C013604

History, despite its wrenching pain
Cannot be unlived, but if faced
With courage, need not be lived again.

—*Maya Angelou, "On the Pulse of Morning,"* 1993

# CONTENTS

# WHO IS SEAN COMBS?

**WHO IS SEAN COMBS?**

It's an impossible question, and the answer shifts depending on who you ask and when. He's a guarded man who has spun the wheel of reinvention, emerging as a larger, better version of himself with each passing decade. He wouldn't dream of having the word *comeback* near his name, because in Combs' mind, he is forever planted at the center of culture. His face has long been a fixture at awards shows, industry mixers, and cultural events. His voice, as distinctive as those of the legendary artists he helped elevate, is instantly recognizable. He was handed the keys to New York City and Miami Beach, and his name is cemented on the Hollywood Walk of Fame. Thousands of broadcast interviews and magazine profiles have celebrated his triumphs across music, business, fashion, nightlife, and media.

Over the three decades that Combs has been in the public eye, he's been known by a handful of nicknames, each defining an era. Those who first encountered Combs in the late eighties and nineties stick with his early moniker, Puff or Puffy. He was the excitable and brash Uptown Records intern who, as a teenager, spun an unpaid job into a director-level position, in which he was responsible for making R&B cool again by shepherding Jodeci's daring look and crowning Mary J. Blige as the Queen of Hip-Hop Soul. Through his iconic record label Bad Boy, he transformed an unknown kid from Brooklyn's Bed-Stuy into The Notorious B.I.G., one of rap's most enduring icons. When Combs stepped into the spotlight as an artist himself in the late nineties, he embraced the larger-than-life persona of Puff Daddy, readily adopted by scoop-hungry gossip columnists and bemused profile writers as they marveled at his around-the-clock work ethic, Bentleys, diamond pinky rings, and extravagant parties. In the aughts, he became a commercial success as Diddy, earning his place among the handful of icons who require only one name. In addition to taking hip-hop mainstream, he helmed reality shows, won a prestigious fashion award for his Sean John clothing line, and became the face of then little-known vodka brand Cîroc. As Combs transitioned into moguldom in the 2010s, launching a media company, donating millions to charities, and declaring himself a billionaire (a rarefied status that *Forbes* would later dispute), he went by the stately Sean Combs. And at fifty, he wanted the world to call him Love, a testament to his stature as a respected elder in the music industry, generous philanthropist, and doting father of seven children. But to his oldest confidants, family members, and many lovers—those who have been closest to him throughout all his name changes—he is and always has been Sean.

As the saying goes, there is power in a name, and Combs has always understood that controlling one's name is the first step in steering a narrative. It began with Puffy. In one of his first explanations, to *Jet* magazine in 1998, Combs said the moniker was bestowed upon him by a childhood friend because Combs' thin frame would often balloon in anger. "It's a silly reason," he explained. "Whenever I got mad as a kid, I used to always huff and puff. I had a temper." His mother, Janice Combs, also claimed to have given him the pet name, regaling rooms with retellings of how her son's youthful cherubic cheeks expanded in anger. In later years, Combs has been evasive about how he came to be known by the nickname. A former Howard University classmate said there was a rumor it came from his alleged sneaky habit of instigating fights, "and next thing you know, puff, he's gone." Combs himself called it a "secret" and played bashful when Oprah Winfrey pressed him on its origins in 2006. "I've never told anyone that," he said. "I know you get people to tell you everything, Oprah. But I can't look you in the eye and explain that one." When she teased him and pushed him to elaborate, Combs held firm. "I'll answer every other question," he responded, and Oprah moved on.

In the history of Combs' legacy, the question of the veracity of the tale behind his infamous sobriquet seems like a mere blip. Does it really matter how, as a kid, Combs came by a cartoonish nickname, one that personal assistants would eventually wearily whisper to music executives when he incessantly rang their offices? That early, enigmatic nickname was a telltale sign of Combs' ability to shape and manifest his own personal story, even if it defied reality. It was the first of many instances in which Combs would skillfully take an opportunity to tweak, twist, and flat-out dominate a narrative to serve his interests, no matter how small. And it would make the details he purposefully left out or shied away from all the more telling.

In many ways, Combs has been one of New York City's closest real-world parallels to a Jay Gatsby figure. Through the music he produced and created, as well as the looks and attitudes he helped shape, Combs has long been part of the cultural zeitgeist, an omnipresent figure who transcended hip-hop. He's charismatic and ambitious, an unapologetically self-serving chameleon. He counts the legendary showman and ringmaster P. T. Barnum as one of his heroes, marveling at the businessman-turned-politician's ability to become a human embodiment of the mythical Wizard of Oz, pulling strings for a dumbstruck crowd transfixed by an otherworldly spectacle. But beyond the mythmaking and the unrivaled successes, there has always been a sense that something untamed lurked underneath Combs' perfect polish. When the party lights dim and the rapturous applause falls silent, who is Sean Combs?

To his peers in the music industry, Combs is a kingmaker with a golden ear and the innate ability to discern what people unknowingly craved. To many of his employees, he was an inspiration, taking chances on kids straight out of school and teaching them discipline at an intensity they had never encountered. Even his rivals seemed to respect Combs' ingenuity, determination, and ferocious work ethic. His inner circle of lifelong friends, from Harlem to Howard University, credit Combs' generosity in ushering them into his expanding empire and opening doors they had thought shut to them. To his children, Combs is a superhero, a loving father who prioritized traditions and making cherished memories together. To the wider Black community, Combs is a fierce advocate of Black excellence, championing the idea of "for us, by us" and founding companies that reflected this ideal, filling key roles with talented Black men and women. And to the general public, Combs was a trailblazer, responsible for the tracks that scored some of their fondest memories.

For decades, Combs' sterling reputation held firm, despite the occasional nick. He survived scandals that might have ended other careers: a fatal stampede at City College of New York in 1991 that left nine people dead; the bloody beatdown of a fellow music executive in the man's own office; the mayhem of a Manhattan nightclub shooting in 1999 that left three injured; and other run-ins with the law. Conspiracy-laced rumors circulated around the deaths that began to stack up around Combs, including of Death

Row Records rival rapper Tupac Shakur and The Notorious B.I.G. Potentially reputation-damaging lawsuits were quickly labeled as false then settled out of public view. Susurrations of his explosive temper cropped up as asides in otherwise glowing profiles and on anonymous forum pages, yet Combs almost always addressed his publicized mistakes head-on, apologizing and vowing to do better. Each time, he emerged not only seemingly unscathed but also somehow wealthier, more powerful, and even more broadly celebrated.

But in one fell swoop, the carefully crafted image Combs spent the majority of his life perfecting was supplanted by a different portrayal. In November 2023, his former long-term girlfriend and ex–Bad Boy artist Casandra "Cassie" Ventura alleged in an extremely graphic and deeply personal civil lawsuit that she lived in a nightmare of physical violence, emotional abuse, financial control, and sexual coercion. The entirety of their relationship, she claimed, was stained by rampant domestic violence, with beatings so severe that she once needed a plastic surgeon to stitch her face back together. Ventura was only twenty-one years old when she began dating Combs, who introduced her to a different kind of sexual relationship, one filled with drugs and unvetted random men brought into their bedroom for sex marathons that he called freak-offs. She would later categorize them as acts of sex trafficking. An endless, substance-hazed cycle dominated her life and kept her music career at a standstill as their relationship deteriorated, ending with an alleged act of rape in 2018.

As the world collectively recoiled in shock and disbelief at the horrific allegations, Combs publicly disavowed the claims. His attorneys described the complaint as "riddled with baseless and outrageous lies" and accused Ventura of "aiming to tarnish" her ex-boyfriend's upstanding reputation. Still, Combs directed a $20 million settlement into Ventura's bank account within twenty-four hours. It did little to curtail what came next.

Ventura had filed her lawsuit under the Adult Survivors Act, a special one-year look-back window in New York State that provided survivors of sexual abuse the opportunity to file civil complaints for their previously time-barred claims. While Combs was able to promptly shut down Ventura's case, there were still a few days left on the clock, and two more women filed sexual assault lawsuits against him under the statute before the window closed for good on November 24, 2023. And in the months that followed, more than eighty people—men and women, relative strangers and ex-partners—would make use of New York City's Gender-Motivated Violence Act, California worker protection laws, and federal statutes to come forward with assault allegations spanning from the early 1990s to 2024. As evidence, they submitted photos of themselves with Combs, including one woman's snapshot of herself as an excited seventeen-year-old sitting on Combs' lap. Another produced old pictures of herself hanging out with Combs at his Florida house. Their friends submitted sworn affidavits of their own memories as corroboration, and one woman said she kept her unwashed clothes from the night of an assault in a plastic bag at the bottom of her closet.

Ventura's lawsuit also caught the attention of federal prosecutors at the Southern District of New York, one of the country's toughest prosecutorial offices. They claimed Combs ran a sex trafficking and racketeering conspiracy from the shadows of his iconic record label over a period of twenty years. Towering bodyguards and friendly assistants served as Combs' alleged co-conspirators, according to the government, catering to his every whim and protecting him at any cost. They helped him satisfy his desires with a pharmacist's cabinet of pharmaceuticals to fuel freak-offs for days on end—and allegedly went to extreme lengths to shield him, including arson, bribery, and kidnapping. The backstory to the government's weighty accusations seemed almost fantastical in the face of Combs' public persona. Yet, his attorneys had no choice but to concede some undeniable truths at trial: Combs' taboo sexual tendencies, the closely guarded secret of his prevalent physical abuse of Ventura, and an all-consuming twenty-five-year addiction to painkillers. The well-paid lawyers offered a range of defenses to minimize and bat away the accusations: All the sex was consensual; domestic violence is not sex trafficking; his accusers were, at best, money-hungry opportunists and, at worst, vindictive liars. They played to the jury's sympathies, hinting at Combs' unresolved trauma from his father's murder when he was a toddler, compounded by the losses of numerous close friends, like The Notorious B.I.G. and his beloved long-term partner Kim Porter.

Combs was acquitted of sex trafficking and racketeering conspiracy charges, but the additional accusations included other forms of abuse. In Combs' rise to fame, people whom he'd discarded in the course of his tremendous trajectory now felt emboldened to make public their own experiences with someone who, until that point, had been perceived as untouchable. More than a hundred people—those who intimately knew Combs, grew up with him, worked for him at one of his many companies, and even were his ex-girlfriends—formed a chorus of encounters and anecdotes that further slashed at Combs' unraveling persona and instead painted a picture of a dangerous, conniving man with a narcissistic personality. They used words like *abusive*, *cold*, *selfish*, *calculated*, *violent*, *controlling*, and *mercurial* to describe the mogul. They said he was a man with two warring sides, a charmer capable of overwhelming affection one moment and explosive rage the next, a benefactor who could give generously and then take perverse joy in ripping everything away. "*Generous* is absolutely a word you should never use when talking about Diddy," said Danity Kane member Aubrey O'Day. "There is nothing generous about him. If he ever gave something to anybody, it was out of self-interest, it was self-motivated or some type of payoff that you aren't even understanding."

More than a dozen former employees described Combs as a tyrant who created a toxic working environment. They braced themselves for his whiplash moods and frequent verbal outbursts, acutely aware that he had the capacity to escalate any confrontation to a physical level. Industry acquaintances knew he was someone to be feared, with a notorious temper and sidekicks ready to do his bidding. Forgotten former Bad Boy artists spoke of their careers being stifled as Combs became more concerned about elevating himself above the musicians who entrusted him with their precious dreams. Although some found ways to fight their way out of their contracts, many claimed that no other label wanted to touch them after they left Bad Boy, and they became convinced they had been blackballed by their former champion. Women who found themselves being pursued by Combs initially felt flattered by his unrelenting attention, then gradually noticed a chilling shift in his demeanor when he wouldn't take no for an answer. Those privy to activities within his inner sanctum witnessed him engineer public sympathy and weaponize the media with tried-and-true tropes to ensure his narrative drowned out every other version of the truth. For all of Combs' bravado and macho alpha posturing, those who were allowed close enough recognized him as an insecure man afraid of rejection and abandonment. And they watched as he tried to keep these ever-present fears at bay by controlling, manipulating, and dominating others. "The act of leaving can bring about vicious results," Bad Boy cofounder Kirk Burrowes said. "And the women catch it the worst."

If victims, lifelong fans, or impassive bystanders to his career expected a reflective apology from Combs during his moment of reckoning, it didn't arrive, apart from a brief show of remorse made in court as Combs begged a judge to sentence him to time served and let him return home to his waiting family. Otherwise, Combs refused to concede an iota of wrongdoing. He was adamant that he was innocent of any and all accusations of sexual assault. Anything that didn't register on the civil or criminally liable scale didn't warrant a public concession from him. "He truly doesn't think he's done anything wrong," said Deonte Nash, a fashion stylist who worked for Combs and Ventura and was around the couple for a decade. "I mean, he does feel bad, but it's like a child. . . . Once you take away everything, and then all of a sudden, they feel bad, they feel remorseful."

---

The sheer scale of the disturbing accusations, contrasted with the sanitized persona Combs ensconced himself behind, provokes the question: Who is the *real* Sean Combs? And has anything the public has been fed over the duration of his career been truthful? Is he a creative genius who became so enthralled by the limelight that he was led astray, or is he a master manipulator whose endgame was always platforming himself? Is he a combination of both? A close examination of old newspaper archives, early internet articles, anonymous forum pages, and quickly settled lawsuits indicate that Combs' fiercely guarded nature was already hiding in plain sight long before any allegations broke. There have now been investigations, documentaries, exposés, and an outpouring of people who knew Combs both personally and from a distance, all attempting to capture the breadth and full spectrum of his multifaceted character.

Tim Patterson, who grew up with Combs in Mount Vernon, New York, said he understood some things about his childhood friend from an early age. Top of mind is that Combs always seemed to keep a wall up. "If you would sit Sean down, he'd probably tell you, 'I'm not a good friend,'" Patterson said. "I guarantee you;

he'd say something to that effect. He wasn't here to be your friend. He was here to be Liberace, the Ringling Brothers, to be the best Black man that ever lived. He really believed it. So, he didn't really take steps to be friends. He didn't know how."

Eventually, questions will move past the specifics of what Combs has done and to whom, and they will shift to why and how a man who was at the epicenter of so much abuse and terror was permitted to spiral out of control for decades. How could Bad Boy executives and security staff help lure his girlfriends back into his orbit after he hit them, or music industry executives and artists continue eating after seeing Combs punch Ventura in her stomach during a dinner, causing her to leave in tears? Junior personal assistants rarely lasted longer than two years; how was there no whisper network that warned newcomers to stay away from the company? When Combs ranted and threatened people's livelihoods, was there no one who felt they could stand up to him? From the very beginning, no one stood up. "We were young women in our late teens, and he wasn't famous," said an eyewitness who saw a teenage Combs unleash a brutal and unrelenting assault on his girlfriend while at Howard University in the late eighties. "It's heartbreaking this cycle never stopped, and that he was able to abuse so many women."

Everything Combs has told the world about himself is now open to further inspection. Behind every name change and rebrand, was Combs looking to erase a version of himself? It was obvious when he dropped Puff Daddy for P. Diddy in 2001, admitting he needed a fresh start following a nightclub shooting where three were injured. When his team expedited a *Vanity Fair* cover story about his rebrand to "Love" in September 2021 despite having nothing solid to promote beyond yet another vibe shift, was there an ulterior motive behind his talk of the #MeToo movement and posing with his three adolescent daughters? The life story he's been selling to the world has now begun to be augmented and asterisked with additional context from dozens of people who claim they were silenced for years.

Combs' touch on culture is undeniable, present throughout almost every decade since the nineties. The hundreds of songs he produced scored the soundtracks of the most defining years of late baby boomers, Gen Xers, and millennials. His antics on *Making the Band* and *I Want to Work for Diddy* helped usher in the dominance of reality TV. Ordering overpriced champagne and bottle service at nightclubs was part of the P. Diddy effect. Even if inadvertently, people danced to his music, wore his clothes, drank his booze, and ultimately contributed to making Combs a mogul who believed the rules didn't apply to him.

As Combs entertained and dazzled the world with his music, his stunts, and the sheer spectacle of Puff Daddy, who was the real man he seemed hell-bent on hiding?

# PART I

# CHAPTER 1 | PUFFY

**ON ANY GIVEN DAY AT** Mount Saint Michael Academy in the Bronx, after scarfing down their lunch, a crowd of young men would loosen their ties and gather on the pavement. Squared off from three school buildings with a baseball field across the way, the parking lot, known as the Quad, served as a makeshift stage. Students at the private, all-boys Catholic school would spend the remainder of their brief recess verbally sparring as they practiced freestyling.

It was the mid-1980s and hip-hop was barely past its infancy. A little over a decade earlier, just a few miles south of where the students stood rhyming and beatboxing, Clive Campbell, better known by his stage name DJ Kool Herc, had ignited a genre that would carve out a unique lane for Black storytelling and produce some of the most influential voices in music. A somewhat happy accident, Kool Herc was playing at a casual back-to-school party when he looped the instrumental break of a track and MC-ed over the beat. The practice of rapping and rhyming over a beat-focused track caught wind and spread throughout New York City before whipping across the country. Kool Herc and fellow pioneering

DJs Afrika Bambaataa and Grandmaster Flash were crowned the "Holy Trinity" of hip-hop, paving the way for the Sugarhill Gang's 1979 breakout "Rapper's Delight" and early stars Kurtis Blow, Run-DMC, and a sixteen-year-old LL Cool J. Unlike traditional pathways into the music industry, there wasn't the typical barrier to entry for aspiring hip-hop artists. MCs didn't have to be soulful vocalists, nor did they have to know how to read sheet music or even play an instrument. Instead, they needed only a currency that most street-smart city kids were already rich with: wit and a sharp tongue.

And so, on the Quad, the uniformed and clean-shaven scholars of Mount Saint Michael Academy tried their hand at freestyle battles. Among them was a teenager named Sean Combs. He had a slim frame and an excitable nature, and he carried a leather Louis Vuitton briefcase instead of a nylon backpack like the ones his peers slung over their shoulders. Teenage Combs was the conductor of the rap cyphers, helping determine who would battle who. Even in his youth, Combs had the beginnings of the brilliance that would power his rise: instinctiveness and an uncanny ability to put himself at the forefront of what was cool. They were telling traits that Combs would perfect just a few short years later: shaping platinum records and influencing the zeitgeist on a global scale. But, for now, Combs was just Sean.

---

Years earlier, before those lunchtime rap battles, Janice Combs decided she needed to leave Harlem. Her husband had died a brutal death while her son was just a toddler, but she refused to be a weepy widow.

Her situation had changed drastically from when she was pictured as a grinning twenty-nine-year-old cradling Sean, her chunky baby, and leaning into the side of her smiling husband, Melvin

Combs. His dark hair was cropped close; hers swooped into an exaggerated yet chic bob, a style popularized by the Supremes. The attractive couple met at a party in the Bronx and got married there in 1963. The doe-eyed beauty had modeled and organized splashy fashion shows, once offering a poodle as the grand prize of an "Elegance in Autumn" show that she hosted in 1965. "My mom was modeling," Combs told *Rolling Stone*. "She was always like the fly girl of the neighborhood, and my pops was the fly guy of the neighborhood. That's what attracted them. That's how they got together." Combs was born six years later, on November 4, 1969, on an unusually warm Tuesday.

The Combs family lived in an apartment in Esplanade Gardens, a sprawling high-rise of middle-class co-ops once called the "Jewel of Harlem." Janice worked part-time at a daycare center, and Melvin—who previously served in the US Air Force—pulled shifts as a stylist at a hair salon and as a driver before he eyed a more lucrative income stream: drug dealing. "Melvin liked our lifestyle," Melvin's old friend and small-time hustler Claude Helton told *Vibe*, reminiscing about the plentiful foreign cars and Bahamas vacations his buddies would enjoy. "[It] wasn't long before he started selling drugs." Melvin became affiliated with heavyweight Harlem dealer Willie Abraham, who was rumored to be in league with the Gambino crime family, one of the most notorious mafia organizations in New York City. Although Melvin was once described as a "major dealer" by the New York *Daily News*, he wasn't considered a kingpin in a sprawling criminal operation. Still, he did well for himself. Within a few short years, Melvin had two flashy hot rides, an apartment in Yonkers, and a twenty-two-year-old girlfriend on the side named Cassandra Sullivan. But Melvin wasn't "a hard nigga," Helton clarified. "He was flamboyant and suave. I used to say he was part hippie and part hustler. Real outgoing."

Handsome and charming, Melvin was also friendly with some other infamous Harlem names: crime boss Nicky Barnes and imposing heroin kingpin Frank Lucas. "Melvin was the flashy but good-hearted guy that I'd been cool with for years," Lucas wrote in his 2010 memoir, *Original Gangster*. Speaking with music journalist and author Roderick McNeil before his death in 2019, the gangster said Melvin would bring a toddler-aged Combs over to his home during weekly social visits. "My daughter had one of those little rocking horses," Lucas fondly recalled. "She wouldn't let him ride on it. She used to push him off the ride horse. I said, 'Look at him now; he can build that ride out of million-dollar bills.' That guy got rich, man. He played good, man. I'm proud to see him like that. That was Melvin Combs' son."

Melvin's delusions of grandeur imploded in January 1972, when a police sting operation found him holding a felony amount of heroin and between $10,000 and $45,000 in cash. Two weeks after the bust, at thirty-three years old, Melvin was found dead, his bloodied body slumped over in his new Lincoln Continental. At least two bullets had been fired into his head at close range, just a few miles south of the family's apartment. A clear motive was never pinned down, and conflicting reports from the time offered unsubstantiated motives. One theory was that someone with considerable sway in the larger drug organization had put a hit on Melvin, fearful he'd rat out his co-conspirators. Another news article speculated that Melvin had already flipped on his crew. And a third claimed he owed his bosses nearly $100,000 that he couldn't pay. Police never charged anyone with Melvin's murder. In 1973, a jury eventually convicted Melvin's boss, Abraham, and nine others of raking in $5 million a year by slinging heroin across New York City. At Melvin's funeral, held in the dead of winter, Janice bundled herself in a floor-length chinchilla fur coat, matching the miniature mink pelt worn by a teetering Combs. The

Harlem community mourned "pretty boy Melvin [a] classy, stylish man [who] took all the glamour of Harlem's nightlife with him" when he died, *The New York Amsterdam News* columnist Yvonne DeLaney Mitchell wrote.

Combs was barely two when Melvin was gunned down, and Janice was determined for her son to maintain an idyllic fantasy of his father. When he was old enough to ask about Melvin, Janice told a lie of omission. An adolescent Combs believed Melvin had died in a car accident, and Janice shared no further details about the grisly nature of his death. Melvin's murder left Janice in the lurch financially. Money was tight after his illicit cash streams no longer padded the family's bank account. But now that her son was robbed of his father, Janice was determined to ensure that he would miss out on nothing else in his life. With some money stowed away, Janice would later move into 111 Dell Avenue, a modest brick duplex in Mount Vernon, a suburb in New York's Westchester County. Property records show Janice acquired the plot of land in August 1972 and built the home in 1973. One floor doubled as a separate unit that Janice rented out for extra income. In this tree-lined neighborhood, Janice built a haven for her young family.

It wasn't easy, but Janice would be damned if someone saw her sweat. She managed to stretch twenty-four-hour days and seven-day weeks to jam in three jobs, pinballing between driving a school bus in the morning, looking after children with cerebral palsy at night, and picking up sales shifts at a clothing store on weekends. She often relied on her mother, Jessie Smalls—or Mama Duke, as Janice affectionately called her—who lived in Harlem to help with Combs and her five-year-old niece Keisha, whom Janice adopted after her brother died of an overdose in the late 1970s. Janice kept it a secret from Combs, but she also worked at an "after-hours spot," giggling as she confessed to *Inside the Actors Studio* host James Lipton in 2010 that men found her "glamorous" and tipped her generously for pouring their drinks. Combs was visibly annoyed by Janice's revelation, but attempted to play it cool as the audience laughed along. "I wasn't going to be homeless," Janice told *The New York Times* in 2001. "I wasn't going to be on welfare, if I had to work all day and all night. Never, never."

Image conscious, Janice believed appearance was paramount. "We had a Cadillac car and a house, and [Combs] liked life like that," Janice told *The New Yorker.* "I always made things nice in my house. I'm a fashionable-type person. My husband was a fantastic dresser. It seems to have worn off." Her pursuit of perfection and glamour trickled down to Combs, who was always dressed to the nines. He boasted of wanting for almost nothing in his youth, crediting Janice's devotion not just to his needs but also to his whims. He told a *Vibe* reporter a tale of being crushed when his white neighbors refused to invite him over to swim at their pool. That Christmas, he woke up to his own. "My Moms made sure she got me a pool that was two times bigger than theirs," he said. "It took her like a year to save for it."

Janice sought out extracurricular activities and the best education for Combs, enrolling him in a Montessori school when the teaching style was experiencing a revival. She signed Combs up for Little League baseball and arranged for him to serve as an altar boy at the Parish of St. Charles Borromeo in Harlem. She took advantage of nonprofit services for low-income New York City youth, and thanks to the Fresh Air Fund, she sent him to spend a summer with an Amish host family in Lancaster, Pennsylvania, where he learned how to milk a cow. All work and little play made Combs a mischievous boy; he once took an Amish family's wagon on a joyride and nearly crashed it into an electric fence.

What some would call rambunctious or rebellious behavior Janice had another word for: Her son was a natural "ham." Janice nurtured Combs' knack for entertaining by plunking in front of the camera for modeling jobs and having him audition for plays. As a toddler, Combs nabbed the role of George Washington in a school production, Janice bragged. In the May 1975 edition of *Essence*, a school-age Combs grinned up at *The Wiz* Broadway actress Stephanie Mills as part of a photo shoot promoting a range of children's denim. While his early talent was rooted in dancing, even leading him to take tap lessons, it was the music that seemed to be a draw for Combs. By his teens, he was experimenting with beat making, much to Janice's annoyance. "He was blasting me out of the house with his mixing kit I bought him when he was 13, making that noise, scratching those records," Janice told *Vibe*.

The Combs family's well-manicured appearance and flashy belongings made a lasting impression on Combs' peers. His old childhood friend Tim Patterson recalled being struck by his first impression of Combs, who couldn't have been more than six years old. "I can remember this so clearly," Patterson said. "I can't tell you what I ate for breakfast, but I can remember the first time I saw Sean. I thought he was famous. When I saw his mom, I thought that was Diana Ross." Patterson grew up with Combs, his mother renting the lower floor in Janice's duplex. In a time-aged, sepia-colored photo, a young Patterson wears checkered flared pants, a red sweater, and a neat Afro, befitting the seventies style. Opposite Patterson, with his little leg hiked up on a short stone wall, is an elementary school–age Combs. His wardrobe resembles that of a dapper man in his prime more than a kindergartner, accessorized with a bowler hat and tyke-sized watch. "He stuck out," Patterson added. "He didn't wear the same clothes as me. His Afro was perfect. He had jewelry on. His shoes were white. His socks were brown or black. I had reverence for him from day one, even though he was younger. I really thought this kid was special in some way."

Despite Janice's best efforts, there were moments of struggle in Combs' seemingly charmed childhood. He recalled once waking up in a panic, shaking off a dozen cockroaches that wriggled across his face while he slept. One of the few moments that Janice couldn't grant Combs' wish—a pair of new sneakers that he was desperate for—was a wake-up call for him as to the lengths she was going to in order to create a picture-perfect life for him. "She almost started to cry," he told CNN in 2016. "My hustle was born. I never wanted to see her face like that again." It was through Janice that Combs learned the true meaning of hustling and working, he said, speaking of the many sacrifices she willingly made for him. Combs seemed to revere her for putting him first, even above herself. The shoe denial spurred Combs into taking matters into his own hands. At twelve years old, he cleverly dodged pesky child labor laws to establish a lucrative newspaper-route operation, brokering a deal with older kids about to leave for college. "I told them to let me deliver their papers, and I'd send them half of the money. By the time I was 13, I had six routes," he told *The Washington Post*, claiming he was pulling in $1,000 a week. Combs would never be without an income stream after that, working as a busboy at a Mexican restaurant and dutifully scrubbing gas station bathrooms. His later accomplishments made him all the more appreciative of Janice's self-denial in his childhood and, over the decades, he dedicated himself to repaying the enormous debt he believed he owed her.

---

Through the thin walls of 111 Dell Avenue, Patterson could hear sharp yells and soft blubbering. It was the sound of Janice beating Combs. "I remember that really vivid," Patterson said. Growing up in the same duplex, the boys had become fast friends. Nearly three years older than Combs, Patterson saw himself as an older brother to his neighborhood playmate, as well as a protector. He was already fending off bullies who mercilessly teased and rough-housed a school-age Combs, who, Patterson said, was targeted for being a "nerdy" type and thought of as "the rich kid."

The cries Patterson overheard from his younger friend as Janice delivered stinging blows disturbed him. With no father figure in the house, a strict Janice molded herself into a disciplinarian responsible for correcting any transgression or perceived flaw in her son's behavior. She tolerated no bullshit. Living in Harlem and Melvin's premature and violent death had shaped Janice's determination that it was necessary, if not imperative, for her son to be tough. He needed to be a fighter. "My mother was, I guess, raising me for the real world," a somber Combs said in a raw, all-nighter interview with director Derek Cianfrance for the short 2006 documentary *Black and White: A Portrait of Sean Combs.* "She always telling me, if somebody hit me, make sure I hit them back harder, make sure they never hit me again. Make sure I fucked them up." In one story Combs recounted, his grandmother sent him to the corner store to buy her a pack of cigarettes, but on the way he encountered a bully who demanded that Combs cough up the cash for the smokes or face a beating. Combs chose the former and returned home empty-handed. Upon his arrival, Janice decided her son needed to learn a lesson. She marched a crying Combs back outside and told him that he needed to return with the money or else he wasn't welcome at home. Combs, obedient and resigned, confronted the antagonist and was walloped. Yet he still pleaded and fought to recover the funds. It was a lighter punishment than what would've awaited him at home. "My mother was dead serious," he said. "I could have stayed out there for days."

Janice's discipline style went beyond tough love, according to Patterson and two others. Combs would later speak ambivalently to his inner circle about his mother's heavy-handedness with him when doling out punishment. "He was basically alluding that his mom was a strict parent, and she would get physical with him, like spanking," a woman who dated Combs in the 2020s said. While a hard swat on the bottom is a common form of chastisement for children in many Black households—a 2020 study found that 89 percent of Black parents admitted to spanking their children, often justified by the biblical proverb "spare the rod, spoil the child"—Janice allegedly went a step further. From Patterson's vantage point living alongside the Combs family, Janice ruled with an "iron fist," and her form of corporal punishment veered toward the excessive. Combs would often get his "ass beat," Patterson said. "She didn't want no princess," he said measuredly, choosing his words deliberately. "And there were all signs of a princess being developed." Patterson wouldn't explain further why Janice didn't believe her young son was manly enough but said her stance was firm: "'Better get that shit up out of you quick. This ain't what we do here, we from Harlem.'" Any puffy eyes or a smarting bottom would be soothed with an extravagant apology in the following days, Patterson added. A new toy or article of clothing was a wordless sign of remorse from Janice, a nonadmission of guilt to erase the stings of the night before. Grand gestures and deflection would be how Combs learned to apologize.

Other sounds also emanated out of Janice's modest Mount Vernon home, telltale signs of raucous parties. Positioned just one house away from the street corner, the house was easy to find: By the time a visitor turned off the main road and pulled onto Dell Avenue, they knew they were at the location of the night's festivities because of the glow of lights welcoming them to the well-maintained residence. Inside, there were both familiar and new faces. Friends made the twelve-mile journey up from Harlem—Mount Vernon was easily accessible whether by car or train—and acquaintances tagged along for the late-night get-togethers. When asked, those who knew Janice from Mount Vernon and

Harlem were cagey about some of her business affairs, disclosing only that she often kept a wad of cash on her and frequently paid short visits to establishments around Harlem. Everyone seemed to know her. "Her survival skills are impeccable" is all someone who later worked closely with Janice in the 1990s would offer. "She's so resilient, baby. She is the rose coming out of the concrete of Harlem."

With an open-door policy, social butterfly Janice welcomed everyone to the get-togethers she hosted at her family home. Her guests, from all walks of life, made an eclectic crowd. Among them were the wide-eyed Combs and Patterson, who served as the night's jesters. In the corner of the living room, Janice built a mini-stage where Combs would show off for her friends. "We'd be the entertainment," Patterson said. "We'd go on the stage and dance to Donna Summer."

"Everybody was welcome," Mount Vernon native and Combs' childhood friend Lee "DJ EZ" Davis said in the 2025 Peacock documentary *Diddy: The Making of a Bad Boy.* Although Davis never attended one of the gatherings in his youth, he acknowledged that he heard rumors about what type of partying was occurring. "[Janice] had little cool chicks that would come around, and . . . she made sure everybody was comfortable," Davis said coyly, throwing in a nervous chuckle. Patterson described the scene a bit more bluntly: "It wouldn't be a thing to mistakenly walk into one of the bedrooms, and you got a couple in there, butt naked." That was the environment the boys "were privy to; this is what we were fed," he added. "Was it desensitizing us? I'm sure it was. Were we aware of it? No, that was just Saturday night."

Combs said his interest in sex began at a very young age, bragging he tried to lose his virginity when he was seven years old. When Combs was in his tweens, he discovered *Midnight Blue*, a late-night softcore TV show that featured interviews with porn stars and ads for escorts and New York City brothels. "When I was in junior high, I used to strategize how I could turn that on after my mother fell asleep," Combs told *Playboy.* Combs remembered tuning in to see adult actress Vanessa del Rio every Thursday night. "I was masturbating so much I started feeling bad, because I was going to Catholic school and believed it was a sin. As soon as I would bust off, I would be on my knees asking for forgiveness." At age thirteen, Combs claimed to have succeeded in his "mission" of losing his virginity and said he frequented seedy Bronx hotels that charged by the hour. "I always had $20 or $30 to take a chick to a hotel," he said. He'd replicate rough moves from adult videos he'd studied. "I was acting just like porn stars act," he explained to *Vibe* in a juvenile retelling. "I was smackin' the girls' ass. I didn't do it on my own; she wanted me to smack that ass. I flipped her over because I saw it on the movie and then she told me to do it again, so, you know."

Navigating mixed messages at home, fending off bullies at school, and with hormones raging in his body, Combs missed his dad. He'd only been a toddler when Melvin died, but Combs managed to retain a few fleeting flashbacks of their short time together, like Melvin playfully tossing him up in the air as a baby. Amusement park roller coasters always brought back happy, hazy memories, a feeling of glee intertwined with weightlessness. He'd perk up when others reminisced about Melvin, hanging on to every word as old family friends pointed out the similarities in their personalities, their easy, bright smiles, and how both loved to dance. Combs idolized Melvin, proud of his pop's swagger, hustler spirit, and connections to infamous figures in the New York City street scene. "They say you can't miss something you never had, true, that's only a little ways right," he told Revolt in 2013. "There's definitely been times as I've gotten older that I've missed my father.

His presence not being there and having someone to ask manly advice and things you would ask your father."

Eventually Combs learned the truth about his father's death, after harboring suspicions that Janice wasn't telling him the full story. "I understood why my mother didn't tell me the truth," Combs told the journalist Touré. "Where I was living, I would have probably been one of the biggest drug dealers out there, because the type of person [I am,] I would have wanted to follow in my father's footsteps." Adulation for his father aside, Combs saw Melvin's trajectory as a cautionary tale for himself, vowing to learn from his father's mistakes to achieve their shared goals of success, influence, and wealth. "I'm definitely like him," Combs added. "But I'm just doing it in a legal way."

---

By the time Combs arrived at Mount Saint Michael Academy in the mid-eighties, he was starting to find his footing; it helped that he'd landed at the well-respected private school. Founded in 1926, the school suited Janice's and Combs' more refined tastes. Its Latin motto, Ad astra per aspera, translates to "To the stars through difficulties," and the school held its students to high standards. The administration required the young men to wear collared shirts and ironed ties, with the dress code loosening as they gained seniority.

While Combs might have struggled with bullying in his youth, high school at Mount Saint Michael Academy was different. He was friendly with most of the students in the racially diverse school. His former classmates said Combs stood out among the graduating class of nearly three hundred students. "Sean was always dancing," said Sheldon "Preacher" Francis, who played on the varsity football team with Combs and recalled how Combs would use his spare cash to hook up his buddies with fries in the cafeteria. "He was just an all-around cool kid. He's a hell of a dancer. Back in the day, he had a high top. You could always see his head going from side to side. He was just a very affable person. Some people come to a party, and you notice they say hi, but there's that one person who comes in, and they just bring a certain energy. He always brought energy and life. And I tell you, that smile, man—he always had that Puff Daddy smile."

Combs hung out with a clique of football guys after making the school's league-winning varsity team, alternating between defensive back and cornerback. He made lifelong friends with fellow teammates, including ladies' man Derek Osorio, better known as Chuck Bone, and the suave Corey "Buck" Jacobs, even though they initially clashed. "I was a wide receiver. He was a defensive back," Jacobs told iHeartRadio host Tezlyn Figaro on *Straight Shot, No Chaser* in 2021. "We bumped heads on the football field. At the end of the day, we had to fight, but we have been best friends ever since."

Combs' former teammates said he wasn't a star player, chuckling as they remembered Combs throwing his slender frame around on the field. Yet despite his size, Combs' resolve impressed them. "He would put everything into those tackles," said Francis. "He did it with gusto." It was an early flash of Combs' determined, "can't stop, won't stop" personality, which his classmates watched him grow into. "The character shift was his confidence," Francis added. "He was outgoing, but he became much more decisive. When he said no, he meant no."

Although others would later refer to the famous Combs by various nicknames, in high school, Combs was known to his classmates by his birth name. "He was always Sean," said a football teammate, Roy Rodriguez, who quickly dismissed the notion that Combs was known to his football buddies by any of his later aliases at the time. "Puff Daddy?!" He laughed incredulously. "Never, ever."

Combs and his friends sought out parties in Manhattan, swigging cheap liquor while riding the train to events in the city. A subset of the group named themselves the 7-Up Crew, sharing an interest in battling, both in rap and fashion. "He got with the popular guys in Mount Vernon, the guys who danced," Patterson said. "He started to feel himself. He was feeling his personality, girls liked him." Together, they snuck into nightclubs, including the legendary Studio 54 after it reopened in the 1980s. The hypnotic house, disco, and hip-hop beats would have Combs on his feet, dancing for hours, perfecting the running man and the electric slide. Although Combs had spent time with his grandmother in Harlem, the excursions into the city with his newly formed crew opened up a new world for him. Running with a pack of fly, handsome young men made him finally feel like he belonged. It made him feel untouchable.

Despite Combs' newfound social circle, he left high school unsatisfied. His senior yearbook photo caption summed up his time there: "It was a great experience, but it could have been better!" he wrote. Among his teammates one episode stands out as a possible reason. During the varsity football team's much-anticipated "Turkey Bowl" game against its rival, Cardinal Hayes High School, a Bronx school for boys, Mount Saint Michael's head coach was said to have benched Combs for the entire game. (Combs has long maintained he broke his leg during his high school football days, cutting short his dreams of playing for the Pittsburgh Steelers and leading to chronic pain.) According to gossip, "He held a grudge," his teammate Rodriguez said. When he became a millionaire, a philanthropic Combs openly supported organizations from his youth like the Fresh Air Fund, established inner-city charter schools, and awarded $1 million checks to outside institutions. Mount Saint Michael Academy, which Combs rarely publicly acknowledged, has received a noticeably smaller but still impactful annual donation between $10,000 and $30,000, according to tax records from his nonprofit from 2018 to 2024. Over the years, Rodriguez tried to reach out to Combs for donations or support for their alma mater's men's football team, but he said his calls went unanswered.

---

Arriving at Howard University, a prestigious historically Black university, in the fall of 1987, Combs pursued a degree in business. Like many teenagers departing their hometowns for college, Combs stepped into his own at Howard. He found himself surrounded by like-minded, ambitious peers. "The whole institution is structured that you're not exceptional, you're just part of an exceptional group," explained his Howard classmate Tunji Turner. "This is the first time, especially for Black men, that you're not going to be singled out as that smart Black boy." There was a sense of freedom and pride in being inducted into a storied institution, a pillar of Black excellence. To students and its alumni, Howard was a mecca.

Within months of his setting foot on campus, there would be few who didn't come to know or at least recognize the name Puffy.

Wearing stylish, flashy clothes and cruising around campus in a convertible, Combs went straight into hustle mode, secretly selling old exams, hawking T-shirts, and organizing a cheap shuttle service to and from the airport during the holiday season. When students protested Republican strategist Harvey "Lee" Atwater's appointment to the school's board of trustees in 1989, Combs took photos of the three-day sit-in and turned them into posters, selling them for ten and fifteen dollars a pop.

He seemed to always be in the mix, whether on the dance floor with his fellow Bumptoe crew—a nickname for the shoes they'd wear—or out on the yard with a wider clique of young men who hailed from New York. On sweaty dance floors at popular Washington, DC, nightclubs like Kilimanjaro, the Roxy, and ClubHouse in the late 1980s, he sported a clean-cut, high-top haircut and donned silky shirts as he moved in the middle of dance circles. Whether it was house music, go-go tunes, or hip-hop beats pulsing throughout the speaker system, the crowd cheered as they hyped up the floor's clear star, chanting the name Puffy. While some of Combs' classmates recalled him as a good-time maker, others rolled their eyes at his antics, describing him as brash, arrogant, and an "asshole" with a short fuse. But a majority agreed: His presence was undeniable. "Puff had a swagger that was unmatched," said former Howard classmate Kevin Parks. "I remember the first time seeing him on the yard—there was no way you were gonna deny, like, this dude is different."

Howard was formative for Combs in other ways as well. On his second day of school, Combs found himself in the university's library, flicking through microfilm of newspaper archives to learn about the circumstances surrounding his father's death. Combs read about the undercover police bust, the sprawling drug ring allegations, and his father's life claimed as unfortunate collateral in the bloody heroin empire that dominated New York City in the sixties and seventies. "It changed the course of my life forever," Combs said in 2014, when he returned to his alma mater to give a commencement speech and receive an honorary degree. "Right there in that library, I realized there is nothing greater than a mother's love and desire to protect her child." Combs decided that his classmates and friends from the Washington, DC, area would become his new chosen family. He bonded with a group of ambitious, smart young men who would become the foundation of Bad Boy Records and future of hip-hop, producers Ron "Amen-Ra" Lawrence, Chucky Thompson, Deric "D-Dot" Angelettie, Harve "Joe Hooker" Pierre, and future president of RCA Records Mark Pitts, among others.

Parties would become Combs' calling card. Already immersed in the nightlife scene—and schooled by his mother on how to create a good time—Combs teamed up with Angelettie to create a party promotion group, which they titled A Black Man and a Puerto Rican Productions. Combs and his circle of friends would hand out fliers promoting their events, which were sometimes attended by popular artists passing through Washington, DC, including bona fide hip-hop celebrities like Uptown's Heavy D and Doug E. Fresh of the Get Fresh Crew. Combs' parties quickly became renowned, with students jockeying to cram into the spaces, once drawing a crowd of more than 4,500. "For the next two years, we threw one damn [party] near every week," Angelettie told Ronin Ro for his 2001 book *Bad Boy: The Influence of Sean "Puffy" Combs on the Music Industry.*

Students flocked to Combs' parties to dance. "What made his parties dope is that when you went in, it was packed," said Howard alum Darrius Gourdine. "The party started at 8:00—by 8:45, it was crowded. Everybody was dancing; the sororities were stepping; the frats were stepping. Nobody was standing around. When you left, you were sweating. Your clothes were wet from sweat." Howard classmate Michael Graham added, "I don't know about everybody else, but back then, I used to stretch out before we went to the party." The gatherings were harmless fun, several Howard alumni said. Many remember Combs being mostly sober at his events; his focus was on ensuring the night ran smoothly. The notoriety from the parties and Combs' own hyperactive charisma made him a hot commodity on campus, with a bevy of pretty young women paying him attention. It didn't hurt that the odds were skewed in his favor. Female students at Howard heavily outnumbered their male counterparts. "[If you went] into a Puffy party, it was like fifty [women] for every dude," Graham said. "If you didn't have a number at the end of the night, it's because you had zero game." Loving a spectacle, Combs leaned into the attention. Once before campus closed down for spring break, he wore a box of condoms around his neck, the foils up for grabs to anyone prepared to let loose for the week. Combs routinely hung out around the all-women dormitory, the Harriet Tubman Quadrangle, better known as the Quad. Gourdine chuckled as he recalled one homecoming week when Combs and a crowd of men gawked at models in bikinis lounging on the yard to promote a fashion show. Gourdine snapped a photo of Combs wearing square shades, a black-and-white polka-dot tie, crisscrossed patterned suspenders, and a cheeky grin and positioning himself next to the model in the most revealing number.

Another day, someone pulled the Quad's fire alarm, sending all the women flooding outside. As they waited for the all-clear, Combs "start[ed] dancing in front of all seven hundred of them girls," Tunji Turner said, laughing, refusing to speculate about whether it was Combs who pulled the alarm in the first place. Either way, Combs "had the best captured audience," Turner added. "I thought he was special that night."

Amid all the attention, one pretty young woman in particular caught Combs' eye. She was elegant and poised, and she hailed from a well-connected West Coast family. Combs fell hard. But their romance was Shakespearean, ill-fated from the start. Combs would claim the woman's parents intervened because they believed he wasn't good enough for their refined daughter. The heartbreak, he said, left him scarred. "Her parents didn't like her messing with me because she was an A student and her grades began to slip," Combs told *Essence*. "She started getting Bs, and her parents bugged out and pulled her out of school. Then they said, 'You can go back to Howard if you don't deal with him.' So, she said she wasn't going to be with me anymore. Then I found out she had a new boyfriend. That hurt so bad. It's one of those things in life that everybody goes through, but the pain was so intense it was hard for me to handle. After that, I just closed up." But Combs' version of events omitted the main reason why his girlfriend's parents were concerned. They didn't withdraw their daughter simply because of her slipping grades. They did so after learning Combs had beaten the young woman in front of her dormitory.

Combs already was known to have a temper and, prone to jealousy, he also wasn't afraid to rough up other men who showed interest in "his" woman. And one day in 1988, he was furious. A belt in his hand, Combs turned up to his girlfriend's dorm and began calling for her to come outside, angrily whipping a nearby wall. Timidly, the woman appeared, and Combs pounced, striking her repeatedly with the belt. The woman's cries could be heard from inside the building, as students yelled from their windows for him to stop. "Several of us watched [her] screaming 'No Puffy, no Puffy,'" said one Howard eyewitness. Combs wasn't finished. He grabbed his girlfriend's hair and "looked like he was dragging her," the eyewitness added, noting that Combs' girlfriend cut her hair afterward. "She was a sweetheart. She didn't deserve that." Word reached the young woman's parents, who immediately decided to bring their daughter home. "They were trying to get her away from him," said a third person who knew of the incident. "That was the straw that broke the camel's back. That spanking was the straw that broke the camel's back." The incident upended the woman's studies, but Combs would face no serious repercussions; it was unclear whether anyone had even attempted to call the police. It was an early indicator that he could wriggle out of moments of serious jeopardy with ease. Combs even tried to win the girl back, believing the assault was something they could move past. The altercation soon faded in his classmates' memories as Combs continued throwing his parties and basking in his minor celebrity on campus.

"I think Puff was always searching for what it meant to be

a man," said one former male classmate. "If you don't have the proper guidance, you think that controlling a woman, controlling other people, or putting people down makes you bigger."

---

As had been the case with his time at Mount Saint Michael Academy, something was missing at Howard for Combs. Being the big man on campus had its perks, but he was itching for more. Combs was unsure exactly what he was in search of, apart from knowing where he wanted to end up: rich and powerful. He claimed to have had a short-lived stint as a drug dealer, sick of scarfing down ramen noodles and swiping food items off 7-Eleven shelves while jealously eyeing some of his slicker friends rolling around in BMWs. "I thought, 'I need to get some money like y'all have,'" Combs told *Playboy* in 2010. "I go out on the block, the strip where they're selling drugs, and my man says, 'OK, I'm going to give you this. You wait there. They'll come up to you.'" Within minutes, Combs claimed, three police cars pulled up to the corner and started chasing him. He gave up hustling the same night. "I told my friends, 'Thanks, y'all, but no thanks. This game is not for me.' I walked out that door, and I ain't been around nobody with no drugs. I don't want to see no drugs. I have the corniest drug dealer story of all time. I'm probably the shortest-duration drug dealer in history."

The music industry was what Combs truly had his sights on. In New York City and DC nightclubs, he had caught the eyes of casting directors scouting for attractive young talent to dance backup in music videos. Spry and fluid in his movements, Combs booked roles with Diana Ross, Babyface, Doug E. Fresh and the Get Fresh Crew, and the United Kingdom pop-rock band Fine Young Cannibals. In Stacy Lattisaw's 1989 video "What You Need," a young Combs is one of the music video's leads, flashing his unmistakable megawatt smile as he teaches Lattisaw a step combo. Since his childhood, Janice had primed Combs for the spotlight, and now that it was at his fingertips, a few seconds and cutaway glimpses wouldn't suffice. Combs watched with interest as record label bosses called the shots on sets and controlled the purse strings of seemingly bottomless budgets. They decided what was hip, who became stars, and, importantly, what people would dance to at sweaty nightclubs. Why should Combs settle for being relegated to the background of other people's music videos if he could find a way to be in charge?

Combs began working his limited connections to make some inroads, trying to secure a gig at Def Jam before he made contact with "Moneyearnin' Mount Vernon" Heavy D. At the time, the smooth-talking rapper—born Dwight Myers—was one of the biggest names in hip-hop with his group Heavy D and the Boyz. An early pioneer of laying down raps over danceable R&B beats, Heavy D was undeniably cool. He wore color-blocked suits and tinted square shades, and his 250-pound frame didn't deter him from cutting up the dance floor. In awe of his hometown celebrity, Combs staked out the town's local pizza spot to badger Heavy D about a job, even having the balls to ask the star to let him be his manager. Won over or exhausted by Combs' relentless persistence, Heavy introduced Combs to Andre Harrell, founder of Uptown Records, an imprint of parent label MCA. Uptown was one of the few Black-owned hip-hop record labels at the time. A former rapper himself as one-half of the duo Dr. Jekyll & Mr. Hyde with schoolmate Alonzo Brown, Harrell would coin the concept of "ghetto fabulous." Charismatic and debonair, Harrell blended rap and hip-hop with a luxury aesthetic. His world was filled with Cristal champagne, tasteful bling, and well-cut suits. That specific vision resonated with Combs, who was desperate to find a way in, even if that meant being Harrell's unpaid intern.

Determined not to let this golden opportunity slip away, Combs managed to juggle both the internship and his classes down in DC, stacking a full course load on Monday, Tuesday, and Wednesday in order to catch the 5 a.m. train to New York on Thursday morning and be back to throw his parties by Friday and Saturday nights. "When he first accepted the internship at Uptown Records, I remember a bunch of us giggling on him about it," said Howard classmate Jam Shakwi. "It was like, you're at Howard University, the mecca of Black intelligence, and you're taking a free internship back home in New York? You're hiding out on Amtrak trains and struggling for money to get back and forth from New York to DC? Now I salute it. There was a magic about Puff, regardless of his character flaws."

Harrell sensed it too, clocking Combs' determination to make a lasting impression. He would literally sprint to complete tasks, panting, sweat dripping from his forehead, as he breathlessly informed Harrell of their completion. His grind paid off sooner than expected. Harrell offered a nineteen-year-old Combs a full-time job in 1989, leading him to drop out of Howard before his junior year. "I really was so disappointed about that," Janice told *The New Yorker* in 2002. "A person works day and night just to educate a kid, and to be able to have a roof over your head and a school uniform. He was a fine student, and when he left college, it was hard for me." But Combs knew what he was doing. "I wanted to get my hustle on," he told the magazine.

By the time Patterson returned from serving in the military in 1989, Combs had found his stride, and he reveled in his minor fame from his music video appearances, his Uptown gig, and the residual clout earned from his cool parties. Patterson greeted his old friend Sean upon his return home. But he was cut short. "Call me Puff," Combs instructed.

There was a noticeable edge to Combs' confidence, one that

Patterson connected to an incident he observed between Combs and Heavy D's entourage. Combs had been hanging around the Uptown star more frequently, irking the rapper's friends, who thought of him as a hanger-on "punk" and would bully him. They were up to their usual antics one day when one of Heavy D's buddies whacked Combs up the side of the head, a clear sign of disrespect. Combs finally snapped. "Something just went off in him, and he went nuts," Patterson said. "It was a possessed type of nuts. It was just really some crazy shit. From that point, [Combs] just was not having it no more."

The only way to interpret his old friend's new nickname and this hardened, take-no-shit attitude was that it was the beginning of a deliberate reinvention. One that would become Combs' fabled next chapter. "He buried Sean because Sean wasn't made to feel important," Patterson said. "Sean had no esteem. His innocence was taken. It's not worth pursuing that persona, so I'm going to become these others. That was the beginning of Puffy."

# CHAPTER 2 | PUFF DADDY

**PERFORMING SHIRTLESS** with modest gold chains collecting droplets of sweat from their glistening, toned torsos, the four young men of Jodeci were the newly minted sex symbols of R&B. Their army fatigues, leather vests, and combat boots were a far cry from their clean-cut, suit-and-tie contemporaries Boyz II Men and New Edition, whose shtick looked corny in comparison to the provocative newcomers. They bore the first signs of the Puff Daddy stamp.

After being entrusted to Combs at Uptown, the two sets of good-looking brothers—K-Ci and JoJo Hailey, and DeVante Swing and Mr. Dalvin DeGrate—looked nothing like the "country bumpkins" former Uptown A&R vice president Kurt Woodley had first encountered in 1989. Squeezing into DeVante's Ford Escort to make the road trip from Charlotte, North Carolina, to New York City, they planned to turn right back around after making sure their demo tape got into the hands of an MCA Records executive. Directed to Uptown's offices, they waited in the office's lobby for a full six hours to catch Harrell's ear. They finally earned an audience with Harrell, along with that of Heavy D, singing their original songs "Come & Talk to Me" and "I'm Still Waiting" a cappella. The group had all the makings of stars. Their harmonies and vocals were impressive, DeVante wrote most of their tracks, and, to top it off, they were handsome and charismatic. Harrell and Heavy D took the giddy young men out for dinner, and by the time the bill was settled, Jodeci had a recording deal.

Harrell sent the young men to Combs after the newly minted A&R head had shown promise in his first executive producer role with Father MC's 1990 debut album, *Father's Day.* They were already working with Uptown star, singer-songwriter, and executive producer Al B. Sure!, and gravitating to a new jack swing sound, a fusion of hip-hop beats, light raps, and soulful, gospel-like vocals. In February 1991, Jodeci's first single "Gotta Love," was instantly danceable with a catchy beat backed by a snare drum and synthesizers. Although other groups, like Guy, founded by new jack swing pioneer Teddy Riley, were also flirting with combining R&B and hip-hop, Jodeci's pitch-perfect vocals put them in a league of their own sonically. In May 1991, the full album *Forever My Lady* arrived, with soulful ballads like the title track; "baby-making music" in "Stay"; and the sexually charged, up-tempo number "Play Thang." *Billboard* praised the men's "lush vocal harmonies that provide a convincing foundation for the raplike delivery."

Combs saw Jodeci as his way to make his indelible mark, and he earned credit for making the men the "bad boys of R&B." Combs' calling card would be his prolific and ingenious use of techniques like remixing tracks to extend a song's life cycle and sampling already popular songs, tricking people into nodding along to the familiar tune before they realized it was an entirely new song. Combs struck gold for Jodeci with a remix of their slow-jam hit "Come & Talk to Me." He added not only a drum loop from funk band the Honey Drippers' 1973 song "Impeach the

President" but also a bass line from EPMD's "You're a Customer," making the fourth single more suitable for the club. (He first tried the trick with Father MC's 1990 single "I'll Do 4 U," which sampled Cheryl Lynn's feel-good hit "Got to Be Real.")

After tinkering with the remix to reflect the new hip-hop horizon, Combs figured Jodeci should look and act the part, too. Combs understood that how an artist was packaged could help expand their potential audience. Originally styled in oversize suits, the Jodeci boys looked exactly that: boys. Combs felt Jodeci should mirror the type of male listener they hoped to attract and wanted to overhaul their image. Assisting Combs in the styling department was his girlfriend, Misa Hylton, a firecracker from Mount Vernon. Still in high school when she began dating Combs, she had a cute baby face framed by peroxide-blond hair and a dainty studded nose ring, and she wasn't afraid to get scrappy. She was cool and dressed the part, and Combs tapped her to help dress Jodeci for their very first music video, which was for their single "Gotta Love." Harrell was resistant, and it took her and Combs two hours to secure his blessing for the group to wear bumblebee-yellow rain suits, matching beanies, and heavy boots while dancing in subway stations and outside brick warehouses.

When they performed, Jodeci took their provocative image a step further, dry-humping the stage during performances, sending their female fans into a tizzy. Critics sniffed that a vain Combs was only styling the members after himself. "I wouldn't say they're exactly like me, but it's a combination of me and young Black America," Combs admitted to *Vibe*. The trifecta of the group's charisma, sound, and looks was electric. Within six months of *Forever My Lady*'s release, the album sold five hundred thousand units.

As Combs helped turn the Jodeci boys into superstars, another new Uptown signee was put on his development plate: Mary J. Blige.

The eighteen-year-old's karaoke-style rendition of Anita Baker's single "Caught Up in the Rapture" wound up in the hands of an impressed Harrell, who signed her in 1989, making Blige Uptown's youngest artist and the first female soloist on the label. The epitome of a laid-back Uptown girl from Yonkers, Blige was effortlessly cool, radiating a quiet confidence. She had a tough and somewhat reserved demeanor, almost coming off as blasé and standoffish in televised interviews. But when Blige opened up her mouth to sing, she became expressive, her captivating voice capable of cruising through mid-range raspier notes before escalating into goosebump-inducing cries in an easy upper register. Unlike her R&B contemporaries, whose vocals tended toward sultry and smooth, Blige possessed a huskier, rawer edge, which neither Combs nor Harrell wanted to tame. On her first credited recording, Father MC's "I'll Do 4 U," Blige's growly runs were an instant standout.

Combs saw an opportunity to harness Blige's natural fly girl aesthetic by introducing a feminine take on the new jack swing sound. The first experimentation came in October 1991 with "You Remind Me" on the soundtrack for the Halle Berry and Tommy Davidson–led comedy *Strictly Business*. The song became a hit and the first single off Blige's groundbreaking debut album *What's the 411?* Combs helped Blige look the part, too, with Hylton styling a honeyed-blond Blige in oversize jerseys, Timberland boots, baseball caps, and large hoop earrings. "If I was a honey, I would probably be just like Mary J. Blige," Combs told *Vibe*. "A bitch—not in the negative connotations of the word, but like, 'That's a bad bitch.'"

By summer 1991, Combs was happily throwing his newfound weight around Uptown's offices. Buzz around Blige grew in anticipation of her debut album release date, Father MC was still charting, and Jodeci's *Forever My Lady* continued to climb, eventually going platinum three times over. It was premature to call it a hat trick, though Combs had struck lightning twice and he believed that ought to count for something. To Harrell, it did. Combs was a wunderkind in his eyes. Harrell nurtured Combs' hunger and raw talent by investing a sizable amount of confidence in his new protégé, making high-powered introductions on his behalf. He was only nine years older than Combs, but he became a fatherlike figure to the eager, rambunctious youth. He granted Combs an extremely long leash and even became his landlord in 1990. "He told me he and his mother were arguing, and [asked if he] could move into my house," Harrell told *The New York Times*. What was supposed to be just a week stopgap turned into a monthslong non-rent-paying roommate for Harrell as Combs bunked at his boss's newly purchased Norwood, New Jersey, mansion, which Harrell nicknamed Mohawk Stadium.

He may have been favored by Harrell, but to Combs' colleagues he could be a flat-out nuisance. "I'm gonna be honest with you," Kurt Woodley said. "He could be a little difficult. Puff was starting to get arrogant, but at the same time, he was blowing up." Combs had been a few months shy of his twentieth birthday when he cleverly maneuvered himself into taking over the A&R director position for Uptown by October 1989, after Woodley transitioned into another role. Soon Combs' name became the only one listed for Uptown in the music trade magazine *New on the Charts*' annual "Who's Who of A&R" list. Combs was a fast-talking, conversation-dominating know-it-all. He pushed for exorbitant marketing budgets, like $20,000 to plaster advertisements in the subway and cash by the fistful to pay his street team promoters to drive up hype for an artist in various cities. Combs' version of business casual more resembled the looks he dressed Jodeci in than a Midtown executive's suit and tie. His enthusiasm could be excused, though Combs veered toward being straight up obnoxious. Around studios, an opportunistic Combs was known for trying to bully his way onto songwriting and production credits, which would impressively pad out his résumé while also securing a sliver of the song's publishing revenue. "From a business perspective, we all saw and heard what Puffy did daily, or let's just say, was part of his protocol in terms of being extroverted," said Jacqueline Rhinehart, a marketing director at Uptown. "I would call it 'He's doing the Puffy dance.'"

A version of that dance could be seen in the background of his own artists' music videos. Cutaway shots in Father MC's "Treat Them Like They Want to Be Treated" show a suited Combs jiving with other backup dancers. Drunk on the seemingly unlimited opportunities that were suddenly before him, Combs wasn't going to let a single opening for himself go to waste. After his day job at Uptown, he would head straight from the office to Manhattan nightclubs before finishing what was left in the day at a recording studio.

He also decided to keep throwing parties. It was a quick way to earn himself the same elevated status he had commanded in Washington, DC, as well as maintain a pulse on what music people were responding to. Turning to some of his buddies—including his childhood friend Tim Patterson—who were part of the party-promoting group Butt Naked Entertainment to pull off his initial events, Combs kicked off his homecoming with a Christmas party in 1989.

During his nightlife escapades, Combs met Jessica Rosenblum, a blond door girl known for turning away hundreds of hopefuls a night at Nell's, a West Fourteenth Street velvet-rope hotspot that mixed uptown money with downtown cool. Andy Warhol, Prince, Bono, Mike Tyson, Warren Beatty, Mick Jagger, and Calvin Klein were just some of the A-listers who all dutifully paid the five- to ten-dollar cover to people watch and groove to a wide range of music, from house and funk to soul and hip-hop. A straight shooter, Rosenblum granted or denied eager clubbers entry based on their footwear. She was so notorious for being a stickler that she felt compelled to deny a persistent rumor that she'd once sent Cher stepping. Like Combs, Rosenblum understood that a good party required a mix of guests from diverse backgrounds. The two hit it off and established Daddy's House, a weekly invite-only hip-hop event that landed at the Red Zone, a Midtown club on West Fifty-Fourth Street, a few blocks from the old Studio 54.

There were some early hiccups. Many clubs refused to host parties associated with hip-hop, racially stereotyping both the genre and its accompanying fans as loud troublemakers. It was imperative to Combs that his parties be set apart from the other hip-hop functions that were being caught up in bad press. "Come: in peace, early & correct!!!" one of Combs' neon fliers instructed, adding that it was "no joke" that hats and flashy gold pieces were banned. Another noted in all caps: "IT'S UP TO Y'ALL. PLEASE COME IN PEACE."

Beyond attracting a cool, mixed crowd, Combs took seriously the task of hiring DJs. Unlike the modern trappings that became associated with nightlife and club culture—buying tables and bottle service and posing for social media—the music was the main draw of the crowd. The DJs had to be adept at spinning the newest tracks across a range of genres: disco, house, hip-hop, and even reggaeton. Combs made sure he secured the best DJs to keep the dance floor packed. Radio host and DJ Funkmaster Flex, real name Aston Taylor, credits his success in part to Combs inviting him to spin at Daddy's House beginning in 1991. "Puffy sent me a bottle of Moët," Flex told journalist Thomas Golianopoulos in 2006. "He said, 'The crowd loves you.' I came there every week for ten weeks in a row."

Daddy's House parties quickly became the spot to be on Wednesday and later Thursday nights. Even Combs' senior colleagues at

Uptown—who openly grumbled about him—were more than happy to buddy up to him in order to secure a slot on the guest list. Combs reveled in becoming a man about town, throwing additional celebratory events throughout the year. His birthday parties were always grand affairs, each one trying to top the last and always packed with a who's who of the New York City music scene and nightlife. "It was like a Camelot," said Michelle Patrick, who was known at the time by her promoter name, Lady Justice. Patrick attended at least a dozen events hosted by Combs throughout the 1990s and reminisced that each one felt "like a movie." "You could be on a dance floor, and Tupac is right there to the left and Michael Bivins, he's trying to dance with you," Patrick said. "You're like, 'What is this?!' Everybody's on the dance floor, everybody's just having a good time."

Red Zone club bouncer Robert House, who would later provide security for Combs, said the events at the West Fifty-Fourth Street venue would draw crowds of up to two thousand people. Combs was likely raking in serious cash from the weekly parties. House said if he himself frequently walked away from a night of manning the door with $400 in his pocket from impatient guests palming him $20 to skip the line, he only can imagine that Combs' pockets were padded with four- to five-figure sums. "Because of his arrogance and his work ethic, if you didn't know him, you would have already thought he was rich," House said. "Meanwhile, he's jumping on the train to get there like the rest of us."

Combs was in the thick of it all, commandeering the mic to introduce tracks, especially if they were from his Uptown artists, to keep the atmosphere electric. And though party drugs floated into the nostrils and mouths of attendees, Combs seemed to be above partaking in anything that would be considered hard drugs. He had more refined tastes, preferring expensive chilled champagne like Cristal and Veuve Clicquot. "I never saw him wasted," Patrick said. "He was always in control. People around him would be [inebriated], but I never saw him sloppy drunk." It seemed like a rejection of what he observed in his upbringing, swearing off the thing he hated. "We didn't smoke or drink for a long time while we were in the industry, and we didn't know why," Patterson said. "We didn't like being around it, didn't like to be around cigarette smoke. We would hold one glass of champagne all night, just for pictures."

Although Combs stressed that there was no place for violence at his events, fights managed to break out. House recalled intervening to stop a widespread brawl between a Mount Vernon posse and a rival group. Eventually, the Red Zone stopped hosting Daddy's House, and the party moved to another Midtown disco, whose general manager told a *Daily News* columnist that he canceled an upcoming hip-hop night after Combs' event sent the club's security into a tailspin. "They had guns, they had knives; my security guard told me he caught some of the guests lighting up crack pipes in the balcony," the manager claimed of Combs' revelers in November 1991. A defiant Rosenblum denied the accusation, and said that NYPD officers on the scene didn't bat an eye at any ongoing activity, adding that the cops were actually enjoying the party for themselves.

After a good run, Combs wanted to wash his hands of the endeavor. His Uptown responsibilities became more time-consuming as he oversaw production of Jodeci's remixes and Blige's album. He was already a name in the nightlife circuit; now it was time to enjoy his local celebrity status.

---

For all of Combs' magnetic charm, boundless energy, and relentless ambition, a sharper, crueler edge was starting to emerge. It was noticeable to anyone who worked in day-to-day proximity to him. He had a vicious temper that could be triggered with little warning. And when it came to women, Combs was developing a reputation for being pushy and aggressive. A manager for Spike Recording Studios risked losing future business dealings with Uptown when he decided to ban Combs after receiving roughly three complaints about his behavior toward women in the early nineties. "There was one incident in an elevator where he accosted one of my staff," the manager said. "It freaked her out. [He was] coming on to her, 'Don't you know who I am?' Just cornering her in the elevator for twelve floors." He phoned Uptown's studio booker to warn that Combs was no longer welcome and "after explaining the situation, she understood completely and indicated that this type of behavior was previously known."

Women were something of a sport to Combs, and sex was akin to a trophy. He found the chase intoxicating and would pour his energy into winning over his latest crush. It wasn't necessarily lust that fueled him; it was possession, macho ego, and the subconscious need to impress the men around him. The latter was evident in Combs' habit of deliberately pursuing women whom his rivals and industry associates had dated, as if claiming them proved something about his own virility. (Combs' early girlfriend stylist Misa Hylton was also linked to EPMD's Erick Sermon.) Combs delighted in showing off his conquests for his boys. At least two women claimed Combs videotaped their sexual encounters without consent and then showed them to his buddies, and another two women claimed Combs took turns assaulting them with his friends. He always played the part of a gentleman at first, until he felt his efforts entitled him to something more.

Liza Gardner recalled Combs being overtly flirty and handsy as he fed her drinks throughout a night in the second half of 1990. The then-sixteen-year-old had road-tripped to New York City from North Carolina with two girlfriends to hang out with their Charlotte friends, the Jodeci brothers Mr. Dalvin and DeVante Swing. They ended up at an event hosted by MCA, which owned Uptown Records, where the girls smoked marijuana and mingled with Combs, Blige, Queen Latifah, and Guy member Aaron Hall. A self-professed lothario, Hall hosted an impromptu after-party at his New Jersey apartment, inviting Gardner, her friends, DeVante, and Combs back to the two-level bachelor pad. Gardner's friend, then-fifteen-year-old Monica Case, distinctly recalled being able to see the twinkling Manhattan skyline and the Hudson River from Hall's balcony. As she took in the view, Combs and Hall led Case's older sister and Gardner downstairs. DeVante hung back to keep the high school student company and away from the scene unfolding below her.

Downstairs, Gardner found herself in a bedroom alone with Combs, whom she accused of forcing her into having sex. Afterward, she "laid in bed, shocked and traumatized" before gathering herself together, tugging down her black miniskirt. That's when Hall "barged into the room, pinned her down, and forced Gardner to have sex with him." Meanwhile, Case grew bored and wandered downstairs, asking, "What's going on?" and insisting it was time for the group to leave. She encountered Hall, who was wearing nothing but a towel around his waist. He forcibly kissed her, then scurried off into a bathroom with her sister. "I started raising hell about wanting to leave," Case wrote in a sworn affidavit. Looking around the apartment for her friends, she walked into a bedroom and saw DeVante "watching whatever Puffy was doing to Liza," sending her into a full-blown meltdown. Case said she "started losing my shit" and demanded that the group go back home, threatening to get the doorman or call the police.

Eventually, DeVante, sullen over the night's abrupt end, took the teenagers back to his apartment. The next morning, an "irate"

Combs turned up at the apartment, paranoid that someone would tell his girlfriend about the night before. He began "assaulting and choking Gardner to the point that she passed out." Case awoke to a "crazy atmosphere in the house," according to her affidavit. "I know that Liza was upset, and she was like, 'He came over here, and he choked me, he choked me.'" The girls quickly packed up and headed home to North Carolina.

A few months later, Combs began insisting that Joi Dickerson-Neal let him take her on a date. An undeniably pretty girl from the Bronx with a bright smile, Dickerson-Neal was exactly his type. The two ran in similar circles, which drove Combs even crazier when she turned him down. They had met at a 1990 party when Combs was still crashing at Harrell's house in New Jersey. Combs was smitten and cast her on the spot to appear in a music video for Uptown's duo Finesse & Synquis. Dickerson-Neal needed a ride back to Manhattan and accepted a lift in Combs' maroon Volkswagen Cabriolet. A few hours later they were on set for the "Straight from the Soul" video, portraying lovers arguing in Combs' car, Dickerson-Neal in the same clothes she'd worn to the party. Off camera, Combs began his charm offensive, badgering her for a date.

Dickerson-Neal's guard was up thanks to activist and rapper Sister Souljah, who warned her to stay clear of Combs. (A few years later, Sister Souljah would serve as the director of Daddy's House Social Programs, Combs' inner-city youth charity.) But Dickerson-Neal gave in by January 1991 and suggested a meal at Wells' Restaurant, a Harlem hotspot. It's known as the birthplace of chicken and waffles, and more importantly, it was on her home turf. At the time, Dickerson-Neal was working shifts at the restaurant to help pay for her psychology degree at Syracuse University, and she felt it was a safe environment to grab a bite with Combs.

Dickerson-Neal didn't know if it was leaving her drink

unattended at dinner with Combs or his insistence that she take a small hit of a blunt that would cause the blanks in her memory, but after the restaurant her recollections are spotty. She recalled blips of Combs driving to a recording studio, but her legs felt like rubber and she couldn't stand properly. Suddenly, she was outside an unfamiliar residence, Combs was ringing a doorbell, and a mutual acquaintance of the pair was opening the door for them. It was inside this friend's home, Dickerson-Neal claimed, that Combs sexually assaulted her.

Incapacitated by an unknown substance, Dickerson-Neal didn't necessarily know the specifics of what Combs did, though the morning after Dickerson-Neal told her best friend about the alleged assault. The circumstances were made clear when her friend, DeVante of Jodeci, later informed her that Combs had recorded the assault and showed it to "everyone" at a recording studio. When Combs found out that Dickerson-Neal knew about the tape, he panicked and dropped to his knees, insisting to her that he hadn't recorded anything. Jessica Rosenblum, whom Dickerson-Neal later worked under at Stress Management, happened to oversee the strange interaction between Combs and Dickerson-Neal at one of her parties and pressed Dickerson-Neal on what happened. Dickerson-Neal declined to give specifics because she knew of the party promoters' close friendship. She only disclosed that Combs had "wronged her."

Despite the trauma, Dickerson-Neal did her part. She claimed to have filed police reports in New York and New Jersey and to have spoken to law enforcement and prosecutors, hoping to press charges. She struggled with suicide ideation and sought treatment at a psychiatric unit. She reluctantly confided in her mother, who awoke one night to Dickerson-Neal screaming, trapped in a nightmare about Combs. Distraught at her daughter's agony, Dickerson-Neal's mother drafted a letter to Combs' mother. "I'm writing to inform you of something that your son did to my daughter that has greatly decreased the quality of her life and wreaked havoc on our entire family," the letter, dated November 25, 1992, read. "One weekend while visiting my daughter's apartment, I awoke to her screaming in the middle of the night. When I ran to her bed to ask her what was wrong, she told me that she was dreaming about Puffy. I asked her why she was screaming and who is this Puffy person that he would cause her to have nightmares. I was shocked and mortified to hear her story. She told me that several people have come to her to inform her that your son has an obscene videotape of her. I asked what kind of a videotape, and she said that he, without her knowledge, videotaped my daughter having sexual intercourse with him. He has also showed this videotape to several people. When I say several people, she said that she suspects it to be at least 60 or more. Apparently, your son shows these tapes to all of his friends at parties on large screen televisions. From what I understand, he has done this to several other girls. I realize that this may be hard for you to believe, but if I hadn't heard this story from my daughter's own mouth and looked into her eyes, I would have scarcely believed that any individual would compromise another person's dignity in this manner." (It's unclear if Janice ever received the letter.)

A few years later, Mike Nice Lewis, who worked with Dickerson-Neal at PMD, rapper Parrish Smith's short-lived record label, recalled a conversation in which Combs came up. Her demeanor abruptly changed and she became "very standoffish," so Lewis asked about her reaction and Dickerson-Neal confided that she had a "very bad sexual experience" with Combs. "She didn't really go all the way into detail," Lewis said. "I just knew from what she's telling me that it still affected her even two years later." Dickerson-Neal's claims would lie dormant for thirty years.

Amid his many pursuits, Combs became fixated on an ethereal young twentysomething receptionist working the front desk of Uptown Records in the early nineties. Her name was Kimberly Porter, but everyone called her Kim. Porter radiated elegance and had a smile that rivaled Julia Roberts'. She hailed from Georgia, landing in New York City at the behest of talent scouts from top agency Wilhelmina Models after she beat out three hundred other women for the title of Model of the South in 1987. "Regardless of what happens in New York, I still plan to attend college after graduation," Porter told her local newspaper, which kept tabs on the homegrown star. She had her sights set on Howard University and becoming a corporate attorney. But while modeling and appearing in music videos in New York, Porter met her boyfriend, Uptown star Al B. Sure!, and would have their child, Quincy Brown, in 1991. At a recording session for Jodeci, Combs first laid eyes on Porter, who was cradling Quincy, as she tagged along to a studio session with Al B. Sure!, who worked closely with the band on *Forever My Lady* and movie soundtracks. "I wasn't trying to holler at her or anything, but I was admiring her—her lips, her eyes, her mouth, her shape, her energy—and thinking, 'I wish I had a girl like that,'" Combs said of their brief meeting, disregarding the fact that he had his own beautiful girlfriend in Hylton. It would take a few more years, but Combs always got what he wanted, and winning Porter's affection was no exception.

---

"I feel like Misa and Puffy aren't good friends to me," Sonya Williams confided to her sister-in-law, Cynthia Williams, in a two-hour-long phone call on December 28, 1991. The twenty-year-old needed to vent and had some time to spare before she begrudgingly headed out for a charity celebrity basketball game being held at the City College of New York later that night. It seemed like everyone in New York City—especially hip-hop fans from Harlem, Brooklyn, and the Bronx—was vying for the twelve- to twenty-dollar tickets to the star-studded fundraiser for HIV/AIDS education, which was being hosted by Combs and Heavy D. Members of Jodeci, Boyz II Men, Run-DMC, and Big Daddy Kane were all due to be in attendance and even to square off in the game. LL Cool J and boxer Mike Tyson were also expected to show their faces.

Sonya hadn't planned on attending, but her close friend Misa Hylton called her last minute. The young women ran in similar circles, dating men in the same friendship group before ditching the guys and becoming friends instead. Thick as thieves, Hylton and Sonya resembled each other with their baby faces and petite builds, though their feisty personalities meant they could hold their own. When Hylton started dating Combs, she brought Sonya along for the ride, sticking together as they navigated the high-flying lifestyle Hylton was suddenly brought into. Sonya even began dating Father MC, but she had broken up with him shortly before Hylton invited her to the nearly sold-out basketball game.

Combs heavily promoted the event, spending $2,000 to advertise on KISS-FM radio station and a further $650 on bright orange fliers with Combs' and Heavy D's faces printed on them to further spread the word. DJ Funkmaster Flex would be on the decks, and the handout warned prices would increase at the door. The tickets "sold like hotcakes," a seller told the New York *Daily News*. City College that Saturday night was the place to be, and as the charity match neared, radio adverts said those without tickets might still be able to purchase them at the door.

Concerned that she'd bump into Father MC after their split, Sonya was reluctant to go. She phoned Cynthia, who was married to Sonya's older brother Sonny, to get her frustrations off her chest. The women were close, more like childhood best friends. Sonny and Cynthia had been elementary school sweethearts, and Sonya took her role as auntie to their two little girls seriously, smothering them in affection and popping in for visits between college classes. As Sonya got ready, she explained to Cynthia how she feared her friendship with Hylton was slipping away as the stylist pursued more glamorous pals, like Mary J. Blige. The last-minute invitation and Hylton's insistence on her coming added to Sonya's annoyance. But she wanted to be a good friend, and a free ticket was a free ticket. A supportive Cynthia listened until Sonya finished getting ready and had to hang up in a hurry to run out the door. It was their last conversation.

That night, nine people—including Sonya—were crushed to death in a stampede. More than five thousand people turned up to the event, with the demand for tickets at the door exceeding the gymnasium's 2,700 bleacher seats. In the stairwell to the court, a line of attendees surged toward the gym, suffocating those at the front who were pushed against locked court doors. Dozens were injured in the pandemonium. "Imagine a plane crash without a plane," a first responder told *The Washington Post* of the scene. "Bodies everywhere, people were screaming, but no blood at all. People were grabbing on you to help them."

Footage from the fatal event shows a shell-shocked Combs standing amid bodies and trampled hats, shoes, and other belongings. He and his friends claimed he began administering CPR to victims that they pulled into the gymnasium, but other witnesses placed him standing idly by the bolted doors with money in his hands. Later, it emerged that the city couldn't find the event's listed charity, AIDS Education Outreach Program, among registered state organizations. There were also mounting questions about the proceeds. Combs and the organizers said that they only netted $24,500, despite claims of the event being oversold by at least a thousand tickets at twenty dollars apiece.

Newspapers and city investigators placed partial blame on

Combs, labeling him a clueless recent intern who lacked the experience to organize an event of such scope. In a city investigatory report, he was accused of overselling the event and spending more money on promotion than security. Now people, including his friend, were dead. Trying to keep litigation at bay, likely at the advice of his recently hired attorney, Combs expressed his remorse at the tragedy while distancing himself from responsibility, saying police ignored his pleas to help control the restless crowd. "My dream for this evening was to bring a positive event together about AIDS," Combs said in a press conference in the days after the tragedy. "We've had constant thoughts of all those who suffered."

But in an early example of Combs' public declarations not aligning with his actions behind closed doors, Combs didn't attend Sonya's funeral, her older brother Sonny said, and despite Sonny following up with Combs about a memorial to honor the victims, there would be no statue. Instead, Sonny recalled being summoned to an informal meeting with Combs, who offered him $50,000. "He didn't say what it was for, and I was not in the headspace to even process his agenda—if he was trying to just pay me off," Sonny said. He put the funds toward a charity event in Sonya's and the others' memories. (A bronze plaque bearing the names of the nine victims was eventually placed outside the Nat Holman Gym. A few lines from a poignant poem by Pulitzer Prize winner Gwendolyn Brooks are inscribed: "we are each other's / business: / we are each other's / magnitude and bond.")

The bad publicity threatened Combs' job at Uptown, and Harrell asked Combs to lie low and stay away from the office until the dust settled. Waiting for the turmoil to subside, an anxious Combs holed up with his mother, Janice, in a hotel. A clean-cut man in his mid-twenties hovered nearby. “I thought the world was coming down on him,” Kirk Burrowes said. “I knew how fragile he was from the inside of that hotel, and how hard it was for his mother to keep his spirits up.”

Combs had first met Burrowes, then a movie marketing executive for Orion Pictures’ East Coast division, only a few months earlier, in early fall 1991. Bankruptcy loomed over the film company, and a pragmatic Burrowes was entertaining opportunities elsewhere. One floating offer was from Harrell, who was looking to expand into film and television production and attempting to lure Burrowes to a marketing role at Uptown. Entertaining the offer, Burrowes invited Harrell and some of the Uptown team to a screening he was running for Orion’s upcoming comedy *Married to It*, starring Beau Bridges and Stockard Channing. As part of the movie’s marketing, Burrowes gave away a Rolex watch right before the movie, with one lucky attendee finding a winning number under their seat. “That caused a lot of hoopla from that section,” Burrowes laughed, referring to the Uptown crew. As people departed the screening 112 minutes later, a curious young man approached Burrowes. “Hey, do you have any more watches?” Combs wondered.

Beyond luxury timepieces, Combs was on the hunt for something just as rare. As the fallout of the City College stampede continued to reverberate and friction with Uptown staff was on the rise, Harrell encouraged his restless mentee to form his own production company under the Uptown umbrella. Combs would be able to rule over his own dominion free from outside interference, sign his own artists, and work with outside musicians who would come knocking for his Puffy production flair. Excited by the prospect, Combs was looking for a levelheaded and savvy businessperson to run the operation. After crossing paths with Burrowes at the screening, Combs recruited him to run his new venture. “It’s one of those chance encounters that changes the trajectory of your life," Burrowes said solemnly.

As Combs soldiered through the legal matters surrounding the City College tragedy—a yearslong battle in which he would end up paying $750,000 as part of a wider $3.8 million settlement (the rest paid by Heavy D and New York State) to the victims' families in 1999—he and Burrowes began establishing the foundation of what would become Bad Boy Entertainment. On June 9, 1992, Combs formally incorporated Bad Boy Entertainment as a record label, production arm, and management company. Burrowes stuck with Combs throughout the rocky start-up period, forgoing a salary. He sustained himself with the golden parachute he had received from Orion and by maxing out his father's Amex credit card. Burrowes was rewarded with the title of general manager, and he signed paperwork that gave him a 25 percent stake in the company and a 15 percent share of its annual profits.

Combs returned to the Uptown office in spring 1992, skirting any serious consequences for the deaths of nine people, only to find a new set of rules in place. In an effort to shield Harrell from the day-to-day nature of Combs' antics and to keep him at a healthy distance from any City College blowback, Combs was assigned to report to general manager Mark Siegel, who would keep an eye on him and a tight grip on the label's purse strings. That did not go over well with Combs, a notorious overspender who had a bad habit of running up expensive studio time on the company's dime. Combs chafed at the idea of suddenly having to go through a middleman to reach Harrell. His benefactor was still a staunch supporter, but Harrell felt he was spending more time babysitting Combs than running a music label and pursuing his own interests. It was time to set up some long-overdue guardrails.

Knowing he was on thin ice after the City College tragedy, Combs did his best to bite his tongue and keep his head down.

He moved his fledgling Bad Boy operation into a small corner of Uptown's offices, where coworkers who were "jealous" of Combs' favored status would flip the bird as they walked by, Burrowes said. As he worked to kick start Bad Boy, Combs simultaneously buried himself in finishing the production of Blige's debut, *What's the 411?* Released in July 1992, the album skyrocketed to the top of the charts, pioneering the sound of hip-hop soul and turning Blige into an overnight star. Tracks like "Real Love" and "Reminisce," rich with emotion, cemented Blige's superpower. "I went on a mission to create a female artist that young kids of the hip-hop generation could like," Combs gushed to *Billboard*. "Black females don't have young female heroes, someone they could relate to because of the hip-hop beats. Then the whole concept developed into 'ghetto avant-garde,' a combination of hip-hop beats with soul and jazz undertones." It was the undeniable R&B album of the year, earning platinum status within three months. "She, without a doubt, will become to us what Aretha and Gladys Knight are to our mothers," a critic from *The Source* correctly predicted.

Combs rebounded professionally from the stain the City College stampede left on his reputation, and his pager buzzed nonstop for work. He produced singer-turned-actor Christopher Williams' sophomore record, *Changes*. Heavy D requested Combs' ear on his fourth studio album, *Blue Funk*, as the established artist wanted to veer into a harder sound after growing tired of haters accusing him of being too soft. And Combs was the executive producer of the soundtrack for the 1993 buddy cop comedy film *Who's the Man?*

He was still unfulfilled. Getting Bad Boy off the ground was at the top of his mind, and with it, Combs wanted to break from the confines of R&B and segue into pure hip-hop. It was still the early years of the genre; the Grammys only integrated a rap category in 1989. The East Coast was carving out the early laid-back, shoot-the-shit, party sound of hip-hop. Music mogul Russell Simmons was instrumental in introducing pioneering stars Run-DMC, Kurtis Blow, and DJ Jazzy Jeff & The Fresh Prince. Alongside legendary producer Rick Rubin, Simmons cofounded Def Jam Records in 1984, discovering talent like LL Cool J, Public Enemy, Beastie Boys, and Slick Rick. At Uptown, Harrell's small stable of rappers, like Heavy D and Father MC, were making dance-based tracks about good times and fly honeys. Then there was the fast-rapping Big Daddy Kane, the intellectual social commentators A Tribe Called Quest, funk sample masters EPMD, and female pioneers Salt-N-Pepa and Queen Latifah. Out in California, a harsher tone was emerging in gangster rap and G-funk, with Ice-T, N.W.A, Snoop Doggy Dogg, and Tupac Shakur from Death Row Records.

Combs wanted to prove himself in a league beyond his peers by creating a hardcore rap superstar. He found him in the Unsigned Hype pages of *The Source* magazine in spring 1992: a nonchalant Bed-Stuy rapper who dropped out of George Westinghouse CTE High School to sell crack cocaine while hoping to launch a hip-hop career. His name was Christopher Wallace, but the twenty-year-old had taken to calling himself Biggie Smalls. Combs heard Wallace's demo tape and immediately brought him in for a meeting, making him freestyle on the spot. As Wallace effortlessly did so, Combs was silent, thinking and assessing his future artist. Standing six-foot-two and heavyset, with a lazy eye, Wallace wasn't a ready-made sex symbol like the pretty boys Tupac Shakur and LL Cool J. Plus, Wallace's bluntness and vulgarity were enough to make even Combs blush. His street credibility was legitimate, although maybe too much so. But for all of Wallace's harsh exterior, Combs saw a diamond in the rough. Wallace was seriously skilled and had an effortless flow, having learned how to glide over rhythms and beats from his neighborhood saxophonist, the renowned Donald Harrison. His storytelling about the realities of hustling in New York City was unparalleled, raw, and poetic.

Even before Wallace finished his freestyle, Combs was dead set on signing him. A few weeks later, over plates of soul food at Harlem staple Sylvia's, Combs and Harrell sat across from Wallace and his pseudo-manager Calvin "Mister Cee" LeBrun to finalize a deal. "I remember . . . Puff telling me that he needed me to go with him to convince Big to sign because he wanted Big to sign to Bad Boy, and Biggie needed to know that Bad Boy was connected to Uptown Records and would have all its services and energy and commitment from me," Harrell told *Fader* in 2011. "So, I went and big-brothered that with Puff." And on July 14, 1992, in a careful scrawl, Wallace inked his record deal with Uptown. Combs put the new signee to work, having him lay down verses for Heavy D's "A Bunch of Niggas" and for Blige's *What's the 411? (Remix)* album in 1993. Wallace's introductory one-liner on the remix for "Real Love" became an all-timer: "Look up in the sky, it's a bird, it's a plane, nope it's Mary J, ain't a damn thing change." Less than a year after his signing, Wallace came out of the gate swinging with the hard-hitting "Party & Bullshit" in June 1993. It was a lyrical and rhyming somersault. Although he lacked a high school diploma, Wallace was a "master" of the English language and its key literary devices, Burrowes marveled: "Biggie could manipulate words, and that's why his rhymes are so vivid and alive." Though the song failed to chart, the single put Wallace on the map, catching the ears of his local contemporaries and becoming a nightclub staple at hip-hop joints.

Then there was Craig Mack, whom Combs scouted outside a Manhattan nightclub and signed on the spot after the Long Island high school dropout freestyled for him. Mack was goofy, loudmouthed, and cocky, with a tendency to act before he thought, which rubbed people the wrong way. Still, there was something raw and magnetic about Mack's brash mannerisms, booming delivery, and in-your-face flair. The artists were stark opposites.

Wallace was calm and collected compared to Mack's frenetic energy. He had discovered a duo that could appeal to both sides of the coin. Combs was especially proud of both men's rough-around-the-edges reputations. "My artists are bad boys, bad boys for life, and basically depict that type of image," Combs told *The New York Times* of the men's backgrounds. "It's the confidence they have about themselves."

After Combs added Heavy D and producer 3rd Eye as signees to Bad Boy's management roster, Combs felt his momentum should afford him some leeway around Uptown. Harrell agreed, promoting him to vice president of A&R at Uptown—making a freshly twenty-three-year-old Combs one of the youngest people in the industry to hold such a title. "I wanted to gradually start my own thing, but not because I was having problems at Uptown," Combs told *Billboard* in the announcement about his new role. "I had to totally conform to making records for radio. My stuff will be designed for the young, the person that's more on the edge and has been in hip-hop culture for the past 10 years and has grown and wants the real flavor."

The promotion only fueled Combs' ego. He continued to butt heads with his colleagues, especially Siegel, over blown budgets. "I noticed he would always get into challenges about marketing, promotional stuff," Woodley said. "I don't think everybody really had the vision that he had as a marketer. But as time went on, he started to rub people the wrong way. He started to get pushy." Harrell held out until he couldn't take his Puffy headache any longer. Woodley recalled speaking with Harrell, who was gearing up to give Combs the boot. "He said, 'I'm gonna fire Puff, he's getting a little too big for himself. He's getting really irritating. He's bothering people,'" Woodley said. Adding fuel to the fire was a stunt Combs pulled at a music convention, jumping on the microphone and making disparaging remarks about the uptight MCA label heads, who made their displeasure known to Harrell.

Just after the July Fourth holiday weekend in 1993, which Combs rang in by hosting a barbecue at the new house he'd just moved into in the affluent Westchester neighborhood of Scarsdale, Harrell fired him. Combs was blindsided but in Harrell's eyes, he was doing Combs a favor. "I knew it was time for him to grow, and the only way he could grow was if he was gonna have the same kind of corporate compensations that I was subjected to," Harrell told *The Wall Street Journal*. Harrell offered Combs a string of generous concessions. The offer still stood for Uptown to oversee the making and release of Wallace's first album, but Combs was also free to take the Brooklyn rapper and his nascent Bad Boy label out from under the MCA umbrella.

It would prove to be the best possible outcome for Combs, but the abrupt termination was soul-crushing, and he cried "buckets of tears" while sitting behind the wheel of "Milky," his company-leased white BMW. "He loved Andre," Burrowes said. "He loved Uptown. He just loved everything that it was meant to be. He didn't understand what Bad Boy was going to be at that point in time." Combs told *Rolling Stone* in 1995 that when Harrell fired him, he "cried for a couple of days and felt like I wanted to jump off a building. I felt like I didn't know everything to be able to make educated decisions," he said. "I think at times I was hard to work with. Possibly I was doin' shit that an asshole would do, just abusing the power. But that was only a little bit of the time."

Combs' despair would be short-lived. "This is just another chapter," he told *Vibe* three days after his ousting. "This ain't no sad ending."

# CHAPTER 3 | BAD BOY

**IN THE FALL OF 1993,** across the way from a golf club and tucked behind a blanket of trees, Combs was using his basement home office for a serious meeting with a team of green A&R associates and music producers. It was less than ideal, but he didn't have much of an option. Only a few months had passed since the twenty-three-year-old's abrupt firing from Uptown, and Combs was still smarting from his headline-making dismissal, which served as the lead for his first-ever profile with *Vibe*. "Puff Daddy: This Is Not a Puff Piece," the title declared, as other trade journals discussed how the former mentor and mentee would finalize their professional breakup. The firing sent Combs into a brief spiral; he was so distraught that he turned up at Harrell's house to plead for his job back. His previous benefactor stayed firm: Combs was out for good.

Cut loose from Uptown and MCA, Combs had no immediate backing to operate Bad Boy. "We actually had no money when we left Uptown," Burrowes said. "We were starting over again." Adding to Combs' troubles was the precarious financial position he found himself in. He was expecting his first child with girlfriend

Misa Hylton and had recently moved into his 3,600-square-foot Scarsdale bachelor pad but was without a steady paycheck when rent was due.

Soon, initial despair and panic gave way to determination. Combs refused to let the setback become a death knell on what risked being a flash-in-the-pan career. The new CEO got to work. He set up shop from his home, hosting artists, producers, and anyone he could recruit to join his skeleton crew. "We started with one phone, one computer, and we slept on the floor," Harve Pierre, a Howard alum who rose from producer to Bad Boy president, said in the documentary *Can't Stop, Won't Stop: A Bad Boy Story.* "A music company at that time, you probably wouldn't find in any basement of any house." Combs worked the phones, milking any connection to secure backing. By August 1993, he found himself at Arista Records, home of musical greats Whitney Houston, Aretha Franklin, Babyface, and Dionne Warwick. Combs was there to meet with the kingmaker Clive Davis. "I saw L.A. Reid bringing Puff up to Clive's office," recalled former Arista senior vice president Lionel Ridenour. "I was literally ecstatic, jumping for joy, because at that time, Arista did not have rap. We did not have a foothold in that game, other than the stuff that was beginning to bubble up out of LaFace [Records]. So, L.A. bringing Puff to Clive—that's one of those magic moments."

It was the golden age of hip-hop, and major record companies were desperate to cash in. A hawk-eyed Combs saw an opening for himself. Although he respected and admired his mentors Harrell and Simmons, his confidence bordered on outright cockiness, and he couldn't help but take some swipes in their direction over what he believed set him apart: passion and youth. "I don't just listen to the music with my head; it has to give me a rush," Combs told *The New York Times.* "That's what separates me from Russell and Andre: I live for the music. I think they live for the money. I stay up longer than either one of them." Combs knew a bolder hip-hop sound was the future of the music industry and recognized an opportunity for Bad Boy to fill a gap in the market with tracks that blended clever, hard, streetwise rhymes with beats as thumping as they were danceable. He wanted his label to represent a distinct sound and personality with mass commercial appeal for both Black and white audiences. Combs' conviction in his vision was infectious. "I didn't know that much about Puffy," Clive Davis admitted in *Can't Stop, Won't Stop: A Bad Boy Story*. "I did take the meeting. And it was no question that he had the vision that a hip-hop revolution was coming."

Combs left his meeting with Davis with a lifeline from Arista. According to a two-page agreement in August 1993, Arista would give Combs a one-time signing payment of $1 million; a quarterly $150,000 contribution toward Bad Boy's office and overhead costs; and a $250,000 yearly salary to Combs for his "artist development/executive producer services." It was a crucial investment, for which Davis would take credit in coming to Combs' aid. (Arista would invest another $10 million and became the label's distributor in 1994.) But allegedly there was another source of money behind Bad Boy in the early years. "Puff was getting money from street dudes, they was helping him," a Queens-born affiliate said. Just as traditional label heads spotted profit in the emerging genre, hustlers were beginning to recognize hip-hop's potential, and they wanted in on the action. In exchange for the "investment," the "agreement is you gonna take care of us when you make it," the affiliate explained.

One man in particular helped Combs in Bad Boy's early years, though he chose to remain hidden in the footnotes of the label's origin story. "Fuck it," said an old confidant. "Buck was the one giving Puffy the money to start Bad Boy." A few years after graduating from Mount Saint Michael Academy, Corey "Buck" Jacobs still resembled the dapper young man who, in his black-and-white senior photo, wore a standard tuxedo with a trendy razor cut line at the top of his fade. "To the MSM posse, be cool," he wrote in his 1987 senior yearbook. Combs and Jacobs remained close after high school, though their dispositions were polar opposites. Both were whip-smart and forward-thinking, but Jacobs was calm, smooth, and confident, compared to Combs' bumptious, restless, and shrewd demeanor. Parting ways to attend college in the fall, each molded himself into his own version of what he believed a man should be in the pursuit of success. Whereas Combs dropped out of Howard to chase a music career, Jacobs ditched a technical engineering degree after a few semesters to become the head of a drug-dealing enterprise in Virginia.

Federal prosecutors in Norfolk pinpointed the summer of 1988 as the first year Jacobs started dealing cocaine with college friends to make some extra cash. At first, he was small-time, accused of distributing approximately eight ounces of cocaine per week to a local middleman buyer. By 1990, however, Jacobs was alleged to have grown into a far more substantial player, with his own close-knit crew. Jacobs' operation oversaw the transportation of narcotics from New York to Virginia, regularly delivering up to five pounds of cocaine. The next year, the enterprise grew. Jacobs and his team were funneling both drugs and money to and from safe houses in New York and Virginia, using cars bought under bogus names to make the six-hour drives and purchasing more than thirty firearms. The volume of drugs meant serious money was passing through Jacobs' hands; with one witness telling investigators they had once watched Jacobs count out $112,000 in cash, separating the bills into stacks of $1,000. A conservative estimate of the street value of Jacobs' operation was north of $1 million.

Although Jacobs' criminal enterprise was based in Virginia, he maintained a presence in New York and was associated with the

Butt Naked Entertainment party promotion crew. Described as a gentleman with serious flair, Jacobs cruised around Manhattan in a Porsche, wore heavy mink fur jackets, and paired a thick pinky ring with a green-faced Rolex watch. Combs and Jacobs' go-to spot became the Shark Bar, a swanky Upper West Side soul-food restaurant that was the prime watering hole for young Black professionals, celebrities, and Knicks players. "Everything seemed so secretive," said the old confidant, who met Combs through Jacobs at the Shark Bar, remembering how Combs seemed standoffish when it came to welcoming newcomers.

After a few short years in the game, Jacobs' eyes were opened to the many risks that came with the lifestyle. He lost his number two in a shoot-out over a drug-related debt, and police began intercepting some of his money runs. By the time Combs was serious about launching Bad Boy in June 1992, Jacobs was angling to make a clean break from dealing, figuring he could pivot into the music business alongside his friend. While Combs began developing Wallace for Bad Boy under Uptown, Jacobs seemed content on the periphery. In the music video for a remix of "Dolly My Baby" by reggae dancehall artist Super Cat, Combs is visible jockeying for camera time alongside The Notorious B.I.G., as Jacobs lingers in the background.

---

The pressure on Combs was only slightly eased by the influx of cash; it was now his turn to hold up his end of the bargain: pumping out certified hits. And fast. By January 1994, Arista had questions about where its money was going. In particular, the $150,000 quarterly checks that Arista was cutting. In a curt letter, Arista's vice president of business and legal affairs, Philip Wild, wanted to know what overhead the label had, given that Combs was currently running Bad Boy from his basement. "We feel strongly that a 'contribution' towards overhead costs is just that—a contribution. If actual overhead costs do not total $600,000, we should be entitled to a refund," Wild wrote. "The reason why we are contributing overhead money is based on the assumption that Bad Boy will be taking certain responsibilities off our hands which are normally an overhead cost. It was never intended as a general advance; otherwise, it would be characterized as such (and would have been 100% recoupable). This leads to questions I asked you yesterday. Who has Bad Boy hired? What are their functions? Which record company tasks is Bad Boy prepared to handle now? Please let me know."

Needing to show progress, Combs and his team holed up at Bad Boy's temporary headquarters in Scarsdale, desperate for beats that could serve as the foundation for Craig Mack's debut album, *Project: Funk Da World*. As they shuffled through beats from the in-demand producer Easy Mo Bee, the now-iconic off-kilter "bum-bum" melody began to reverberate through the speakers. The room erupted. "Everybody was going crazy. We were like, 'Oh, my God!'" said Jean Nelson, Mack's first comanager and early hype man. There was a slight hiccup; the beat was already spoken for, tentatively reserved for Apache of Flavor Unit. Combs didn't care. "I will cut you a check for that beat right now," Easy Mo Bee recalled Combs telling him. "And in my mind, I was like, sold." That two-note beat would anchor Bad Boy's first certified hit, the Grammy-nominated "Flava in Ya Ear," in July 1994. The track proved to be what its title promised, an irresistible "earworm," said Tracy Cloherty, the then music director of Hot 97, an early influential radio station that would become synonymous with hip-hop. "From the minute the beat dropped, it was danceable."

Combs unveiled the song at the historic East Village hot spot the Palladium, passing the record over to DJ Funkmaster Flex. "I can still picture that moment," Misa Hylton recalled in an Instagram post. "We were at the bar patiently waiting for the record to be played. The crowd response was going to tell us everything we needed to know." The needle dropped and the one-two beat blared out of the nightclub's speakers. "Everyone went CRAZZZYYYYYY," Hylton added. "Puff looked at me and said, 'You see this shit, Mees!!' I just smiled."

On the other side of things was Wallace, whom Combs had just coaxed back to New York City. After Combs' firing from Uptown, a dejected Wallace believed his career was over before it had really begun. His first single, "Party & Bullshit," was a success by early metrics, but Wallace's widespread commercial viability was still uncertain. Combs was Wallace's biggest champion at Uptown and staying at the label without him seemed untenable, so Wallace took off for North Carolina to link up with his old dealing buddies. Combs called Wallace, begging him to come home and finish his debut, *Ready to Die*, under Bad Boy. Wallace ultimately agreed. Harrell kept his word to Combs, allowing Wallace to part ways from Uptown in a separation agreement dated May 16, 1994. The only stipulation was that Wallace had to pay MCA $326,000 for the costs associated with making "Party & Bullshit" and "Flip That Shit," a 1993 track Wallace recorded for the *Who's the Man?* soundtrack. It was a clean break for both sides, and Wallace got back in the booth.

Combs was also fielding requests for outside projects. L.A. Reid, cofounder of the label LaFace, asked Combs to take a promising new artist, a dimple-faced fifteen-year-old named Usher Raymond, under his wing. Reid had signed the sweet-voiced Atlanta transplant after he was discovered on *Star Search*. Then puberty hit, sending Usher's voice into a fluctuating identity crisis. Reid hoped Combs could do for Usher what he had done for Jodeci, helping him shed his cutesy heartbreaker image for a more mature look and sound. Combs readily accepted and moved Usher into his Scarsdale bachelor pad for roughly eight months, welcoming the teen to "flavor camp."

Combs made good on his promise to Reid. "The prince of new jack swing," *Vibe* declared upon the release of Usher's self-titled debut album in August 1994. He had graduated lyrically from being a "mack" to being a grown lover. Critics praised Usher's smooth vocals and the high-level production from Combs, Al B. Sure!, Jodeci's DeVante Swing, and producer Chucky Thompson. In terms of looks, Reid also got his wish. Usher emerged as a Combs mini-me, rocking Bad Boy merch, weighty diamond studs, and a chain gifted to him by Combs.

Combs molded Usher in other ways, too. "I always wanted a little brother and God blessed me with Usher. He was the *only* little nigga who was able to hang with the big kids," Combs told *Vibe*. Usher would later clarify what Combs was referring to. "Puff introduced me to a totally different set of shit—sex, specifically," Usher told *Rolling Stone*. "There was always girls around. You'd open a door and see somebody doing it, or several people in a room having an orgy. You never knew what was going to happen."

That summer, Combs ran himself ragged juggling a series of projects—including Blige's tour de force sophomore album, *My Life*—that were all lined up to drop in quick succession. Wallace's debut was slotted for release on September 13, 1994, and Mack's *Project: Funk Da World* would drop the following week on September 20. Combs initially envisioned Wallace and Mack as a package deal and wanted the rollouts for their singles "Flava in Ya Ear" and "Juicy" to be linked. He and his team had a stroke of genius with a ready-made pun playing off McDonald's iconic Big Mac. According to Bad Boy's first director of marketing, Michelle Joyce, her team spent hours fashioning promo material of look-alike hamburger packaging with "B.I.G. Mack" stamped on the front. Mack, Wallace, and Combs took over a Burger King counter and posed up with the clever boxes for promotional photos.

Combs' infant son, Justin, born December 1993, made a special appearance.

Fueled by Hot 97 putting the single on a power rotation, "Flava in Ya Ear" became the song of the summer, going certified platinum after four months and staying a record-setting fourteen weeks in the number one slot on *Billboard*'s Hot Rap Songs. Then, in October, Combs assembled Wallace, LL Cool J, Busta Rhymes, and Rampage on an epic remix of the song. The accompanying black-and-white music video made it instantly memorable. Combs commands the opening shot, clinking two empty glass bottles together and, in a singsong voice channeling the 1979 film *The Warriors*, taunts, "Bad Boy, come out and play." The single's popularity earned Bad Boy its first Grammy nod for Best Rap Solo Performance, nominated that year alongside Snoop Doggy Dogg's "Gin and Juice," Coolio's "Fantastic Voyage," and Queen Latifah's winning "U.N.I.T.Y."

Wallace's single "Juicy" came in August. It was a rags-to-riches Cinderella story that would become one of the greatest hip-hop songs of all time and earn Wallace his first of many gold certifications. Decidedly softer than the hardcore "Party & Bullshit," "Juicy" features Wallace rhyming over a sample from the slow-jam funk song "Juicy Fruit" by Mtume, with the hook sung by then-unknown Total, the female R&B trio that signed to Bad Boy earlier that year. "It was all a dream," the song begins, and then Wallace takes listeners on a journey through his childhood, when he was toughened by judgmental teachers and struggle meals, like sardines for dinner, while harboring fantasies of becoming a rap star. Together, "Flava in Ya Ear" and "Juicy" marked Bad Boy's quick ascent into mainstream consciousness, paving the way for the label's decade-long run dominating the charts. "[Combs] came in there with fire, hot records. I mean, it never stopped," Arista vice president Lionel Ridenour said.

Even while he was focused on Wallace and Mack, Combs began investing heavily in a new crop of artists. Around 1994, he added to his growing lineup sultry soul singer Faith Evans and sleek girl group Total, followed by their slick male counterpart, 112. Envisioning Bad Boy as a one-stop shop for all his production work, Combs opened Daddy's House, his very own state-of-the-art recording studio on West Forty-Fourth Street. It doubled as a hangout spot for Combs' in-house producers, an all-star group aptly named the Hitmen. Combs worked all angles to promote his artists, especially Wallace, taking him on the road to perform at smaller shows, including Howard's annual Yardfest, for practice and exposure. The campus was a perfect breeding ground for new music. Not only were the students the epitome of cool and Black culture, but they also hailed from across the country. Playing there was like hitting Los Angeles, Atlanta, Philadelphia, Chicago, and New York City in a single show.

In January 1995, giddy about the future of his label, Combs brought MTV cameras to the new Bad Boy headquarters, a legitimate setup in the heart of Midtown and a huge step up from his suburban basement office. Giving a personal tour of the floor to *Yo! MTV Raps* host Fab 5 Freddy, Combs beamed, standing between Wallace and Mack. "This is my foundation, my life right here," Combs solemnly said. "We all need each other to live and breathe. That's the way we treat each other." Combs wasn't posturing. To him, Bad Boy wasn't simply a record label but a family. He'd heavily cross-promote newer artists on established singers' songs to build up their profiles before officially unveiling them. Combs had tested the waters with Wallace and Mack on Blige's and Heavy D and the Boyz' numbers while at Uptown, and he implemented the same playbook at Bad Boy. The Total trio, Kima Raynor, Keisha Spivey Epps, and Pamela Long, were introduced via "Juicy." Wallace's future wife, Faith Evans, cropped up on his remix for "One More

Chance." And 112, a quartet comprised of Atlanta natives Michael Keith, Marvin Scandrick, Daron Jones, and Quinnes Parker, had Evans featured on their self-titled debut album.

Combs' artists became a cast of recurring characters within his Bad Boy universe, and Combs positioned himself as the center of it all, the patriarch of his growing family.

---

Wallace easily surpassed Mack as the undeniable star of Bad Boy, thanks to the monster success of *Ready to Die*. It was praised critically, had three iconic singles, including "Big Poppa" and "One More Chance," went gold by November 1994, and was double platinum the following October. On the album, Wallace delivered an even balance of tracks that party people could bump and grind to at nightclubs and that spoke to the sobering realities of life on the streets. He was vulnerable, frankly addressing thoughts of suicide, yet he remained undeniably tough in his gruff sound, lyrics, and persona. The combination worked. "Biggie Smalls, Rap's Man of the Moment," *The New York Times* declared in December 1994.

Much as he had fashioned Jodeci and Blige, Combs was equally controlling with the looks of his Bad Boy artists, especially New York's first gangster rapper. In Wallace's first music video, "Juicy," he wore a yellow mesh Bad Boy basketball jersey in flashbacks to his days on the block, but for "Big Poppa" and "One More Chance," Wallace threw on Versace shades, turtlenecks, and Kangol flat caps. Rapping about champagne and sexy women, Wallace conveyed a hint of an untouchable Italian mafia boss mixed with a cool uptown street cat, leaving behind the Brooklyn dealer hanging out on the block. "We were trying to damn near make him a sex symbol," Wallace's manager Mark Pitts told *Vibe* in 2006. "I didn't even know what a Coogi sweater was until he said it."

Combs was even tougher on his female artists. He decided Faith Evans' role at Bad Boy was a "mature balladeer," meaning the New Jersey native needed to class up her look to appeal to the "grown and sexy folks." Evans was self-conscious about lingering baby weight from her first child, so Combs hooked her up with a prescription for diet pills. Total's Keisha Spivey Epps recalled that when Combs discovered that she had broken one of his edicts—none of his singers could smoke cigarettes—he followed her into a bathroom and screamed that she was messing up his money. Combs sent Epps home from the studio, warning that if she smoked again, she'd be banned forever.

---

Within a few short years, Combs had taken his label from an unknown venture to an industry powerhouse. He filled the Bad Boy office with familiar faces from Howard, Harlem, and Mount Vernon, people who were loyal to Combs and his vision. It felt like a true family operation; Combs' sister Keisha worked as the receptionist, and his mother, Janice—whom everyone affectionately called "Mama Combs"—was also a frequent face. Wearing her platinum-blond hair in a cropped style, Janice became chummy with the extended Bad Boy family, particularly Lil' Kim. She'd sometimes tag along on the road, seen smiling, with a young Justin happily plopped on her lap, backstage at a Hampton, Virginia, tour stop for "The Phattest Concert in the '95." Janice wasn't just hanging around. Agreements between Bad Boy and Arista are cosigned by "Janice Smalls"—her maiden name—identified as the label's vice president. Although she had no background in music, Janice was no figurehead, and Combs routinely used his mother as a sounding board. In the mid-nineties, Janice established her own artist management company and signed the girl group Triple Flavor in 1995. "She was his confidant, good, bad or ugly," said

Mimi Carpenter, a Triple Flavor member. "I admired the relationship of how close a mother and son can be, how he really trusted and valued her opinion in business."

Combs similarly entrusted eager, fresh graduates with responsibility for everything from A&R to production and marketing. There was a hunger these first staffers had—not just to make Bad Boy a success but to cement hip-hop as a mainstream genre. Anytime a record sold or a song charted, it could be linked back to their hustle and devotion. "While the world did not understand the power of hip-hop," Bad Boy's first marketing director Michelle Joyce said, "I was working in it and watching it unfold. I knew beyond a shadow of a doubt that it wasn't *how* it was going to pop, *if* it was going to pop—it was only *when* it popped." Combs saw his employees as an elite task force, working side by side in the trenches, bound by the belief they were building something extraordinary, a philosophy that traced back to his brief time at Howard.

It was a brutal grind. Routinely running on only a few hours of sleep, Combs was a workaholic, and he expected his staff to follow his lead. "Our motto is, sleep is forbidden," Combs would say. "When most are sleeping, we are working." Any given day at Bad Boy's office was unpredictable, except that staffers could expect to put in ten- to twelve-hour workdays. In this fast-moving environment, Combs required his team to make the impossible possible. A black-tie party in another city could be sprung on the team with a week's notice. Part of Combs' genius was his shrewd eye for understanding how to capture his audience's attention, something that went back to his party-promoting days. His expectation of perfection made him an extremely demanding boss. It was essential that his staffers be fluent in "speaking Puffy," multiple former employees said, or risk being on the receiving end of an expletive-filled lashing. Many took his tirades on the chin. Combs could be difficult, but he was also a genius. His passion was infectious, and his team trusted his vision wholeheartedly. And while they may have left the office exhausted, they were convinced they were on the verge of making history.

Just how far Combs would go to remain in absolute control finally crystallized for Kirk Burrowes in May 1996. While he was sitting in his office, Combs barged inside wielding a baseball bat. He was there to force Burrowes to sign away his 25 percent stake in the company "or face violent repercussions." To Burrowes, Combs was erasing his contribution to Bad Boy, wanting the glory and profits to belong to him and him alone. "Kirk is the one responsible for Bad Boy's success and making it the professional, young, Black-run company that it has become," Combs proudly told *Billboard* in 1997. Yet, in modern tellings of Bad Boy's founding, Burrowes is seldom mentioned. "He has done me so dirty, and he has continued to try to put his foot on my neck," Burrowes said.

It took Burrowes two decades to confess a secret aspect of their unusual friendship. In 1995, he alleged in a later lawsuit, Combs began gradually exposing him to sexual behavior in the workplace, like summoning Burrowes to a meeting and then having him watch as he masturbated; putting Burrowes in compromising positions with third parties; and even groping him and asking him for sexual favors. Yet Burrowes remained naively committed to Combs, who drilled into the entire staff that family, loyalty, and unity were the founding tenets of Bad Boy.

---

The intense atmosphere at Bad Boy was so charged that situations teetered on the edge of becoming physical. "I saw a few [incidents that] could be categorized as violent outbursts, but no one was ever hit," Daddy's House first studio manager Felicia Newsome recalled. She herself went on strike when Combs called her a "bitch" in front of her entire team in the first few months of setting up the studio.

Refusing to be disrespected, Newsome gave Combs a deadline to deliver a genuine apology in front of everyone who had overheard the derogatory remark. When Combs missed his window, she closed up shop for the day. Realizing Newsome was serious, Combs apologized to her in front of the Daddy's House team. "From that moment on, he never called me outside my name," she said.

That didn't mean he behaved well toward other women. Newsome said she physically restrained Combs from jumping into two women's brawl over Wallace. The hot-tempered executive wasn't trying to de-escalate the matter but seemed ready to deliver his own blows. "I'm holding him by his waist, I'm saying to him, 'You need to calm down. This is not your fight,'" Newsome said. "It started not really as a violent outburst, but it took him a minute to get to the point of him getting ready to go . . . beat this girl's ass."

There was also Combs' tumultuous relationship with girlfriend Misa Hylton, which soured after the birth of their son, Justin. One night in early March 1994, according to Mount Vernon police records, officers responded to a fight at Hylton's parents' home, just a short drive from where Combs himself had grown up. Three months postpartum and cooped up with a baby inside her house, twenty-year-old Hylton felt she was overdue for a night out. Combs objected and threatened that he'd take away their child if she dared to leave. Amid the couple's warring, Hylton's mother, Christine, scooped Justin into her arms to shield him from the escalating chaos. Combs launched himself at Christine, shoving her as she clutched the baby. Hylton bolted out of the apartment as Combs yelled and chased after her, only to be held off by a man police described as Hylton's father. At that point, police arrived at the scene and arrested Combs, though the Westchester County district attorney's office declined to pursue charges.

Things deteriorated from there. Burrowes and another early

Bad Boy staffer claimed they had to pull Combs off Hylton at the office in 1994. Burrowes recalled seeing Combs strike his girlfriend, and the second employee ran into the room after hearing high-pitched screams and the sound of glass shattering. Downtown at The Hit Factory, Burrowes and another source acknowledged there was a "knock-down, drag-out fight" between the young couple during a Mary J. Blige recording session for "Be Happy," a track on her 1994 sophomore album, *My Life*. And at Justin's second birthday party in 1995, one associate who knew Combs felt unsettled by the sight of a teary-eyed Hylton. "I remember [Combs] being in one of the rooms with Misa and she was crying," they said. "You don't want to make accusations. But why would she be crying at her son's birthday party?" Those who were accidental witnesses to Combs' temper did their best to bury their emotions; their apprehensions gave way to the momentum of what they were building, and many truly believed these were isolated moments from a creative genius under extreme pressure.

Combs' warring with Hylton coincided with his pursuit of Kim Porter. He had pined for Al B. Sure!'s beautiful girlfriend since catching a glimpse of her in the recording studio a few years earlier. Combs said Porter's relaxed attitude and grounding demeanor made him nervous, and he bided his time until they bumped into each other at a party in 1994. Al B. Sure! recalled things slightly differently: In his telling, Combs was a menace to their relationship. Those who knew Porter described her as a "real-life Barbie doll" and so pretty that people couldn't help but gawk. She had a magnetic charm and was effortlessly stylish. She kept a tight circle of friends, including top model Kimora Lee Perkins—the future wife of fellow music mogul Russell Simmons. Together, they'd dance in kitten heels into the early hours of the morning. A straight shooter, Porter knew how to hold her composure and could seem intimidating, at least until she smiled. It was easy to see why Combs was under her spell. The two became inseparable, indulging in late-night poker sessions and jaunts to strip clubs. She'd hang around his office, and he'd accompany her to photo and music video shoots.

As smitten as Combs was with Porter, he also pursued April Lampros, a pretty blonde studying at the Fashion Institute of Technology who later interned at Arista. After they met in early 1994, Combs love-bombed Lampros, sending her Valentine's Day flowers, showering her with gifts, inviting her to a "Daddy's Day Bash," and flying her out to Miami and Atlanta. Gradually, the adoration turned into "an aggressive, coercive, and abusive relationship based on sex," she later alleged. Combs had a "terrible" temper, routinely threatening Lampros if he suspected she was flirting with other men or didn't answer his calls fast enough. "If anyone is in your apartment, I will beat your ass and theirs" was one of his frequent threats. Years later, she learned that Combs had secretly recorded their sexual encounters and showed the videos to his friends. During their relationship, Lampros alleged, Combs sexually assaulted her three times between 1995 and 1996, forcing himself on the incapacitated, drugged college student at a hotel and shoving her to her knees to perform oral sex on him in a parking garage.

Porter seemed to have an understanding with Combs when it came to him dating other women, though it didn't mean she liked it. A shameless Combs later invited Lampros to Porter's birthday party at the Cheetah nightclub in 1997, the invitation noting a "sexy-formal" dress code and one entry per laminated invite. A year earlier, Lampros alleged, Combs had pressured the women into a threesome. He plopped an Ecstasy pill onto both Lampros' and Porter's tongues and instructed them to swallow. In the early hours of the morning, Combs kicked Lampros out of the house so he could cuddle alone with Porter, leaving Lampros feeling like a used plaything. A resentful Porter held a grudge over Combs' insistence on the three-way, misdirecting her anger at Lampros. When Porter swung by a popular SoHo bar and realized Lampros worked there, Porter allegedly used her celebrity to get Lampros fired in 1998. When Lampros told Combs what happened, he thought the cattiness was hilarious.

---

In August 1995, all of hip-hop convened in the auditorium of New York City's Paramount Theater for the second year of the Source Awards. Hosted by *The Source* magazine, the then bible for all things hip-hop, the night was supposed to be one of celebration, honoring the success of emerging rap groups while mainstream music played catch-up. The live performances of the night were heavily dominated by Bad Boy's roster, including Wallace, Mack, Evans, and Total, but it also had numbers from Snoop Doggy Dogg, Bone Thugs-n-Harmony, Da Brat, Method Man, and Wallace's Junior M.A.F.I.A crew. Amid the excitement, an edge of hostility was in the air. A pissed-off André 3000, one-half of the Atlanta-based duo Outkast, touched on the palpable tension when he accepted the award for New Group of the Year to boos from the East Coast–dominated crowd. "The South got somethin' to say," he exclaimed.

The discord only sharpened when Death Row CEO Marion "Suge" Knight strolled onstage to collect the label's award for Motion Picture Soundtrack of the Year. Menacing in both his cold demeanor and towering stature, the six-foot-two, heavyset Knight was widely feared. The color red dominated his wardrobe, fat Cuban cigars often hung from the corner of his sneering mouth, and he proudly wore a diamond-encrusted pinky ring that spelled out *MOB*. Knight's entire persona would have been a cartoonish mash-up of a slick hip-hop executive and a ruthless mafia boss if it weren't for his connections to the Los Angeles street gang the

Bloods and a string of assault charges. As Knight took the microphone at the awards show, he had a score to settle. The auditorium quieted and Knight scowled before taking the opportunity to stoke the flames of a war in which, by his own crew's account, blood had already been spilled. "Any artist out there that wants to be an artist and wants to stay a star, and don't have to worry about the executive producer trying to be all in the videos, all on the record, dancing. . . . Come to Death Row!" Knight bellowed.

Part of the tension was rooted in a rift between Wallace and Tupac Shakur, a star on the Death Row label. Although the two were pitted against each other as rap's biggest rivals, Wallace and Shakur had once been close. "Tupac took Biggie under his wing to practice," Burrowes explained. "They loved each other as friends." The Bad Boy executives had been fond of Shakur, who was a "master of the commercial hip-hop record," Burrowes said, and Bad Boy execs would "sit around and dissect" Shakur's popular single "I Get Around" "from beginning to end, front to back, inside out." Combs admitted to *Rolling Stone* in 1997 that he even modeled Bad Boy in part after Death Row, admiring the undeniable movement the label was creating. "These were record companies that were the sound of the culture, and we wanted to become another sound of the culture," Combs said.

But as Wallace and Shakur became closer, "there was someone on the sidelines jealous, not wanting that friendship to happen," Burrowes said. Up until that point, Combs was considered the label man. Although he was a young twentysomething, partying late into the after hours with his artists, Combs wasn't considered an actual rapper or MC. Nineties hip-hop photographer Monique Bunn, who was close with Wallace and other Bad Boy artists, said that Wallace, and especially Shakur, saw Combs as essentially a "corny executive" who liked to hang around and adlib on tracks. "Puffy recognizes talent, knows how to work with talent, and knows how to get people's talent and use that, but he's not talent, he's not an artist," Bunn said. Yet, Combs had no intention of being shoehorned into a single role, let alone that of a stuffy executive. He wanted to be an artist, designer, entrepreneur, and an all-encompassing celebrity figure. He particularly admired how deftly Shakur maintained his street credibility while achieving mainstream commercial appeal. Shakur could rap about violence, his disdain for law enforcement, and the harsh reality surrounding him in Los Angeles, and still build a glittering Hollywood career, booking movie roles alongside Janet Jackson. Shakur provided a blueprint that Combs wanted to follow: a bona fide cultural icon who transcended hip-hop.

As Wallace and Shakur forged a genuine friendship built on mutual respect for their craft, Combs tried to needle his way in, too. Shakur wasn't interested. "Pac didn't have any kind of respect for Puff," Bunn said. The repudiation stung. "[Combs] was jealous of Tupac," Burrowes observed. "If you're jealous of [someone] and their magnetism, their charisma, and you're studying them, their songs—you want them to be your friend, not your artist's friend." Rejection was triggering for Combs. That uncomfortable yet familiar feeling stirred up an insecurity that he believed he had outgrown in his youth. Who was Shakur to snub him and his offer of friendship?

Then, in November 1994, Shakur had arrived at Quad Studios in Times Square to lay down a track for an Uptown Records–Bad Boy affiliate when three men in army fatigues jumped him on the way upstairs and shot him five times. In Shakur's eyes, the ambush was a setup, and Bad Boy operatives had some hand in it. (Combs has long denied that he had any part in the robbery and shooting.) "When we got upstairs [after I was shot], I looked around, and it scared the shit out of me," Shakur told *Vibe* in an early 1995 cover story from behind bars. "Andre Harrell was there, Puffy was there,

Biggie. . . . There was about 40 niggas there. All of them had jewels on—more jewels than me. I saw Booker [the artist Shakur was supposed to be recording with], and he had this look on his face like he was surprised to see me. Why? I had just beeped the buzzer and said I was coming upstairs." As Shakur was bleeding, waiting for help to arrive at the studio, "nobody approached me," he added. "I noticed that nobody would look at me. Andre Harrell wouldn't look at me. . . . Puffy was standing back, too. I knew Puffy. He knew how much stuff I had done for Biggie before he came out."

Shakur's anger only festered as he spent time at Riker's Island and another facility after being found guilty in December 1994 of groping a fan a year earlier in New York. (He was acquitted of more severe charges stemming from the nineteen-year-old woman's accusations that Shakur forced her to have oral sex with members of his entourage.)

The Quad shooting caused an immediate rift between Wallace and Shakur, and for Combs, it presented the perfect opportunity to capitalize on a feud that had been held at an impasse due to the men's friendship. But Combs was strategic. As the Source Awards crowd jeered Knight off the stage, Combs decided to play peacemaker. When he approached the podium later that evening to hand out a trophy for Solo Artist of the Year, Combs was hyperaware that the slightest encouragement might push the excitable crowd over the edge. "It was the scariest situation of my life because of the level of power we had," Combs said later. "At that point I was scared because I knew the wolves that was with me were real live wolves." Attempting to dissolve the tension, Combs hugged the award's recipient, Snoop Doggy Dogg, and spoke of unity. "All this East and West—that needs to stop," he admonished. "So give it up for everybody from the East and the West that won tonight. One love."

It was a calculated play: Combs positioned himself as the

sensible adult, trying to broker peace, which cast Knight as the unreasonable thug. But that narrative wasn't reality. While Knight's Death Row and the Bloods were inseparable, Combs similarly had his own connections to the streets, which doubled as his personal security. His right-hand man was Anthony "Wolf" Jones, a member of Valley Mob, a low-level Bronx crew. Jones, who was tight with Corey "Buck" Jacobs, had slid into the picture after Jacobs needed to disappear. Prosecutors in Virginia started building a sweeping case against Jacobs and at least five other associates on drug and firearm charges. Jacobs' alleged second-in-command, Kenneth W. Kemp, was arrested in New York in September 1993, and officials accused their crew of running a trafficking operation dating back to 1988—one that grew to distribute as much as fifteen kilograms of cocaine a week in the Norfolk area, recruited couriers from New York, and acquired up to fifty firearms. In court papers, Jacobs was accused of twenty-nine counts of conspiracy and narcotics offenses, and a warrant was issued for his arrest. "Buck was on the run for a couple of years," said an old confidant. Jacobs quietly dipped out of New York and resurfaced in California, going by the name Derrick Andrews and evading officials until his arrest in 1999. At thirty years old, Jacobs was sentenced to sixteen life sentences. (President Barack Obama granted Jacobs, a nonviolent offender, clemency in 2016.)

While Jacobs lay low out west, Jones became Combs' silent partner and secret keeper. He had spent just shy of two years in state prison after being convicted in 1991 of attempted murder and criminal possession of a gun, and the time had done little to blunt his intimidating presence. People called him "Wolf" for a reason. Jones was watchful and alert, and he was known to handle disputes with his fists or something that packed a little more power. He was also a looker, muscular and handsome with sharp features. "He was a silent figure around Puff," said one Queens-based associate who was close with Jones and his family at the time. "[Jones] was a strength from the streets. . . . He was able to navigate places for Puff." Adding to his formidable reputation, Jones was tight with Demetrius "Big Meech" Flenory, founder of the notorious Black Mafia Family drug empire based out of Detroit.

But instead of flaunting these affiliations like Knight, Combs wanted to keep the two worlds separate in the public eye. He wanted to be viewed as the clean-cut music executive who rose above the roughness of street life. Still, that separation didn't always hold, and there were incidents where the facade came close to slipping into public view, like in January 1995 when Combs menaced a clueless Georgetown University cafeteria worker. Combs had been handing out fliers near a campus dining hall when the worker told him to stop. Combs cursed him out and demanded to know when his shift was over. Two hours later, as the man was heading home, Combs intercepted him in the parking lot and, with a "sly" smile, pulled aside his coat to reveal a silver handgun. Having effectively spooked the worker, Combs and an associate jumped into a car and sped away. Combs was deemed an on-campus threat, and DC police began looking for Combs, who eventually self-surrendered in New York City, where he was arraigned. Charges were dropped within a month, his lawyer said, because "the case lacked merit."

By the end of 1995, Combs was on the New York Police Department's radar following an incident with Gary Miller, a retired New York police detective turned *New York Post* photographer. Miller had been snapping pictures of Combs' fleet of Mercedes-Benz vehicles, which were suspiciously outfitted with NYPD parking cards, when Combs confronted him. Miller attempted to explain the situation, but Combs grew agitated. "I don't give a fuck if you're a current cop, a retired cop, or what you are. Give me the fucking film," Combs allegedly demanded, as his posse encircled Miller on the street. During the course of Combs' tirade, Miller claimed the music executive exposed the butt of a black pistol in his coat pocket, and he warned Miller to "stop shooting my shit." Outnumbered, Miller relinquished the film to Combs, who destroyed it on the spot. Combs was booked on robbery charges, but eventually the charge got reduced to a minor misdemeanor of criminal mischief. Combs pleaded guilty and paid a $1,000 fine.

Combs' impromptu Band-Aid of a speech at the Source Awards might have held off confrontations that night, but it did little to quell the brewing storm that was headed for both coasts. Bad Boy took the definitive first step in escalating the East Coast–West Coast feud. At Combs' direction, Bad Boy dropped Wallace's "Who Shot Ya?" in late February 1995, despite Wallace not "feeling so beefy" with Shakur, Burrowes said. The track was a sucker punch. Shakur had been shot on East Coast turf, and he couldn't even respond—he was only a few weeks into serving his sentence for the sexual abuse conviction. Wallace was adamant that the track wasn't directed at Shakur. An early version had been floating around for months, considered initially as an interlude track for Blige's November 1994 album, *My Life*, before it was scrapped over Wallace's explicit lyrics. "I wrote that muthafuckin' song way before Tupac got shot," he told *Vibe* in 1996. "It was supposed to be the intro to that shit Keith Murray was doing on Mary J. Blige's joint. But Puff said it was too hard." Regardless of when the track was recorded, the timing and title led Shakur to the same interpretation as listeners: Wallace was mocking him.

Days after Shakur was released from a state facility in October 1995, he recorded an early version of what would widely be considered the ultimate diss track, "Hit 'Em Up." However, he waited until completing his fourth studio album, *All Eyez on Me*, to release the final version in June 1996. Holding nothing back on the venom-filled track, Shakur unleashed the full weight of his hatred in a five-minute screed leveled against Wallace, Combs, and anyone affiliated with Bad Boy. "First off, fuck your bitch and the clique you claim," Shakur spat in the opening line. He boasted about sleeping with Wallace's wife, Faith Evans, sneered at the "fat motherfucker" for crashing on his couch in his early years, and made it crystal clear where things stood with his former friend.

The feud between the two stars became an all-out war between the two rival camps with diss tracks and violent music videos ricocheting coast to coast. It felt like violence was ready to break loose at any moment. Threats of retribution kept Combs from attending hip-hop summits in Miami and Philadelphia. A gun was allegedly flashed during a melee following the Soul Train Music Awards in March 1996. And Death Row loyalists giddily spread rumors that Knight, allegedly seen in a photo playing with Combs' son Justin, hooked up with Combs' ex-girlfriend Hylton. In retaliation, Combs was sneaking around with Sarah Chapman, a stunning Spelman College student Shakur had been dating.

---

As Combs' attention was devoted to promoting Wallace and hyping up Bad Boy, Knight was quietly plotting a coup d'état. A distracted Combs had all but forgotten the label's first star, Craig Mack, who was parked on the sidelines as Wallace catapulted to fame. The two artists weren't close. There were flecks of jealousy on Mack's side and sheer annoyance on Wallace's, who scoffed when he was asked if Mack would be featured on his sophomore album *Life After Death.* "No, I don't fuck with that dude," Wallace said bluntly. This was only confirmation of the suspected animosity between the labelmates after Wallace took a swipe at Mack on his track "Big Poppa," boasting that he gets "more mack than Craig."

Mack had spent the past few years fuming, still without a second album and unable to understand why everyone else's star was rising around him while he was struggling to keep his young family afloat in the suburbs of Long Island. Mack wasn't the best at managing his money. There were still royalty checks coming in from his album and cash in hand from shows, but his $25,000 advance was long gone. Mack took the train into the city instead of hired cars, worried the entire way that fans would recognize him and clown him for slumming it. Things became so dire that at an industry event, Mack once asked Combs to spot him some cash. A bored-looking Combs pulled out a thick wad of cash from his pocket and with a "smug, nasty" look, peeled a lone hundred-dollar bill from the stack and handed it to a humiliated Mack, said Mack's then-wife Roxanne Alexis Hill-Johnson.

The artist and label boss were clashing creatively as well. As with all his artists, Combs was heavily involved in shaping Mack's look and sound. Playing into Mack's last name, Combs thought his shtick should be more of a braggadocious, fast-talking player. Mack—who prided himself on being a principled Christian, so much so that he refused sizable checks to be in alcohol commercials—fought Combs every step of the way, unlike his fellow artists who readily molded themselves to their boss's vision. It all contributed to Mack's lack of respect for Combs, whom he treated like a peer rather than the man who controlled his career. Mack let his grievances be known, turning up at Bad Boy's offices to complain about money, a lack of studio time, and Combs starring in his music videos, among myriad other frustrations. "He spoke to Puffy directly about shit he didn't like," Mack's former business attorney Paul Insinna said. "Puffy took that as a slight because . . . you always got the impression [Combs'] attitude was, 'You should be glad to be in the same room as me, let alone getting paid.' Craig didn't fall for that shit . . . and that put him in a bad position."

Mack had other points of contention. It rubbed him the wrong way that Combs wanted his own piece of the spotlight alongside his artists. "Puff was not in the seat that [Mack thought] he was supposed to be in," Mack's close friend said. There was no subtlety in the fact that, unlike other record label owners, Combs wasn't satisfied with being confined to his corner office; he wanted to be seen and heard. Combs would throw ad-libs on his artists' tracks and make significant cameos in their music videos, standing on podiums above his singers and puffing on a cigar poolside. Combs rapped on Mack's third single, "Making Moves with Puff," leaving no doubt Combs was the king of a rapidly expanding empire. And it was no democracy. Combs held all the cards, and as new artists jockeyed to sign to Bad Boy, Combs felt he didn't have to pander to Mack.

By early 1996, Mack still didn't have any solid guarantee about the timing of his follow-up album. He was nearly broke and begging to be let out of his contract so he could sign elsewhere, but Combs refused to let Mack walk away. Never one to do things subtly, Mack attempted to strong-arm his way out by filing for bankruptcy in April 1996. It was the same pathway Tionne "T-Boz" Watkins, Lisa "Left Eye" Lopes, and Rozonda "Chilli" Thomas of TLC tried to take in July 1995 with LaFace Records. The trio claimed that despite being at the top of the charts, they were $3.5 million in debt due to costs incurred by signing to music executive L.A. Reid's label. Mack claimed he was trapped in a similar situation, with his deal impairing his ability to financially recover from the debts he was racking up with Bad Boy. He was being billed for the hours he spent in the recording studio trying to put together a nonexistent album, and his budget had been tapped dry from the steep costs of his music videos.

Mack was itching to get his lick back at Combs, and Knight was looking for any opportunity to claim a scalp from his rival.

Death Row was already plotting to open an East Coast division, going so far as to neg Combs by flooding New York City with "Death Row East" T-shirts. (After Combs caught sight of club promoter DeWitt Gilmore in one of the rival shirts while leaving a nightclub in Manhattan, Gilmore claimed, a pissed-off Combs and his driver jumped in their car and tried running him down.) Knight began heavily courting Mack to defect and serve as the face of Death Row East. He flew Mack out to Los Angeles, flashed wads of cash, and wired his family $20,000 every few weeks, Hill-Johnson said. Mack's early hype man Malcolm Johns was privy to the schmoozing, too. "I remember Suge Knight coming in, throwing about $20,000 on the bed, and Craig going, 'Thank you,'" Johns said. That was on top of the unheard-of deal Knight was reportedly dangling: a $1.25 million recording budget with a $200,000 advance. (Knight may have also had a personal motivation for poaching Mack from Combs: In September 1995, his close friend Jake Robles was killed at an after-party in Atlanta, and Knight was convinced that Wolf, Combs' security guard, was involved in the shooting.)

Mack was eager to accept, but he just had to wiggle out of his Bad Boy contract first. Once he filed for bankruptcy, Bad Boy lawyers and executives tried to work out a deal that would keep Mack on board. Finally holding the upper hand, Mack's lawyer Insinna hatched a plan to "ask for everything" they could dream up and put together a proposal with a $100,000 advance and $350,000 in recording funds that Mack would control. And more lucrative in the long run, Mack asked to retain his full publishing and merchandising rights. "It was a crazy deal," Insinna said. "And they gave me everything I wanted." But Mack rejected the offer, adamant that he wanted to be done with Combs and Bad Boy. No deal—no matter its perks or advances—would beat the price of his freedom that he had cleverly maneuvered. Plus, Mack secretly had Death Row in his back pocket, but it was a risky move: Prematurely flirting with other labels could nullify the bankruptcy process.

Stubborn to a fault, Mack couldn't resist scheming with Knight to pull the ultimate fuck-you on Combs. In September 1996, he had yet another covert meetup with the Death Row crew in Las Vegas. Everyone had descended upon Sin City to catch the highly anticipated boxing match between heavyweight champions Mike Tyson and Bruce Seldon. The hyped-up fight attracted the likes of actors Forest Whitaker and Jenny McCarthy and the Reverend Jesse Jackson, as well as the Bad Boy crew and the Los Angeles hip-hop faction. But newspapers would gloss over Tyson handily knocking out Seldon in the first round. Instead, the top story of the *Las Vegas Review-Journal* that weekend would read, "Rapper Tupac Shakur, notorious for his controversial lyrics and brushes with the law, was fighting for his life late Sunday at University Medical Center after being gunned down on the Strip." After the fight, as Shakur and Knight rolled their BMW to a stop at a red light, on their way to a nearby after-party, unknown assailants in a white Cadillac sprayed their car with bullets. Knight suffered a wound to his head, while Shakur took the brunt of the fire. He died six days later on September 13, at age twenty-five.

Shakur's murder remained a cold case, though officials had one suspect in mind for decades: longtime Compton Crips leader Duane "Keefe D" Davis. Between 2008 and 2009, Davis laid out the circumstances that he claimed led to Shakur's death during hours-long interviews with Los Angeles Police Detective Greg Kading. (Davis agreed to speak with law enforcement as part of a proffer agreement, which granted him free rein to discuss the murder, without the fear of the government using the information against him.) Davis described the shooting as a moment of street retaliation, with significant risk-reward margins, claiming Combs had put a bounty on both Knight's and Shakur's heads. (Combs has vehemently denied Davis' claims.)

Davis was not particularly close with Combs, but he was in business with Eric "Von Zip" Martin, a known Harlem drug lord who was friendly with Combs and Wallace. Through his hustling partnership with Martin, Davis was introduced to the Bad Boy family. It was largely an informal relationship born of the ongoing hip-hop feud, Davis explained to detectives. When Combs and his entourage rolled through the West Coast, Davis and his Crips crew served as their local protection. It was during the ongoing feud, Davis claimed, that Combs twice floated the idea of taking care of Knight, later adding Shakur to his short list after the release of "Hit 'Em Up." "That pissed him off," Davis told Detective Kading. An informal deal was struck one evening at Greenblatt's Deli, an iconic Jewish locale on the Sunset Strip. "All of us [were there]," Davis said in the proffer interview. "When we got there we was laughing at him, cause he was with this broad that sucked dick, and sucked every dick in there, and he's all held up kissing with her. We was laughing like a motherfucker. He's like, 'Man, what you laughing at dog?' Man, don't just come out here and get any broad, dog. . . . He took me downstairs and he's like, 'Man, I wanna get rid of them dudes, man.'" Davis claimed he assured an emasculated Combs that his guys could "wipe their ass out quick" like it was "nothing," but the price was $1 million.

Davis said the perfect opportunity arose in the aftermath of the Tyson fight. Exiting the MGM Grand, Shakur had spied Orlando "Baby Lane" Anderson, a Crips affiliate who also happened to be Davis' nephew. Anderson had his own beef with Death Row from earlier that year, when he had tried to yank a heavy diamond-studded chain off a Death Row member's neck. Payback came in the form of Shakur, Knight, and the label boss's pals attacking Anderson in the hotel's lobby.

Street code required an immediate response, and Davis said he recognized this as a chance for retaliation and to secure his payday. But Davis and his crew came to Sin City without weapons for what was supposed to be a social gathering on neutral turf. However, Martin had come strapped, driving his own rigged-up car cross-country. Martin was aware of the bounty, and allegedly confirmed to Davis that it was perfect timing. From a secret compartment in his car Martin pulled out a .40-caliber Glock and gave it to Davis' crew. (Martin died in 2012.) The day after Shakur was shot, Davis claimed, Combs used Martin as a middleman to ask Davis, "Was that us?" Davis then confirmed the deed was done. A partial payment of $500,000—because Knight survived—was supposed to be sent to Davis through Martin, Davis claimed, but it never materialized.

Combs has adamantly denied having any role in Shakur's death, and officials have maintained Combs was never a suspect. Davis was arrested and charged with first-degree murder in September 2023. He denied the charges against him, although he has openly implicated himself in numerous interviews, podcasts, and his memoir, where he bragged about being in the getaway Cadillac the night of the murder. He has issued a range of denials and defenses, including that his proffer was made under duress, that he had exaggerated his involvement for entertainment purposes, and that he wasn't even in Las Vegas at the time of the shooting. Nevada prosecutors were convinced they had their man and scheduled his criminal trial for August 2026.

Shakur's brazen murder rattled the entire industry. Threats and lyrics had metastasized into a dead body. Knight immediately pointed the finger at Combs, and fears of retaliation shook the Bad Boy office. "It got to be a little dangerous at some point," former Bad Boy publicity director LaJoyce Brookshire said. "I didn't recall reading in the employee manual [that] dodging bullets was a part of my job description." Michelle Joyce, still the head of marketing, received a voicemail from an unknown caller who threatened to kill her. She ended up leaving Bad Boy. Out of an abundance of caution, Bad Boy temporarily moved its employees over to Arista's headquarters.

Mack scrapped his plans to defect to Death Row, fearing for his safety. "He was scared," Hill-Johnson said. Word about Mack's plan had already leaked via Hot 97 radio host Wendy Williams, who repeated the juicy scoop on the air. "I started to immediately get calls and faxes from Puffy's lawyers," Insinna recalled, saying Bad Boy's lawyers hauled Mack back into the office. "They had us by the shorthairs." On September 9, 1996—two days after Shakur was shot—Mack filed a notice with the court that he had reached a settlement agreement. Mack was able to leave the label, but he had to withdraw the bankruptcy filing and would owe Combs a cut of any new deal he signed. His career never bounced back, and he turned out to be one of the first of many artists who flocked to Combs and Bad Boy with dreams of success, only to leave disillusioned, broke, and bitter.

---

Tensions seemed to have slowed to a simmer by early 1997, at least enough for Wallace and the Bad Boy team to feel comfortable spending time in Los Angeles as they prepared to roll out Wallace's anticipated follow-up *Life After Death.* Wallace touched down in the City of Angels in February, holding court with reporters and filming the music video for the album's lead single, "Hypnotize." He was more famous than ever, having transformed from an unknown rapper freestyling outside a bodega a few years earlier to an international celebrity who was making hip-hop mainstream, despite his hardcore lyrics. His sophomore album would cement him as an even bigger star with a defined, stylized sound.

But six months after Shakur's murder was too soon. As the leading men of Bad Boy took the stage at the Soul Train Music Awards to read out the female nominees for Best R&B/Soul Single on March 7, 1997, the crowd hissed their disgust as Wallace greeted the West Coast with a simple "What's up, Cali?" before announcing Toni Braxton as the category's winner. (It was an icy reception compared to the previous year when Wallace performed a medley of "One More Chance" and "Get Money." In a dark suit, Wallace had descended from the sky in a cage, as if he were a ghost paying the auditorium a visit from heaven.)

The next day, the Bad Boy entourage hit up a party hosted by *Vibe* and Qwest Records at the Petersen Automotive Museum. Wallace was holding court at a corner table, temporarily dependent on a long black cane following a serious car accident that kept him stationary for much of the event. He still managed to look effortlessly cool in dark wraparound shades as he graciously accepted congratulations from the room when the DJ began blasting "Hypnotize," which had hit radios a few days earlier. Combs parked up next to Wallace, keeping him company until a fire alarm began blaring. Officials shut down the event sometime after midnight, claiming the gathering was overcrowded.

The group split up between several cars to head back to their hotel, and Wallace hopped into a GMC Suburban with close friend Damion "D-Roc" Butler, Junior M.A.F.I.A. member Lil' Cease, and Gregory "G-Money" Young. Half the music world watched as an eerily familiar scene unfolded steps away from the party. While the Suburban idled at a red light, a dark Chevy Impala pulled up alongside Wallace's car and a suited gunman fired several rounds into the vehicle. "We have a man shot, we have a man shot," a 911 caller frantically told an emergency responder. "We have a man shot in our car right now!" In the background of the call, a woman is heard hysterically sobbing and a man shakily asking,

"Yo, Big, you hear me? Big!" The group raced Wallace to Cedars-Sinai Medical Center, but it was too late. Wallace, at the age of twenty-four, was declared dead in the early hours of the morning on March 9, 1997.

Immediately, law enforcement said they couldn't rule out that Wallace's murder "was possibly a hit." Though Los Angeles police and a subsequent FBI investigation sat on the name of a suspect identified by multiple eyewitnesses for years—a man who had a shrine to Shakur inside his house—no person has ever been charged with Wallace's murder.

Anyone who wasn't already in Los Angeles was jolted out of their bed that morning by long-distance calls with the news. Fearing for his own life, Combs fled Los Angeles on the first flight out. News of Wallace's death ripped through Bad Boy's office, but there was no time to grieve. In a state of shock, the publicity director, Brookshire, asked for time off. She had been in Los Angeles with Wallace days before his murder, riding along with him in the same SUV during the trip. Her request was denied. Combs wanted his paralyzed team to pour all their energy into ensuring *Life After Death* was "number one, number one, number one, number one, number one. Top 10, top 10, top 10," Brookshire said. The posthumous album sold nearly seven hundred thousand copies in its first week and went eleven times platinum, and it is one of the best-selling rap albums of all time, according to the Recording Industry Association of America.

The outpouring of sympathy after Wallace's shocking death was overwhelming. Thousands of people lined the streets in the heart of Brooklyn to catch a glimpse of his funeral procession. Fans cheered and cried as Wallace's hearse, adorned with wreaths of flowers, rolled by his Bed-Stuy childhood home. Murals were painted in his honor, and Wallace's premature death cemented him among the greats forever. Leaders within the Black community, including Nation of Islam's Louis Farrakhan, Minister Benjamin Chavis Muhammad, and civil rights activist Kwame Ture, stepped in by April 1997. They feared further escalation and were calling for talks and truces. But at that point, it was already too late. Momentum had already been moving in one direction: tragedy.

As the shock subsided and grief settled in, Combs was left at a crossroads. He still had a solid lineup of R&B artists—Evans, Total, and 112—but Bad Boy had become synonymous with The Notorious B.I.G. Would Combs be able to evolve his label and stay relevant without its king?

# CHAPTER 4 THE IMPRESARIO BECOMES A STAR

**IN AN ALTERNATE UNIVERSE,** Bad Boy could have suffered the fate of becoming a mausoleum to Wallace's legacy in the wake of his abrupt death. The West Coast was still out for blood, and rival groups were springing up in Atlanta, Houston, Cleveland, and Chicago, all looking to declare their city the new mecca for hip-hop. The East Coast was robbed of its undisputed heavyweight champion, and Bad Boy needed a new star to retain its dominance. Tapping into his uncanny ability to spin untenable circumstances to his advantage, Combs figured, why not him?

It began with Combs' debut solo album, set for release in July 1997. The project was years in the making, a culmination of Combs' long-mocked habit of embedding himself in his artists' music videos and tracks through ad-libs and intros. After enduring taunts from his rivals, he was determined to prove all those cameos were a prelude to his own long-overdue arrival.

A year earlier, Combs had flown the Hitmen, engineers, and songwriters to paradise in Trinidad and Tobago to pump out tracks for what, tragically, would be Wallace's last album. Getting out of town served two purposes: It forced the team to focus on creating hit tracks, and it offered a respite from the tensions of the escalating hip-hop war back home. For six weeks in spring 1996, Combs took over a compound called the Caribbean Sound Basin, spending $4,000 a day to rent it out. Located twenty minutes from the beach, the facility was outfitted with a pool, a sauna, a gym, and a pool table, but Combs had one small suggestion. "I remember specifically his request to put in a basketball court," laughed the studio's owner, Robert Amar. "Which we did." The island air might have smelled of roti, rum, and seawater, but this was no kick-up-your-feet vacation. This was boot camp. "He had a full crew here and they worked twenty-four hours around the clock," Amar said. "When one man went to sleep, another man went to work." Staying on-site, the Hitmen were expected to pump out as many as four new beats a day. Songs were also being developed for side projects, including Combs' album, as well as tracks that could work for other Bad Boy acts. "He was working on, I would say, maybe fifteen to twenty different artists at the time, as well as his own stuff and Biggie stuff," said Trinidad-based recording engineer Sean Poland.

After Wallace's album was completed, Combs took stock of leftover and unfinished tracks from the Caribbean sessions and began pulling together his own record. The concept was to showcase Combs as a rapper in his own right, though he seemed cognizant of his shortcomings. "Don't worry if I write rhymes, I write checks," he'd later rap on "Bad Boy for Life." His delivery was sometimes monotone, and he was consistently off-key when he tried to carry a chorus. Too weak to carry an entire album on his own, he devised a workaround. Artists from the Bad Boy family were known to make appearances on each other's records, so why not make use of them on his own album? Combs' roster of artists, including a handful of new signees, appeared on almost every one of the seventeen tracks on the album.

Mason "Mase" Betha would be the standout among recent arrivals. With a deliberately slower flow, Mase brought a nonchalant and measured swagger to Bad Boy's brash, in-your-face reputation. It was Bad Boy or bust for the nineteen-year-old, who intercepted Combs at an after-party at an Atlanta rap convention and rhymed for him on the spot. "Puff started doing his dance and everything right in the middle of the dance floor," Mase wrote in his 2003 memoir. "When I was done, it was over. I knew it. He knew it. And the whole club knew it." Combs closed the deal as soon as they were back in New York, sliding a $50,000 check across the table. Mase went straight to the bank, then the studio. There were the Yonkers rappers Jason "Jadakiss" Phillips, Sean "Sheek Louch" Jacobs, and David "Styles P" Styles. Fellow Yonkers native Mary J. Blige caught wind of the trio and shared their demo with Combs. He signed the group on the condition that they shorten their name from the Warlox to the more commercial-friendly the LOX. And with his grit, Black Rob, real name Robert Ross, completed the trifecta of heavy-hitting new rappers on the label.

Combs utilized all three new acts on Puff Daddy and The Family's *No Way Out*, hijacking some of their most promising singles—including Black Rob's "I Love You Baby" and two of the LOX's intended solo numbers, "It's All About the Benjamins" and "I Got the Power"—and sticking them on his own album.

Combs envisioned the album as more than a debut; it was a statement of survival. Particularly his own. It told the story of the hustle and grind, fly guys and good times, and how to persevere through struggle and sorrow. He toyed with naming the album "Puff Daddy & the Goodfellas" and "Hell Up in Harlem," and elements can be heard in the album: the siren-wailing intro where Combs whispers a prayer for protection for his family; gritty rhymes about the life of an uptown hustler; and guest artists referring to Bad Boy as a mafia-esque rap family. ("Puff Daddy & Mase" would have also worked, with Mase perhaps outshining his boss on his own album.) But *No Way Out* stuck because it fit, literally summing up how Combs felt at that juncture: He was a man with nowhere to go but forward.

In that spirit, he leaned into the monumental void Wallace left behind and recorded one of hip-hop's most enduring anthems. In "I'll Be Missing You," built around the iconic bassline guitar melody from the Police's famed "Every Breath You Take," Combs created a reverent tribute to Wallace. Emotional and authentic, Combs lets his guard down to openly grieve alongside widowed Evans, who sings in the bridge of longing and the hope of reunification in an afterlife. The song doesn't particularly showcase Combs' lyrical prowess—but then, rapping was never his strength. His true genius lay in knowing what people needed in a single moment. The mourning hip-hop community was aching for healing, and Combs was offering them a salve. Scrambling to meet the moment, Combs released "I'll Be Missing You" as the album's second single in late May 1997.

Despite a few mixed reviews panning Combs for shamelessly ripping off the British rock band, the song flew to the top of the charts. The momentum snowballed into a hit album, fueled by danceable club tracks "Been Around the World," "It's All About the Benjamins," and "Can't Nobody Hold Me Down." Critics bemoaned Combs' tired practice of sampling from popular seventies and eighties tracks, including David Bowie's "Let's Dance," a cover of Al Green's "Let's Stay Together," and other notable songs, but that did little to stymie fans purchasing the record in droves. Selling 560,000 copies in the first week and nabbing *Billboard*'s number one spot, the album won Combs his first Grammy

Award, picking up Best Rap Album and Best Rap Performance by a Duo or Group.

The magnitude of the moment crystallized at MTV's Video Music Awards that September. Backed by Sting, Evans, 112, and a gospel choir wearing saintly white robes, Combs took center stage to command a crowd of thousands to raise a light in Wallace's honor, receiving a standing ovation. This was the moment Combs had been longing for. In that instant, he wasn't the suited label boss, a producer relegated to the shadows, or Bad Boy's incessant hype man; he was the artist, the one commanding emotion, not orchestrating it from the sidelines. It was the validation he had hungered for since his initial foray in the business, and what he'd envied in the very stars he created.

There wasn't a line Combs was unwilling to cross to secure that sensation of glory. Still in the throes of grief, Evans was against joining Combs onstage. "I did the song," Evans wrote in her memoir, *Keep the Faith*. "I did the video. But I'm not ready for that kind of performance." Combs hounded her as she hid from him at the studio and ignored his nonstop calls until he finally managed to get hold of her through a friend. Even before Evans brought the phone to her ear, she could hear Combs screaming. "You not ready?" he yelled. "What the fuck are you talking about!" He then turned menacing. "Faith, listen to me," he began. "You want to give up on your career? Fine. But you WILL NOT fuck up my shit. DO YOU HEAR ME?" Evans gave in, bottling up her conflicting feelings about Wallace and transforming them into raw emotion on the stage. But she was done with Combs. "I knew in that moment," Evans added, "that something was going to have to change."

Watching Combs soak up the attention, it dawned on Burrowes that few things mattered more to Combs than unadulterated fame and the superlative accolades he was finally receiving. Weeks earlier, Combs had commandeered a New York City studio for a *Rolling*

*Stone* cover shoot. The iconic music magazine was crowning him "The New King of Hip-Hop." In the pictures, Combs stands barechested, glistening with perspiration, his face inexplicably streaked with eye black, typically used by athletes to block out glaring stadium lights. Reminiscent of a similar image of Tupac Shakur, Combs' clothing is minimal: a Chicago White Sox baseball cap, a heavy Issey Miyake coat, crisp white Versace briefs, and a heavy gold Jesus pendant. As he stares into the camera, his face is blank, unreadable—in contrast to B.I.G.'s name handwritten on his chest in bold black letters. Combs seems to take no joy in his coronation, reluctantly accepting the title he is bequeathed after the murder of his best friend. If the King of Brooklyn was going to be a martyr of rap, Combs was taking it upon himself to hold the torch for Wallace's legacy.

It's an arresting visual. But what others interpreted as heartbreak and humility Burrowes read differently. He saw a shrewd, calculated Combs using Wallace's death to elevate himself. Burrowes had tried in vain to convince Combs to give the late rapper that very same cover when *Rolling Stone* approached Bad Boy for the August edition. It would have been the ultimate posthumous honor. "I was telling Sean, 'Let's make it Biggie. You still have a chance [to be on the cover],'" Burrowes said. Combs flatly refused, telling Burrowes, "No, he's dead. I'm putting out Puff Daddy and the Family in July. I need to be on the cover of *Rolling Stone*."

As Combs wept publicly for the man he called his best friend, he was allegedly stonewalling police, refusing to answer their follow-up questions. Combs was also able to silence swirling reports that Wallace had been out the door before his death. "[Wallace] was absolutely about to leave Puff," Bunn said. "I know for a fact [because] he told me that." Wanting to strike out on his own, Wallace planned to helm his own label with his crew, Junior M.A.F.I.A. Wallace had also instructed his lawyers to regain control of his publishing rights, which Combs was fighting tooth and nail to retain. And after Wallace died, Burrowes claimed, Combs tried to alter Wallace's recently renegotiated recording contract by removing an entire section that would reestablish more favorable terms to Combs. Burrowes said he refused to tamper with a dead man's deal and claimed that, in retaliation, Combs fired him by the end of 1997. To Burrowes, it was apparent Combs had been angling for his solo moment, and now that he was securing it, he'd be hard-pressed to give it up. And as time would prove, he wouldn't. Wallace's death propelled Combs to such a height that no future artist on the Bad Boy label would eclipse Combs' all-consuming star power.

---

Combs would usher in a new era for Bad Boy, one filled with shiny suits and a sound that would push hip-hop and the culture surrounding the genre even further into commercial territory. He reinvigorated the label with a fresh slate of signees, including R&B singer Carl Thomas, rappers Mark Curry, G. Dep, Loon, pint-sized tween Jerome Childers, and the rock group Fuzzbubble, and positioned himself as the centerpiece. Combs' entire ethos was about keeping the good times rolling, and by extension, his idea of good music was fun and sexy. Some of the biggest hits he had helped steer—"Big Poppa," "Hypnotize," "Flava in Ya Ear," and "It's All About the Benjamins"—had a lighter tone than raps about life in the streets. The deaths of Wallace and Shakur had turned hip-hop dark with senseless bloodshed, and for his own protection, Combs beefed up his security measures. He was always cautious, but he believed it was time to lighten up and have fun.

It began with Mase, who was preparing to release his debut album, *Harlem World*, in October 1997; Combs wanted him to wear reflective green and silver getups in the music video for the head-bopping lead single, "Feel So Good." Mase protested but ultimately acquiesced. Combs had no qualms about cribbing yet another era's songs, this time Kool & the Gang and Miami Sound Machine, rhetorically asking on the track, "Does Puff drive Mercedes? Take hits from the eighties? But does it sound so crazy?" The rest of the record contains banger after banger, filled with cameos: Lil' Kim, Busta Rhymes, Total, Lil' Cease, Jay-Z, Black Rob, the LOX, and DMX. In its first week, *Harlem World* sold 273,000 copies; before the end of the year, it had gone platinum twice over. Combs was on fire, pulling off a hat trick with three number one albums in a single year. That fall, he set out on his nationwide tour, No Way Out, supported by a crew of familiar faces—the Puff Daddy family—Mase, 112, the LOX, and Black Rob, along with friends of the label Jay-Z, Lil' Kim and Lil' Cease of Junior M.A.F.I.A., Foxy Brown, Busta Rhymes, and teenage crooner Usher.

Combs was promoting good times, but he still was on high alert. Whenever he stepped outside, at least two hulking figures seemed to flank him. Some, like Rob House, had once manned the doors of popular nightclubs Combs frequented. Others, like Damion "D-Roc" Butler and Ruben "Rube" Sandy, came up alongside Wallace in Junior M.A.F.I.A. and were folded into the Bad Boy family. A few had a history with the law or were known to carry firearms, including Anthony "Wolf" Jones and a man who bore the same name as a Bronx heroin kingpin. Security was there to anticipate threats before they happened, but over time, their real job became protecting Combs from himself as his bravado bled into recklessness.

One of the first tour stops was in Cleveland, Ohio, in November 1997. After playing at the Gund Arena, Combs took over a block of rooms at the Ritz-Carlton hotel. The Bad Boy crew partied until the wee hours of the morning, and a married couple, whose room was on the same floor as team Bad Boy, were growing frustrated with their rowdy neighbors as the night dragged on. "It was very loud, running up and down the hallways and just carrying on," the husband recalled. "The room next door to us, it sounded like they were having a dice game, throwing dice against the wall. We just kind of put up with it." The couple tried to ignore the noise, but when what sounded like a fight broke out in the neighboring room, they called down to reception to complain. The wife squinted out of the peephole and listened as an apologetic hotel security staffer told the group to settle down, overhearing him identify their room as the source of the complaint.

"It quieted down and we thought, 'Okay, everything's fine,'" the husband said. "We went to sleep and we were woken up by a loud bang and then something dropping on the floor." Exhausted and assuming that an item on the desk must've fallen, they went back to bed. When the morning light slid through the curtains, they saw a gaping hole in the wall across from their bed. Following a faint trail of drywall residue, the couple discovered a 9mm bullet resting on the floor, right next to where they had been sleeping. "I'm 100 percent sure it was a retaliation for calling a message [to the front desk]," the husband said. If the gun had been aimed just three feet over, "I'd have been shot," he added. "It was right about the level of where my body would have been. It was a pretty upsetting event."

The incident caused commotion at the hotel, a former Ritz-Carlton worker recalled, with everyone gossiping about "Puff Daddy" and the stray bullet. A police report concluded the shot had come from the neighboring suite, which had been booked under the name Paul Offord, Combs' longtime security guard whom everyone called Uncle Paulie. By the time local officers arrived at the Ritz to speak with Combs' camp, the Bad Boy tour buses had peeled off on their way out of town.

Law enforcement some five hundred miles west was also looking to talk to Puff Daddy and the Family. A few days earlier, a private driver had ferried Combs and his security around Moline, Illinois, and Davenport, Iowa, where the group was playing a show on November 10. Hours after finishing her shift, the driver received a series of frantic calls. An unidentified man from Combs' camp wanted her to check the car for something they'd left behind. At first, she found nothing but empty champagne bottles and crumpled sweatshirts. The man kept calling and finally specified that he wanted her to check the drawers under the seat. Inside were two loaded handguns—a Glock 9mm and a Llama .45, both of which police later identified as stolen. The driver ignored the man's demand to ship them to him and called the police instead. And four months later, in Washington, DC, a Westin hotel housekeeper cleaning up after Combs and his posse found another set of handguns: a Sig Sauer 9mm and a Bryco Arms 9mm. Both loaded. Both registered as stolen.

---

As Combs was finishing out his tour, he was simultaneously working with his artists on their projects. In January 1998, he rolled out the LOX's first album, *Money, Power & Respect*, and continued to nurture his R&B acts, with Evans, Total, and 112 all releasing their own albums in the fall. For members of the rock group Fuzzbubble, it was surreal to be signed by the man who basically "owned MTV," leveraged his connections to place their track "Out There" on the *Godzilla* soundtrack in 1998, and spared no expense when it came to their music. "He put us up in a million-dollar house on Mulholland Drive, overlooking [the Los Angeles] skyline," said lead vocalist Mark DiCarlo. "If we wanted this producer, boom, we got whoever we wanted to sing on our album."

Combs was also being tapped to produce tracks for outside artists Jay-Z, Busta Rhymes, Aretha Franklin, R. Kelly, LL Cool

J, Soul for Real, and Boyz II Men. He would become instrumental in helping reshape Mariah Carey's career with the release of *Butterfly* in September 1997, pushing the pure pop vocalist to new heights with an edgier hip-hop soul sound. With the help of Combs-produced tracks like the silky "Honey" and sultry Bone Thugs-n-Harmony collaboration "Breakdown," the album flew to the top of the *Billboard* charts. Carey described it as her "magnum opus" that helped her spread her wings amid her split from her husband and guiding force, Sony Music head Tommy Mottola. She had turned to Combs to produce the album after the success of a "Fantasy" remix they worked on in 1995. The two would generate dating buzz, though it's unclear if anything ever materialized. But in singing Carey's praises, a top *Washington Post* music critic also declared Combs "the godfather of hip-hop soul and the hottest producer in pop music today."

By the end of 1998, Combs had already released a greatest hits compilation, only four years after dropping Bad Boy's first album. Except for Combs, every top Bad Boy artist, including Biggie, had only one song featured on the album. Combs had two. That same year, Combs pushed beyond his typical wheelhouse with the rap-meets-rock song "Come with Me," which was featured on the soundtrack for the *Godzilla* remake. Combs sampled Led Zeppelin's "Kashmir" and somehow convinced guitarist Jimmy Page to play on the orchestral-backed track. To top it off, he began working on his second album, *Forever*, which would feature the likes of Jay-Z, R. Kelly, Nas, and Lil' Kim.

As Combs spotlighted himself and his new crop of artists, it helped obscure those who were no longer working with him. Jodeci shrugged off his absence on their sophomore album *Diary of a Mad Band* in late 1993, blaming it on his ousting from Uptown. Blige had a harder time dodging questions about her professional breakup with Combs when he wasn't listed on a single production credit for her junior album, *Share My World*, in 1997. In fact, Blige had made a clean break from her Uptown beginnings. She ended her turbulent relationship with labelmate and boyfriend, Jodeci's K-Ci; defected from the imprint label to parent company MCA by then; and most glaringly, she cut ties with Combs. She didn't breathe a word of what occurred between them. In an interview about the album with trusted journalist dream hampton for *Vibe*, Blige's publicist warned that any questions about Combs were off-limits. In a roundabout way, hampton still managed to sneak a mention in, relaying that Combs had called Blige the "greatest artist I've ever worked with." Blige was floored. "Puff is family," she said. "He'll always be family, even if I see him at a party and don't speak with him."

Yet even as Bad Boy dominated the charts and as Combs became an in-demand producer, raking in hundreds of millions of dollars while basking in the glow of his celebrity, he wasn't satisfied with the unfathomable success he had created for himself before reaching thirty. He wanted to be even bigger. "I'm not going to go down in history as a black music maker," Combs told *The New York Times*. "I'm going to go down as a music maker that was so incredible that he represented all of culture. You're not going to be able to label me. You can't keep on underestimating me and what I can do. Bad Boy is going to go right up there with 20th Century Fox and DreamWorks. There's no other way."

He wasn't being hyperbolic. Combs admired the likes of real estate developer Donald Trump, Revlon billionaire Ronald Perelman, and family dynasties like the Rockefellers and the Gettys. Instead of being relegated to a specific corner of the entertainment industry, Combs wanted to dominate its entirety. The expansion was rapid. He built out an internal marketing branch, Blue Flame, to handle his label's promotion and event needs. He entered the publishing business, investing in the struggling lifestyle magazine

*Notorious*. On the side, he began plotting with Ralph Lauren alum Jeffrey Tweedy to begin developing what would become a multimillion-dollar clothing and lifestyle brand, Sean John, in 1998. He was eyeing Hollywood, whether for acting, launching a media company, or both. Then there was his upscale soul-food restaurant, Justin's, which opened in the Flatiron District in September 1997. Strategically placed between Midtown business offices and trendy downtown clubs, the entire eatery served as an homage to the billionaire-in-the-making. Diners could sip twelve-dollar fruity "Passion Diddy" martinis or tuck into the "Mogul Combo" appetizer platter. Between bites, guests kept an eye on the front door, through which celebrity artists, Knicks players, and industry titans could breeze in with an entourage. Patrons could also interact with Janice, the de facto maître d', who swanned around the restaurant and graciously accepted compliments for her famous red velvet cake recipe. Combs even thought about becoming a sports agent, going so far as to contact the NFL Players Association, the union that represents professional football players, to find out about its requirements to become a certified representative. Each new venture reflected a different piece of the persona he was cultivating: the tastemaker, the businessman, the visionary, the mogul.

Combs also made sure to give back. In the mid-nineties, he founded Daddy's House Social Programs, a nonprofit that worked to provide inner-city children with educational and recreational resources. There was a free two-week summer camp offering, an annual Christmas and Kwanzaa ball, and Thanksgiving feasts that provided hundreds of meals to homeless families. "We did not create Daddy's House as a way to capture the press, nor were we inclined to use it as a tax write-off," Combs said in 1996. "It's because I was blessed to become so successful that I want to give back to the community as well."

There were a thousand plates spinning at once, yet he didn't let that stop him from enjoying his favorite pastime: being Puff Daddy. No longer was it just his record label or his artists being covered by the media—Combs himself was becoming the story. He was a regular staple in his hometown papers. The *New York Post* dutifully kept readers abreast of which late-night haunt Combs partied at each week and who was spotted on his arm as he left. In a feature about the rowdy antics of the rich and famous in St. Bart's, *The New York Times* mentioned Combs four separate times, relating an anecdote in which supermodel Lauren Hutton helped boot everyone off his chartered yacht and rally the guests to go clubbing. Instead of idolizing industry titans, he was rubbing shoulders with them, partying into the wee hours of the morning with heiress Paris Hilton and supermodel Naomi Campbell. He began hosting an annual "White Party" at his newly purchased $2.45 million East Hamptons waterfront residence in 1998, requiring all attendees to come head to toe in bleached outfits. The parties instantly became legendary; they were where the new faces of hip-hop partied into the early hours alongside a more established Hollywood crowd and industry socialites. A young Leonardo DiCaprio giggled in a cuddle puddle with Combs, while fashion designer Vera Wang and famed *Who Wants to Be a Millionaire?* host Regis Philbin posed for a group photo, and elsewhere magician David Blaine performed a card trick for famously imperious actor-comedian Chevy Chase. With free-flowing champagne, the nights could easily slip into debauchery. At one, a trio of topless women clung to the side of Combs' pool as two poured champagne into a third's mouth. At the same event, a fully clothed Combs poured a bottle of Veuve Clicquot over two semi-naked women.

Combs graced charity events, sat courtside at basketball games, and seemed to be everything, everywhere all at once. He managed to corral a who's who of Hollywood to appear in a video invitation for his twenty-ninth birthday party in 1998. Future president

Donald Trump, Oprah Winfrey, Chris Rock, Mariah Carey, Joan Rivers, Derek Jeter, Will Smith, Danny DeVito, Ellen DeGeneres, Sammy Sosa, and Jennifer Love Hewitt rattled off Combs' many different nicknames to invite guests to the grand event. "Sean, P. Diddy, Puff Pastry, Combs," quipped Ben Stiller. Although Bill Clinton didn't participate in the video, he did send Combs his presidential birthday wishes. "Dear Puff Daddy," the typed note, stamped with Clinton's name, read. "Happy Birthday! Hillary and I send our very best wishes for health and happiness in the coming year."

Combs veered toward becoming a caricature of himself with the incessant attention. Not that he minded. It fed his ever-growing, insatiable ego. His status surpassed anything he could have dreamed of. Not only was he a multimillionaire at the head of a high-profile music label, but he commanded respect from the business world, he was an esteemed celebrity figure, and he had become a staple of the socialite circuit.

Then he began dating Jennifer Lopez.

---

The two began their fling after Combs hired the then-rising Hollywood starlet for his music video for "Been Around the World," the fourth single off his 1997 debut album *No Way Out*. The ten-minute video was ambitious and over the top. Writing the cinematic script himself, Combs portrayed himself as a world-class spy on a top mission to save a beautiful Tunisian princess from a deadly assassin. Combs had written roles for legendary producer and composer Quincy Jones, actress Vivica A. Fox, and artist Wyclef Jean. Lopez was selected to be Combs' leading lady after the success of her starring in *Selena*.

If Combs had ulterior motives for hiring Lopez—he had a track record of using music videos and photo shoots to pursue women he was interested in—he couldn't act upon them. He was with Kim Porter, who was pregnant with their first child. And Lopez had just tied the knot with Ojani Noa, a Cuban waiter-turned-restaurateur, in February 1997. But when Lopez quietly divorced Noa in early 1998, Combs sidelined Porter in favor of the rising superstar. "Puff came at me hard," Lopez would later say. "He said he looked at me and fell in love and made me love him, too." A few weeks after Porter gave birth to their son, Christian, Combs and Lopez were caught by the tabloids allegedly doing some X-rated canoodling on the sandy shores of Palm Beach. He began referring to her as "honey," and sightings of the suspected lovebirds became too frequent to ignore, though they swore they were strictly friends.

They still continued to play coy when Lopez posed seminude for Combs' recently acquired *Notorious* magazine in fall 1999. On the cover, her toned body is framed by feathery white wings, and her skin is slick with oil. "The Angel Bares All to Puff Daddy," the headline declared. Combs interviewed Lopez for the cover story, speeding past her string of blockbuster movies and her pivot into music with her smash debut album, *On the 6*, for which Combs helped produce the track "Feelin' So Good" (featuring Big Pun and Fat Joe), to spend a significant portion of the conversation shamelessly flirting. He prodded her to divulge secrets about her sex life, like whether she would have a threesome with two men and if she preferred her lovemaking "rough" or "passionate." He drooled over her "beautiful ass" and wondered if she'd ever give him a kiss. Lopez entertained it all, and at the close of the conversation, both, in a juvenile puppy-love manner, admitted they "liked" each other.

It was catnip for the press. The paparazzi and gossip columnists were relentless in their coverage of Hollywood's newest power couple. Lopez was the sweet, giggly beauty from the Bronx, and Combs was hip-hop's resident bad boy. The attention he got from being linked to Lopez was different from the fame Combs was accustomed to. After nearly a decade in the public eye, he had hardened himself against its glare. He survived scoldings over his scandals and lawsuits tied to deaths. A legion of fans—as well as haters—constantly weighed in on the music he and his artists were making. And Combs smiled through gritted teeth as he threw open the passenger door of his baby-blue Bentley and allowed skeptical magazine writers to trail him for a weekend. His romance with Lopez had nothing to do with any of that. A simple outing would generate its own cycle of press, their photo splashed on front pages of checkout aisle magazines. It was what he craved: the public's eyes firmly trained on him, and for something as innocuous as his love life.

But beneath the celebrity gloss, Combs had met his match. Lopez was as competitive, relentless, and ambitious as he was, hungry to expand her career to its utmost height. Both were perfectionists, passionate and headstrong. They hailed from similar backgrounds, with working-class parents who nurtured their talents and prioritized their education, enrolling them in Catholic high schools in the Bronx. There were some obvious differences. Combs was the nightlife maestro; Lopez was more of a homebody, rarely a drinker and never a smoker. He had a constant rotation of faces coming in and out of his entourage; Lopez kept her clique tight. But they meshed when it came to the draw of the spotlight and their ability to command attention. In their own ways, they were addicted to love. Their relationship, like so many for Combs, was tumultuous, filled with massive, blowout fights and dramatic makeups.

As Combs and Lopez explored Paris, romped on beaches in Florida, and hit red carpets and Oscar parties, Porter was left at home with a baby Christian and an eight-year-old Quincy, her son from her previous relationship with Al B. Sure! No matter how hard Combs tried to deny the obvious, even claiming Lopez was a showmance meant for publicity, Porter was no one's fool.

Refusing to be the weepy, wounded woman, she resolved to teach Combs a lesson. She changed the locks of her Manhattan home, though Combs continued to stop by unannounced and phoned her incessantly—sometimes more than fifty times in a single day. Even when Porter decamped to Georgia to be with family, Combs was undeterred. "It was like my life was not my own," Porter described of the period. "He was very, very intrusive."

Combs spent the duration of his relationship with Lopez bouncing between the star and Porter, insisting to each that it was her he truly loved. It was a messy affair, and he roped his personal team into helping him juggle the two women. "It was definitely a game of trying to keep the one from finding out about the other," said one administrative team member. Combs reveled in the chaos of two beautiful women feuding over him. It was torturous for them. Porter threw a small television at Combs in a fit of anger, and Lopez once furiously banged on hotel doors trying to catch Combs cheating. "I never caught him, but I just knew," she said. "He'd say he was going to a club for a couple of hours and then never come back that night."

Years later, in a single interview, Combs casually let slip two fundamental truths about how he viewed relationships and the power he wanted to exert over his partners. Things weren't working with Porter because she "wasn't really conforming to how I wanted her to conform," and Lopez was able to massage his ego in ways Porter wouldn't. When Combs struggled to justify himself further, he spluttered, "Do you really think that God meant for a man to have just one wife?" In Combs' view, he believed in complete freedom for himself and humble submission from his girlfriends.

Even when they were together, Lopez was reluctant to divulge too much about her relationship with Combs. She wanted to maintain privacy, but what she did disclose of their private lives suggested a deep love between the pair, though it was turbulent.

The two were never married, but Combs would threaten Lopez with divorce, their bond so intense it felt like they had a legal commitment. "It's a lot," Lopez told *Rolling Stone* in 2001. "He'll say, 'So, where do I send the papers?'" In later years, Lopez confessed that she was "totally crying, crazy and going nuts" over the tailspin of their two years together, while being constantly paranoid that Combs was cheating on her. In her 2014 memoir *True Love*, she alluded to enduring forms of abuse, though she never mentioned a partner by name. "I've never gotten a black eye or a busted lip," Lopez wrote. "[But] I know what it feels like for your soul to be diminished by the way your loved one is treating you. . . . Maybe it's a push, a shove, or a nasty word that stays with you. The scars might not be visible, but they run just as deep."

Throughout their on-and-off two years together, Combs' temperamental and possessive behavior would flare up often. He had considerable sway when it came to how Lopez dressed. Though he had not attended the Oscars before, he gave input on Lopez's gown for the 1999 show. He accompanied her to dress fittings, approving a strapless black tiered Badgley Mischka gown for the red carpet. At the 2000 Video Music Awards, Lopez was a walking advertisement for his new fashion line, wearing a bedazzled white crop top with sequins spelling out *Sean John* across her chest. People in their circle at the time recalled Combs being aggressive with Lopez, speaking harshly to her, and sometimes manhandling her when she shot back a fiery response to him. Daddy's House manager Felicia Newsome recalled once walking into the studio's lounge to discuss business with Combs, who was with Lopez. In the middle of their discussion, Combs snatched Lopez's cell phone from her hand and hurled it at the wall, never breaking the conversation with Newsome, as the device clattered to the floor. An unflinching Lopez was silent.

He was often jealous, and the green-eyed monster reared its head frequently. In the early hours of Halloween morning in 1999, Lopez was chatting with a fashion publicist when, without warning, Combs allegedly punched the man in the head, flattening him to the ground. He had a similar hotheaded reaction when he learned Lopez had received an array of flowers from singer-songwriter Marc Anthony, whom she had met during his run on Broadway in *The Capeman* in 1998 and would later marry. The bouquet sent Combs into a rage. "Puff was triggered," a source with knowledge of the event said. A seething Combs threw himself into his chauffeured car with a pistol on his lap. His trusted personal driver weaved through the jam-packed streets of New York City while Combs plotted how best to send a clear message to Anthony that Lopez was off-limits. Fortunately, he never reached Anthony; a distraught Lopez begged her impassioned boyfriend to calm down. Eventually, Combs relented.

---

Come spring 1999, Combs felt unstoppable, emboldened enough to barge into the Midtown offices of Interscope Records music executive Steve Stoute, looking to confront his well-respected peer. Combs' anger stemmed from his appearance in the Hype Williams–directed music video for "Hate Me Now," by rapper Nas. Between shots of the men rapping on top of a bodega, they played biblical martyrs, lugging heavy wooden crosses before being crucified in front of a jeering crowd. Combs reportedly insisted on being part of the crucifixion scene, a crown of thorns crushed into his head. But after speaking with some religious leaders, Combs got cold feet, and days before the video was set to premiere on *Total Request Live*, he phoned Stoute—who was also Nas' manager—with instructions to cut him from the scene. Combs believed it was a done deal—that is, until he watched MTV broadcast the unedited video on April 15.

Stoute was in the middle of a meeting when Combs stormed into his office, trailed by two hulking associates. Without warning, Combs punched Stoute in the face and bashed a corded phone over his head until the executive crumpled to the floor. The assault continued, with Combs and his lackeys taking turns kicking him and cracking a chair over his body. Finally satisfied, Combs flipped over Stoute's desk as he left. "I was lying there on the floor bleeding," Stoute told the *Los Angeles Times*. "My jaw and my head were all swollen. I couldn't move my arm. It was a traumatic experience, and in the middle of it, I didn't know exactly how to feel. I was upset. Embarrassed. Scared. Angry. As far as I'm concerned, this was an attempt on my life. The only reason I'm not dead is because they missed."

Stoute went to the police, leading to Combs' arrest for felony assault and criminal mischief, charges that carried a seven-year prison sentence. Although Combs reportedly took six weeks to apologize by reaching out privately, Stoute was holding firm, adamant that Combs should face consequences. "If this kind of behavior is allowed to go unpenalized, it'll be like an invitation for extortion in the music business," Stoute added to the *Los Angeles Times*. "If somebody can get away with walking into the headquarters of the world's biggest record company and beating up a senior executive over a disagreement, I guarantee you this is going to be a great business for criminals to thrive in."

It took only two months for Stoute to have a change of heart. Combs issued a public apology, saying he was "extremely sorry" and that he took full responsibility. "I messed up," Combs said. "It's nobody's fault but my own. I'm not apologizing so that I won't go to jail or so I won't get sued. I've told Steve I'm truly sorry, and

I mean it." Even still, the mea culpa was padded with some self-justification, and Combs claimed the press "distorted a lot of what happened that day," despite Stoute going on record in multiple interviews with a play-by-play of the events. The apology—and the reported $500,000 out-of-court, private settlement—moved Stoute to ask the Manhattan district attorney's office to drop the case altogether in June. Meanwhile, Combs was in the middle of a media tour for *Forever.* During a stop in Detroit in August, Combs flew off the handle at cable TV host Roger Mills, who had asked Combs to comment on the lingering allegations that he had contributed to Wallace's death. Combs took "immediate and extreme umbrage and terminated the interview," according to Mills' lawyer, and a member of Combs' team tried to buy the unflattering tape from Mills, who declined. When the payout was rejected, Combs decided to switch tactics. He allegedly had his entourage go after Mills; they roughed the host up and physically took the tape, destroying Mills' camera in the process. (Police never arrested Combs over the incident, and Mills lost a subsequent lawsuit he filed against Combs, a jury finding no assault and battery had occurred.)

In September, the charges against Combs in the Stoute case were downgraded to a harassment violation. Combs pleaded guilty and walked away with no jail time, no fine, and importantly, no criminal record. At the hearing, a surly Combs pleaded guilty to the violation and was ordered to attend one day of anger management training. Before Combs departed the courtroom, on his way to a charity event, the judge asked Combs if he happened to remember him. "Can't say I do," came Combs' reply. The judge reminded him that they had met years earlier during the investigation into Combs' role in the deadly 1991 stampede at the City College of New York.

Things reached a crescendo in the early hours of December 27, 1999, when a spontaneous change in Combs' holiday plans ended with him making panicked calls from a New York City police station in the early hours of the morning. The holiday weekend had seemed nondescript, brimming with the usual festivities and errands. Combs spent Christmas Day playing Santa Claus, dropping off gifts for his son Justin in Westchester County and paying rapper Lil' Kim a thirty-minute visit in New Jersey. Then he caught a movie with Lopez and her manager Benny Medina at an Upper East Side theater. That night, Combs, Lopez, and Janice took a helicopter out to Combs' home in East Hampton. The lovebirds had been in the quiet, beachside town for less than twenty-four hours before they got bored and decided over dinner that they were in the mood for some fun. Aware of an industry party at Club New York in Times Square, Combs hired a Hamptons limo service to whisk him and Lopez into the city. It was meant to be a speedy outing; the couple were due back in the Hamptons in the morning to fly out to St. Barts, where Combs had chartered a yacht for the couple to ring in the New Year. "Seemed like a good idea at the time," Combs would later testify.

Arriving in the city shortly after midnight, Combs linked up with his massive entourage at Daddy's House before the group headed to the nightclub. Although the club had metal detectors, Combs' posse, which included his most trusted bodyguard Anthony "Wolf" Jones, breezed past security and were escorted to the roped-off VIP section. Among the night's attendees was twenty-one-year-old Jamal "Shyne" Barrow, one of Bad Boy's most promising acts. Even without a single track out, word of his rich baritone delivery had spread from his local barbershop to Combs, who signed Barrow to a reported million-dollar deal in 1998. Having immigrated with his mother from Belize to Crown Heights, Brooklyn, when he was seventeen, Barrow got tired of the living room doubling as his bedroom in their cramped apartment. He began running with a local gang to relieve his boredom and to scrounge up extra cash. After sustaining a gnarly gunshot wound from a fight, Barrow kept his nose clean, graduating from high school and writing poems that would transform into raps. Combs adopted Barrow into the Bad Boy family, taking him under his wing and hyping him up as the future of the label. When Combs called up his crew about his plans to swing by Club New York, Barrow tagged along.

Combs and Lopez spent the next few hours drinking champagne and dancing. Shortly before 3:00 a.m., they were ready to call it a night. They snaked their way through the crowd of sweaty, intoxicated bodies, and Combs, who was in high spirits, greeted fans and dapped up men who outstretched a hand to him. As the group rounded the venue's large circular bar, someone physically bumped into Matthew "Scar" Allen, a known Brooklyn hothead with a considerable rap sheet. Allen was upset that a drink had spilled on him and, seeing an apparent lack of remorse from Combs' camp, kicked off. "Who the fuck do you think you are," he began shouting in Combs' direction, witnesses testified. "You're not the only nigger with money. Other people have money, too! I'll see you. I'll see you!" Pulling a fistful of cash out of his pocket, Allen flung twenty-, fifty-, and hundred-dollar bills in Combs' direction, people diving for the money as it scattered on the ground.

After that moment, eyewitnesses' accounts varied. Several clubgoers testified that they saw both Barrow and Combs flash guns that had been tucked away in their waistbands. Combs said he instinctively dropped to the floor. Undisputably, pandemonium broke out as the sound of gunshots ripped through the packed club. Attendees dove to the ground and rushed for the exits. Three people were left lying bleeding on the nightclub's sticky floor. Divorced mother of two Natania Reuben had a bullet tear through her nose. City Parks worker Julius Jones was left with a bullet lodged in his shoulder, resulting in permanent nerve damage in one of his arms.

And Robert Thompson of Connecticut sustained a graze wound to the shoulder.

Seconds after the shots went off, Barrow sprinted out the front entrance, running smack into two New York police officers who were out on patrol when they heard the gunfire and made a beeline for the club. Locking eyes with one of the officers, Barrow attempted to change course, ducking right and nearly running straight into an oncoming car. The officer tackled Barrow to the pavement and found a gun; they placed the twenty-one-year-old under arrest.

Police also arrested Combs, Anthony "Wolf" Jones, and Combs' personal driver on gun possession charges following a high-speed police chase through the streets of Manhattan. A sobbing Lopez was also caught up in the nightmare scenario, spending a rough fourteen hours in jail—during which she was handcuffed to a bench—before being released around 4:00 p.m. the following day. She bolted from the precinct alone, dodging reporters as she was spirited away in a waiting town car. "They established she did nothing wrong," her rep said. "Jennifer had nothing to do with the gun or the shooting."

The men weren't so lucky. Police had found an unregistered gun in the car and demanded that someone fess up to owning it. Finally, officials gave up, and all three men were arraigned on weapons charges. By the time Combs left the courthouse around 10:00 p.m., a crowd had gathered. Jostling reporters and photographers thrust cameras and microphones in Combs' face as he prepared to make his first statement. "I do not own a gun. I do not carry a gun," Combs swore. "The charges and allegations against me are 100 percent false. I am confident in the next couple of days I'll be vindicated." Combs' denial was absolute, spoken with a certainty that projected innocence.

But buried in reports from precincts and police stations across the country, a different story sat gathering dust, one that documented a yearslong pattern of firearms accompanying Combs wherever he went. Given this paper trail, Combs knew that if the nightclub shooting case went to trial, he'd have to face his history head-on. For now, denial was his only move. The day after his release, Combs tried to reclaim the narrative. At a press conference inside the W Hotel in Manhattan, he sat beside his attorney Harvey Slovis. Toned down in a simple Sean John pullover sweater, Combs repeated the same line he'd delivered outside the courthouse: "I do not own a gun, nor did I possess a gun that night." But as soon as he left the stage, he needed to fix a big problem. Someone had seen him that night with a gun: his new driver.

---

Wardel Fenderson had been working for Combs for only three months when he found himself in the middle of a nightmare scenario. He'd gotten the temporary gig through an acquaintance, Combs' regular weekend chauffeur, who was recovering from medical treatment and needed a trustworthy fill-in. With three children and the holidays around the corner, Fenderson was glad for the extra $250 per shift.

Fenderson had spent Christmas Day chauffeuring Combs as he dropped off presents like Santa Claus. The following night, he was spending time with his nineteen-year-old daughter when around 9:30 p.m. his peace was interrupted. Combs was headed back to the city, and Fenderson was being called back into work. He jumped into the shower and had Combs' Lincoln Navigator idling outside the Daddy's House recording studio by 11:30 p.m. Fenderson recalled there being a warning in this interim before everyone headed to the club: a glint of metal poking out of Combs' waistband. "What in God's name is he doing holding a gun?" a startled Fenderson thought after catching a view of the firearm out of the corner of his eye.

Fenderson ferried the crew to the club and parked nearby to wait. The next few hours went by without event, and Fenderson passed the time in his typical fashion, listening to music and flipping through the newspaper. Around 2:45 a.m., now in the early hours of December 27, Fenderson received an update that Combs was wrapping up his night and it was time to pull the SUV around to the entrance. Moments later, terrified club goers burst through the doors, screaming. "They are shooting, they are shooting!"

The chaos continued inside the Navigator. Combs, Lopez, and Jones all piled into the car, screaming for Fenderson to start the car as Lopez kept repeating, "Shyne busted off! Shyne busted in the air!" Fenderson didn't need any further prompting. "I hit it," Fenderson said. "We're out of here." Within moments, police were on their tail, and a chase ensued. Fenderson recalled feeling like he was on autopilot as the car jumped a curb and blew past nearly a dozen red lights. Over loudspeaker, an officer demanded that they pull over. It was "like something out of a movie," Fenderson said. "It was just pure chaos. There was a panic, frenzy situation. They are screaming, 'Don't stop, don't stop, keep going!'"

Amid the bedlam and wailing sirens, Combs and Jones frantically began asking Fenderson if he knew how to open a secret compartment in the car. Unbeknownst to him, the luxury vehicle had been outfitted with two hidden safes, accessible only by an intricate switch combination: Twiddle the radio knob, rotate the car's temperature controls clockwise and counterclockwise, hit the rear window defogger, and then pull the front driver's seat lever, and ta-da, the safe doors would spring open. But Fenderson was new on the job and hadn't been filled in on the hidden vaults, let alone the complicated combo.

As Fenderson whipped through the city, Jones tried to open

the safe, grabbing the steering wheel from Fenderson, who spied a gun peeking out of Jones' waistband. At another point, Fenderson believed he saw one of the car's back windows roll down. (A driver for an escort company would later testify that while sipping coffee and patiently waiting for a client to finish up at a hotel with a john, he saw the Navigator fly past him and an object tossed from the speeding vehicle, which clanged against his bumper. It was a Smith & Wesson handgun, which was turned over to the police.)

The Navigator made it more than ten blocks north before a police car pulled out in front of the vehicle on Fifty-Fourth Street. "My exact words were 'Chase is over, I'm stopping,'" Fenderson recalled. Surrounded by officers with their guns drawn, the group exited the car and were frisked and handcuffed. Officers found a gun on the floor of the passenger seat. In those immediate moments, Combs was "formulating a plan" to have Fenderson take the fall, automatically ruling himself and Lopez out. Jones also couldn't cop to owning the gun; his previous criminal record all but guaranteed that he would have to serve time if he made the confession. At the precinct, Combs slyly approached Fenderson, careful to make sure the officers didn't notice. "Mr. Combs then turns to me and whispers in a hush tone," Fenderson said. "His exact words were, 'I will give you $50,000 to say the gun was yours.'" More than a dozen times in various holding cells, Fenderson claimed, both Combs and Jones pressured him to tell officials the gun belonged to him. At one point, Combs slipped off a diamond pinky ring, which had been a birthday gift from Lopez, and offered it to Fenderson. "He told me, says, 'Yo, dog, this ring is worth $300,000. I will give you this as collateral if you don't think I'm good for the money,'" Fenderson claimed.

At first Fenderson thought $50,000 was a reasonable offer, and he reluctantly agreed to say the gun belonged to him. He called over an officer to make the admission; then he told a second officer the same thing. But once he was separated from Combs and Jones, Fenderson started to absorb the gravity of the situation. "I'm thinking to myself, 'Well, you make $50,000 a year. Chances are, you cop to this gun you're not going to have that job anymore, you're going to have a felony criminal record.' And, $50,000 at that point for one day's work did not seem like it was worth all of the trouble," Fenderson said. "And I'm saying to myself, he said the gun was clean. How do I know that? How do I know that two years later, somebody doesn't surface in the swamp in Louisiana, and the ballistics match the gun that you already pleaded guilty to? So at that point, I'm like, I can't take this gun." (In fact, the gun had been reported stolen from Georgia in August.) Fenderson beckoned an officer over and walked back his statement, pleading with the officials not to inform Combs and Jones of the retraction.

After a few hours, all three men were transported via a police van to central booking downtown at 100 Centre Street and arraigned on gun charges. By 10:30 p.m., Fenderson walked free alongside Jones and Combs, his $10,000 bond posted by Bad Boy's CFO Derek Ferguson. Combs made a beeline toward the press, and Fenderson got into a limousine with Jones. He knocked back Rémy Martin cognac and shared "good bud" with Jones, never disclosing he had changed his mind about being the fall guy back at the precinct. He'd wait for the following day to share that information from the comfort of his own home.

Combs did his best to bring him back into the fold, summoning him to his Park Avenue residence, but it was a brief visit: Fenderson wouldn't budge. Combs unleashed his network of staffers to apply pressure to Fenderson, who held firm, ignoring well over a dozen messages from various callers. Eventually, on December 30, Combs called himself. "Hi yo, it's P. I was just thinking about you, dog," a stammering Combs told an answering machine. "Just hit me on my cell 'cause I'm just concerned [about the] news you hit me with earlier. . . . I just want to make you feel, like, comfortable, you know what I'm saying, make your family feel comfortable." Fenderson listened to the message with a tape recorder in hand. Accompanied by an attorney and the recording, Fenderson headed to the district attorney's office on January 3.

The following month, Combs was in sunny Los Angeles preparing for the forty-second annual Grammy Awards. He was up for Best Rap Performance by a Duo or Group for his song with R. Kelly, "Satisfy You." Lopez was also nominated for the first time, anxious to see if her club hit "Waiting for Tonight" would take home Best Dance Recording. It was primed to be a big night. Combs and Lopez were poised to make their splashiest red-carpet appearance together as a couple, effectively killing gossip that they were on the outs in the wake of the nightclub shooting. Hours before Lopez made fashion history by wearing a sheer plunging tropical-print Versace dress—a gown so instantly iconic that it directly inspired the invention of Google Images—Combs was informed that there was news for him back in New York. Prosecutors had just charged him with bribery.

---

Instead of shrinking away from the spotlight in the year leading up to the criminal trial, Combs took center stage. Any absence could leave room for a counternarrative to emerge or risked looking like an admission of wrongdoing. So, he fully embraced his relationship with Lopez, walking more red carpets with her. He forged ahead with his international tour for *Forever* in 2000, making stops across Europe. "I think that in spite of his odds, he kept to himself, but he let go of himself in the music," said Tierra Brown, whose girl group Four Colourz was one of the tour's opening acts. "I feel like that tour was his therapy." During a stop in Vienna, Austria, he met nineteen-year-old Kathi Steininger, a budding television journalist, at an after-party hosted at a nearby nightclub. Steininger managed to get him to agree to an interview, and as the night wound down, Combs led Steininger back to his tour bus, since the club was too loud to talk on camera. The interview never happened. The cameraman was told to hang back, and Steininger alleged that once they were on the bus, Combs gave her a spiked drink and assaulted her. She wound up in the Netherlands, still on the bus as it continued to the next stop on the tour, where, she alleged, she was given another spiked drink, this time a disorienting concoction handed to her by one of Combs' bodyguards. Later she was dropped off at the airport with an envelope of cash and Combs' number scribbled on a piece of paper.

Stranded without her passport, Steininger said she had to obtain emergency documentation from the Austrian embassy in Amsterdam and endured a hellish multiday journey home. "I felt worthless," she said. Steininger went on to have a successful career as a TV anchor in Austria, but "that's how it still feels, and that's how it keeps on feeling." She saved a newspaper clipping of a review of the concert, in which a small photo shows her talking with Combs, as well as Combs' note, a taxi driver's card, and stationery from an Amsterdam hotel as corroboration of the ordeal. "I didn't say anything for a long time," Steininger added. "[But] I know what this man is capable of."

Privately, Combs was a nervous wreck. The gun and bribery charges carried a fifteen-year prison sentence, but the shooting had also brought attention to the disparate and buried incidents that involved firearms in Combs' past. Officials in Las Vegas, as well as the feds, were reportedly quietly investigating Combs, his security chief Paul Offord, and Bad Boy as a company for alleged ties with criminal organizations, including street gangs and an underground gun supply network. (An investigation into Combs and a weapons probe were never formally announced.) He began self-medicating, abusing painkillers he had been prescribed after a surgery in 2000. He hired the country's top defense attorneys: famed civil rights lawyer Johnnie Cochran, who became a household name for helping O. J. Simpson walk free after his own criminal trial in 1995, and the notoriously tough Benjamin Brafman, who later represented Michael Jackson. They didn't come cheap. "He just went into immediate liquidation mode," said Kevin Rogers Francis, who worked at Justin's restaurant and *Notorious*. "One of the first casualties was the magazine." By February, the publication paused its print edition, and freelancers were complaining of missed paychecks. At some points, Justin's would also miss payroll.

Acting like a man on borrowed time, Combs began ticking off items on his bucket list. He landed a role in the crime comedy *Made* after losing out on a part a year earlier to Jamie Foxx in *Any Given Sunday*. He also got back to work: Bad Boy artists who had been languishing on the back burner while Combs prioritized himself finally received the green light for their albums. R&B singer Carl Thomas, who signed to the label in 1997 and consistently served on backup duty for other Bad Boy artists, released his debut album, *Emotional*, in April 2000. Black Rob put out *Life Story* in March 2000, after hanging around the crew since 1996. Shyne also put out his much-anticipated self-titled first album.

Tensions around the Bad Boy office were at an all-time high, according to former staffers. Combs was trying to juggle too many things at once: signing new acts, preparing for trial, managing the Sean John line, and prioritizing his relationship with Lopez. The new millennium had brought a wave of change to Bad Boy's doorstep, and Combs was distracted. The public's music tastes were shifting toward pop with Britney Spears and dance-pop with a touch of R&B with NSYNC and the Backstreet Boys. Hip-hop and rap were branching into rock sounds, with the arrival of Eminem, Linkin Park, and Limp Bizkit. Digital music also arrived, which would decimate the CD and vinyl record industry in the coming years.

Seeing the writing on the wall, some artists began to leave the label. Bad Boy's second-biggest star, Mase, had already abruptly walked away from the music industry at the peak of his fame in April 1999. Disgusted by his hedonistic lifestyle, Mase turned his back on a multimillion-dollar record deal to become an ordained pastor in Atlanta. Mase likened his search for salvation to Moses fleeing Egypt, and Combs to the hardened Pharaoh, unwilling to allow his investment to walk away. Mase hoped his departure would serve as a wake-up call for Combs. "God was removing all these people from him to get his attention," Mase wrote in his memoir *Revelations: There's a Light After the Lime*, tallying up the artists who left Bad Boy and the tragedies that kept befalling Combs. "In the process of me telling him to let the people go, I realized that some of the people didn't want to be free, they were happy living in Egypt. They were happy smoking and drinking. They thought they were happy living that lifestyle. . . . You can't stay around the devil's work and say it won't affect you."

The rock group Fuzzbubble also departed. They had an album ready to hit shelves, but Combs wouldn't sign off on a release two years after they had signed with Bad Boy. It came down to two things, according to lead singer Mark DiCarlo: Combs and his team were out of their depth managing a rock act, and Combs was increasingly distracted by his personal life and spin-off ventures. "He's doing a gazillion things," DiCarlo explained. "I guess we became less of a priority." When the group finally pressed Combs, their boss shrugged. "Do what you gotta do" was his response, and Fuzzbubble was released from their contract in 2000. The band shopped their album around, but no label would bite. They ultimately secured a distributor in the Orchard and put the record out on their own. The record brought in nonexistent numbers, and after their 2002 album, *Demos, Out-takes and Rarities*, the group disbanded. Soul singer Tanya Blount Trotter left the same year. She had signed with Combs in 1996, but the momentum she'd built with her poignant duet "His Eye Is on the Sparrow" with Lauryn Hill in *Sister Act 2: Back in the Habit* and her breakthrough 1994 single "Through the Rain" had petered out after four years with the label. Combs had brought Trotter to Bad Boy because he had plans to release "Thank You," a contemporary R&B gospel album that never saw the light of day. Trotter spent years writing for other Bad Boy artists and featuring on other various projects, while plans for her own album stalled, prompting her departure. (In some cases, the departures had nothing to do with Combs at all. At nine years old, Jerome Childers became the youngest signee to Bad Boy in 1996, but after suffering a nervous breakdown on the set for his music video for "Dear Yvette," he left the label around 1998. "I was treated with a lot of kindness and respect from all the people that were there," he said.)

Eventually, trial day arrived on a frigid Monday morning on January 29, 2001. Combs' well-oiled team acted like they were at war and every arena was a battlefield. Cochran and Brafman were bulldogs in pretrial filings and in front of the jury, and Combs' hovering publicists whispered with quote-hungry reporters in echoing court hallways, feeding them background material and maintaining the narrative that Combs was innocent. Combs packed the courtroom with his famous friends, including Russell Simmons, Faith Evans, and model Tyson Beckford. According to two Bad Boy employees, he also required his staffers to show their support by taking shifts in court, spending tedious days on the court's hard wooden benches. "Most of us didn't want to be there," said one four-year Bad Boy employee. "Every day they would pick a different department, and they'd be like, 'Okay, so today marketing is going, [and] all the marketing staff had to go down to the court and show solidarity towards him, so he could be like 'See, my staff is here. I'm such a wonderful person.'"

One constant face in the courtroom pews was Janice Combs. At sixty, she was still every bit as glamorous as she'd been in her youth, often wearing bright blond or auburn wigs and, at times, piercing ice-blue contact lenses that gave her a Lil' Kim–like look. Over the years, the mother and son remained extremely close, and Janice often appeared on Combs' arm at red-carpet functions. At New York social events, she schmoozed with the likes of Paris Hilton and Drew Barrymore's mother, Jaid; and at Kimora Lee Simmons' Baby Phat fashion show in 2000, Janice strutted down the runway with two of her miniature Yorkies.

Combs had a sense of loyalty to Janice, even naming one of his affiliated Bad Boy companies after her: Janice Combs Publishing. (Incorporation documents from 1997 list Combs as the sole president and the sole owner of the venture.) Eternally grateful for her sacrifices in his youth, Combs loosely employed her, supported her short-lived artist management group, and proudly declared that he had made her a millionaire. But by the late nineties, Combs seemed to be slowly pushing Janice away and diminishing her role in the day-to-day business of Bad Boy.

There was a period, particularly from the 1990s to early 2000s, when Combs "didn't seem to respect her," said one associate who was in Janice's orbit. Perhaps it was a lingering grudge from a fight that caused Combs to move in with Andre Harrell in 1990, but one associate said, "My sense is that she was a tool whenever she needed to be seen." In early 1999, Janice was still living in the same Mount Vernon home where Combs had grown up, while he snapped up a sprawling estate near the beach in East Hampton, purchased a family-friendly mansion in New Jersey, acquired a massive Park Avenue building, and plunked down $3 million for a Beverly Hills home. There wasn't a trace of Combs in the well-maintained Mount Vernon house's main living areas, said an associate who visited and found it strange that Combs was a ghost in his childhood home. He was missing from the bulk of the family photos on display, and his belongings, including his First Communion photos and a Video Music Awards Moonman that Combs had gifted to Janice, were piled into a spare room in the basement.

Janice had her own ways of keeping herself occupied. Every day, she'd drive down into Harlem and pay visits to various businesses, always keeping a stack of cash in her purse. "Miss Combs is Harlem," the associate said. "All the numbers runners knew her. She's like the queen. There's no other way to say it. She ran that." In 2001, she opened her own soul-food joint, Mama Duke—named after her late mother—in Brooklyn's Prospect Heights neighborhood. Whatever rift had come between her and Combs had healed by December 1999, when Janice tagged along on Combs' Hamptons jaunt with Lopez shortly before the shooting. When a *New York Times* journalist stopped by to interview Janice while her son's criminal trial was underway, Janice was living in a waterfront condo in New Jersey, employing a formally dressed maid, her home dotted with photos of Combs. "Sean has manners, he knows the right thing to do," Janice told the reporter, confident Combs would beat the case. "I can pat myself on the back; I can pat anything on me."

Combs was playing his part, as well. Ever the showman, he reminded the world what was at stake for him. He turned up to court wearing his own Sean John gear, signed autographs for adults and children alike, and waved to fans who wore "Free Puffy" shirts and brought signs. He tugged off his chunky diamond studs before the jury was brought in and frequently spent his downtime thumbing through a well-worn Bible. Midway through the trial, as more witnesses claimed they had seen Combs with a gun, his public relations team decided to hijack the headlines.

After weeks of rampant speculation, they confirmed that Combs and Lopez had split—on Valentine's Day no less. The blame was placed squarely on Lopez, a source telling the *New York Post* that her manager Benny Medina and the rest of her team had gotten in her ear. "Deep down, she loves Puffy," the source dished. "This breakup is what everyone in her camp wanted. They thought it was best for her career."

It was a full-scale blitz from every direction. Combs was deploying his entire arsenal of charisma, wealth, and powerful connections to execute both a media and a courtroom strategy. Prosecutors alleged that there were also shadowy bribery attempts and suspicious contact with key witnesses, including the instigator of the nightclub shooting, Matthew "Scar" Allen, who had vanished from New York in the weeks after the altercation. (A spooked Allen quickly took off to Maryland after Combs reportedly intercepted him at a party and delivered a coded message that he understood as an offer of a payoff.) Although Allen was not called to testify, when his handwritten statement, which claimed that he had witnessed Combs and Barrow fire their weapons, was read into the trial record, Combs shook his head in disgust.

Assistant District Attorney Matthew Bogdanos knew what he was up against and baked it into his prosecutorial strategy. He positioned the shooting victims, as well as the government, as the underdog, the biblical David going up against the fearsome Goliath. He chose to try the case solo, sitting alone before the jury, in stark contrast to Combs, who was rolling several lawyers deep. Before the trial commenced, Bogdanos accused Combs of "playing the media like an instrument for a decade" and spinning the narrative in his favor. "There are people who believe that they can use money, power, influence and benefits to change testimony," Bogdanos would emphasize in his closing arguments.

Behind the scenes, the case wasn't precisely shaping up to be what the prosecution had hoped for. As Combs' attorneys feigned outrage at what they described as the ludicrous suggestion that a man of such status would be associated with firearms, Bogdanos needed the jury to see evidence that Combs had previously been associated with guns. The state of New York had dug up Combs' gun-related incidents that were buried in police reports across the country. The husband from the Ohio Ritz-Carlton incident said prosecutors attempted numerous times to persuade him to testify to demonstrate a pattern of reckless behavior. He declined. "I told them, 'They know our name. I'm not going to take the chance of opening up that wound,'" he explained. "[Combs] had a lot of reach. In fact, he had a reputation that if he didn't like you, he could have you hurt." Miller, the *New York Post* photographer who had secured a partial win against Combs over the flashed gun, was kept on standby in case he would be called to testify.

---

Whether to let out the stress from court or simply because he was undeterred by his circumstances, Combs continued to keep his social calendar booked. Unlike those who become outcasts and pariahs amid scandal, he was in high demand: Celebrities like heiresses Paris and Nicky Hilton, designer Tommy Hilfiger, and actors Sofía Vergara, Chris Meloni, and Stephen Baldwin squeezed themselves into the front row for his Sean John New York Fashion Week showing, which was being held in the middle of his gun trial. Combs poured an estimated $1 million into the twenty-minute presentation at Bryant Park, with the metal invitations to the show alone costing $140,000. After a long week at court—and after-hours meetings with his design team—Combs stood backstage and watched as shirtless male models in low-slung jeans strutted down the runway in oversize fur and shearling jackets. The audience was rapturous, giving Combs a standing ovation as he took a bow.

Anna Wintour, *Vogue*'s ultimate tastemaker, gave her stamp of approval: "Sean John is a great designer."

He continued making late-night appearances at clubs and bars. The evening before the verdict landed, Combs partied at the Lotus nightclub until 2:00 a.m. During his cross-examination, Combs made no attempt to hide his disdain for Bogdanos. He was indignant that he was being subjected to such a laborious process, bristling when questioned about his history of prior incidents and tersely repeating that he didn't carry a gun that night. He was adamant that he did not try to bribe Fenderson, testifying that any recorded voicemails that could be interpreted as such were merely him "expressing concern."

Over six weeks, sixty witnesses gave their accounts of that singular night. At least four men and women, including Fenderson and Allen, claimed that they had seen Combs with a gun, and the ballistics report showed a bullet hole in the ceiling above where Combs had been standing. Twenty-five years later, victim Natania Reuben is still confident about what she saw on the night that changed her life. "He had on winter white from head to toe, holding a black gun," she said firmly. "I saw it." Combs' attorneys sowed seeds of doubt about any witness who claimed to have seen Combs with a gun in the nightclub, poking holes in their recollections of events and painting those who were pursuing lawsuits against Combs as greedy contestants on a fictional "Who Wants to Be a Billionaire?" game show. Finally, on March 16, the verdict was in. Combs' hands trembled as the jury filed in and he refused to look over at his co-defendants, Jones and Barrow, who were simultaneously holding their breath. When Jones' and Combs' verdicts were read aloud—not guilty on all counts—there were gasps in the gallery. Combs burst from the courthouse holding hands with a beaming Janice. He planted a kiss on her cheek before declaring that he wanted to be with his children.

Reporters who went to his home couldn't find him there; he had gone to thank God in person from the pews of a church, someone informed the media. Later in the day, he turned up at the Peninsula hotel's penthouse suite to celebrate his acquittal. His mood boosted by the victory, Combs tried making a move on one of his staffers, a freelance graphic designer working with Bad Boy's marketing team. Combs sauntered over to the woman, as she mingled with her boss and his girlfriend, and began massaging her shoulders suggestively. "I'm getting touched on my shoulder, my arms, my back. He's like, 'Oh, yeah, you like that? I know you like that.' Like really, really gross," the graphic designer recalled. "I was like, 'No, not so much,' and I sort of floated my way out of there."

Weeks later, the graphic designer's boss's girlfriend had to get something off her chest and blurted out, "I have to tell you something that [the boss] forbade me to tell you, but I'm telling you because you're my friend." Later in the evening after the graphic designer had rebuffed Combs, he allegedly approached her boss in order to "solicit" her for sex, going so far as to offer payment. "He really did objectify me and then try to buy me through his boy," the graphic designer said. "When people ask me about my days at Bad Boy, it's just overshadowed by his crap. He viewed women as people to accommodate his whims."

As Combs reveled in his acquittal, Barrow wasn't so lucky. The entire weight of the law dropped on the twenty-two-year-old, who stared ahead, reactionless, as the jury found him guilty on five felony counts. (He was acquitted of the more serious charges of attempted murder and intentional assault in the first degree.) Combs' attorneys had muddied the waters just enough to save Combs' skin, but they offered no support to corroborate Barrow's argument that he had acted in self-defense when Allen allegedly opened fire first.

While Combs and Jones jubilantly left the courthouse, Barrow was taken into custody. Combs visited his protégé only once, traveling to the notorious Rikers Island, where Barrow awaited sentencing. Barrow was surprised to see Combs in the visiting room. And furious. "I think I tried to spit in his face," Barrow told *The Breakfast Club*. "I didn't want him to come see me. I didn't want anything to do with him." In Barrow's eyes, Combs had discarded him as the sacrificial lamb necessary to secure his own freedom. There was no apology or excuse Combs could offer that would make things right.

Combs didn't bother to show up at Barrow's sentencing. The baby-faced rapper received a ten-year prison sentence and attempted to console his mother as he was led away in handcuffs. "I love you, Mama" were his parting words. Combs was brief in his statements about Barrow's fate, calling the jail term "unfair and extreme" and offering his continued prayers and support. By the end of the year, Bad Boy had dropped Barrow; the label was trying to diversify and cross over into pop music. It was strictly business for Combs. Barrow served nearly nine years of his sentence, in a mixture of maximum- and medium-level prison facilities around New York State. He converted to Orthodox Judaism while in prison and signed with Island Def Jam for a reported $3 million, releasing his prison-recorded album *Godfather Buried Alive* in 2004. Upon his release in 2009, Barrow was deported to Belize, where he was able to rebuild his life, becoming a political leader in his birth country. His short-lived stint at Bad Boy had upended the course of his life. "Let us not forget what the cold, hard facts are," Barrow said later. "This is someone who destroyed my life."

# PART II

# CHAPTER 5 | P. DIDDY

**"I GOTTA TAKE A BREAK,"** an emphatic Combs stressed in his first interview after his acquittal. "I'm going to take a leave of absence just to be Sean Combs, [to] have time to think about what's the next level I want to play on."

Although he'd emerged victorious from his case, Combs' commercial appeal had taken a significant hit. Arrests, office beatings, and nightclub shootings added an air of street credibility and could bolster album sales, but in the corporate world, criminal investigations didn't go over as well. If Combs wanted to continue his ascent, becoming a household name while simultaneously being welcomed into prestigious business and society circles, he'd have to sever ties with the rougher elements of the lifestyle he had been selling to fans. He decided he needed to soften up, and it began with a name change. "No more Puff Daddy," Combs said. "I'm rockin' with P. Diddy now—my man Biggie gave me that name."

Combs seemed to take his vow of personal betterment to heart, embarking on a multiyear public effort to clean up his act. His Sean John clothing line scaled back on the heavy fur and saggy jeans, adding in more well-tailored three-piece suits and sharp corduroy jackets. He revisited the idea of releasing a gospel album, called "Thank You," that he had shelved in 1997. "It's just about if you believe in one God and you believe in giving thanks for all your blessings and being here," Combs explained of his inspiration. "It comes from the perspective of a sinner. I'm still making mistakes in life. I'm still learning, but I'm on the right path. It comes from the perspective of a sinner that's on the right road, and who's walking the right road and trying to get better every day."

He championed even more philanthropic efforts, including those that fed back into his own charity, Daddy's House Social Programs, which he started in 1995. In 2003, he raised roughly $2 million for various causes while running the New York City Marathon. It was an impulse decision. He wasn't a runner, and he had six weeks to prepare, but he convinced MTV to document his crash-course training in *Diddy Runs the City.* Trailed by at least four bodyguards and cameras, the novice runner finished the race in a commendable four hours, fourteen minutes, and fifty-four seconds.

Elsewhere, Combs pursued more acting roles in his bid to crossover into Hollywood. Two months after his acquittal, Combs landed a part in *Monster's Ball* starring Halle Berry. He received minor praise for his grounded portrayal of death-row prisoner Lawrence Musgrove. (He developed a crush on the future Oscar winner. "He was on a mission for Halle," former security guard Rob House recalled. "He was talking about Halle for like a month straight." The infatuation ultimately went nowhere.) Combs also dabbled in theater, playing Walter Lee Younger in a revival of *A Raisin in the Sun* on Broadway in 2004.

And his annual White Party, the hottest event of the summer, became even more of a spectacle, akin to a promotional vehicle for Combs and his personal brand. "It was more corporate," said celebrity photographer Selma Fonseca, who worked and attended more than two dozen events hosted by Combs over the decades. "People were filming, and [there were] big cameras, and a step-and-repeat with all the sponsors." Absolut Vodka partnered with Combs in 2003 to host the shindig at his East Hampton house, where circulating winged waitresses handed out chilled shots while mermaids with satin tails lounged in Combs' pool. The following year, PlayStation logos were plastered across signage as Combs used his newly founded nonpartisan, get-out-the vote organization, Citizen Change, to drum up more awareness ahead of the presidential election. He turned up with an original copy of the Declaration of Independence, borrowed from screenwriter Norman Lear, as his date for the evening. And while there was always an interesting mixture of people from the music industry, city scenesters, longtime friends, and a sprinkle of Hollywood faces, the gatherings became more eclectic. Esteemed fashion and intellectual figures were seen around the dinner table, including famed photographer Patrick Demarchelier and novelist Salman Rushdie. Combs exported the gathering to Saint-Tropez's moneyed waterfront in 2006, and to the Los Angeles celebrity scene three years later.

Combs continued to draw prominent figures into his orbit, including Mötley Crüe rocker Tommy Lee and It Boy actor Ashton Kutcher. The pair made something of an odd couple, but Kutcher told *Hot Ones* in 2019 that they became "fast friends" after meeting through MTV when Kutcher was hosting *Punk'd*. They seemed joined at the hip in 2003 and 2004, sitting courtside at basketball games, cohosting parties, and going on double dates with Porter and Kutcher's then-girlfriend Brittany Murphy, and his later-wife Demi Moore. "By the way, if you're a single man, there's probably no greater human being in the world than him," Kutcher told James Corden in a joint appearance with Combs on the British comedian's late-night show in 2018. "We were having a lot of fun together." (Former Bad Boy intern Damien Vazquez recalled that at the peak of Combs' friendship with Kutcher, Combs fired one of his personal assistants because she had bumped into Kutcher at a nightclub and introduced herself, saying she worked for Combs. "He said, 'That's my friend. Not your friend. You don't talk to no one.'")

Combs' efforts paid off tenfold. He earned flattering press coverage, and anonymous forum pages on the gossip site Lipstick Alley began tracking his every move. Corporate businesses began approaching Combs with lucrative offers, hoping to be linked with the over-the-top P. Diddy lifestyle brand. His net worth started to rise rapidly when Warner Music Group paid $30 million to acquire a 50 percent stake in Bad Boy as part of a three-year agreement in 2005. Estée Lauder helped develop his first fragrance, Unforgivable, in 2006, netting a purported $100 million in global sales in its first year. By that year, he moved his empire into a massive office space in Midtown. The building neighbored the sceney eatery Serafina, sat catty-corner from the storied Ed Sullivan Theater, and was a few blocks north of Daddy's House. Personnel from Bad Boy Records, Sean John, his marketing agency Blue Flame, and even a short-lived film department were spread across five floors. And in 2007, a thirty-eight-year-old Combs shook hands on a partnership with British liquor giant Diageo, the company behind worldwide brands including Guinness, Johnnie Walker, Tanqueray, and Smirnoff, for a 50–50 joint profit venture with Cîroc, a specialty vodka made with French grapes, that would propel him toward billionaire status. Nightlife and partying, already major components of his image, were now critical elements. For a music executive turned rapper who told listeners early on that "It's All About the Benjamins," the early 2000s were a manifestation of that declaration.

---

One of Combs' personal assistants, who would later testify against him under the pseudonym Mia, was gazing out the window of a plane. Team Combs was hurtling toward yet another city for yet another obligation in the mogul's packed, jet-setting schedule. Mia was used to working on her feet for up to twenty hours a day, so being able to sit still and watch the clouds was a luxury. Combs interrupted her thoughts. "I used to look at the world the way you did," he told her. "[But] what's left if I have done everything?"

It was a rare moment of vulnerability for Combs. "He felt sad to me," Mia recalled later. The honest confession moved her so deeply that in the weeks leading up to Combs' forty-fifth birthday in 2014, Mia spent her free time compiling a scrapbook of magazine and newspaper clippings chronicling his successes dating back to 1991. Accompanying the gift was a heartfelt letter that gently encouraged Combs to reflect. "Sometimes life goes by at catastrophic speeds where you never get to live in and enjoy the 'now,'" she wrote. "Things that used to feel unattainable and symbolic of success can become the 'norm' and lose all the adrenaline and excitement it used to stir up. And life keeps going and going, and each new height reached can lose its celebration moment in the whirlwind of getting to that next goal. All of this to say that I hope on THIS day—you get to sit back and actually take it all in of how much you've accomplished—how far you have gone (+ are still going)—so I put together this book of magazine articles for 1991–1999 that I hope will stir up nostalgic feelings of when you started and how you felt and what a dream to you then that's now an everyday reality. So, your 'self' can tell your 'young self' how GREAT you've become. Not that you'll ever forget your past—but I hope it reminds you of when this world made your eyes light up!!"

At the time, there wasn't much that would make Combs' eyes light up. The sad reality was that for all of Combs' monumental achievements, he was beginning to feel desensitized to his triumphs. Despite the wealth and acclaim, satisfaction never came. The blessings of his success would warp into monomania. Everything that once gave meaning to his life, including the music and artists that brought him to such heights, began to fall by the wayside. Instead, he increasingly sought out excitement in different forms, primarily through sex and drugs. His mood swings intensified, and he seemed to take a perverse joy in being an agent of chaos and instilling fear in others. He felt increasingly lonely and depended on his entourage and staff to keep him busy and amused, or considered them bodies to absorb his frustrations. What followed was an escalating search to feel something—anything.

Combs' partnership with Cîroc gave him the perfect cover to party even harder. He stayed out until the early hours of the morning at nightclubs around the world, attended to by pretty waitresses who served his crew bottles festooned with sparklers. He threw himself into work, halfway joking that he didn't have many close friends because he would always put business first. "I'm not a good friend," he admitted to *The Times* of London. "You need a friend to be there for you. But if people want to go out to dinner and hang out with me, I'm like, dinner? That's four hours! That's four hours of time when I could be working!"

He also used relationships as an escape, embracing his bachelor status. Though Combs would rekindle with Porter in a continual on-off cycle, he was also linked to actress Cameron Diaz, supermodel Naomi Campbell, and several other glamorous women. He would often keep as many as three to four women in the mix. In New York City, he'd have his personal team book rooms at different hotels around the city, where he'd spend time with each woman over the course of the week—and the women would all patiently wait for his return.

It seemed that half of the fun to Combs was the thrill of the chase. He'd laser in on a prospective romantic interest and become hyperfixated on winning her over. A man on a mission, he was not dissuaded by boyfriends or adamant rejections. There'd be over-the-top gestures, invitations to accompany him to various places and events, and a steady stream of compliments. He was a perfect gentleman. Eventually, the honeymoon period would end. He'd grow uninterested and let the romantic connection fizzle into a friendship. Or his controlling side would begin to rear its head, setting off a cycle of high-tempered fights and breakups.

Even with Lopez, Combs dreamed up extravagant stunts to win her back following their final split in early 2001. He ordered the Bad Boy marketing department to design posters that declared in bold red-and-black lettering, "Malito Luvs Bella"—their nicknames for each other and a rough translation of "bad loves beautiful" in Spanish. To ensure Lopez would see his profession of love, Combs sent interns to camp outside *Total Request Live* studios with the signs and plaster them across New York City. "Everywhere she would go, he would have fifteen to twenty people follow her with signs," recalled Vazquez. "Everything from JFK to the city, he had poles with those posters." His efforts also stretched to the West Coast, where he released a hundred white doves and pink balloons over her balcony.

When it came to sex, Combs proudly described himself as "nasty" and "buck-fuckin' wild." He regaled blushing journalists with stories of a ménage à trois in the presidential suite at the Le

Méridien hotel in Beverly Hills. He gloated about his stamina and openly talked about his fondness for tantric sex. "I'm proud to say I love sex," he told *Playboy* in 2010. "You might catch me in a porn store at any given moment—it ain't nothing I'm ashamed of. If they start sending freaks to jail, I'm guilty as charged."

And to fend off the gloom that descended when he felt alone, there was a small nondescript black pouch that was always within reach. Some years it was a leather Louis Vuitton toiletry case that his team nicknamed the medicine bag. Others, it was a Gucci pouch called the VIP bag. The contents remained the same: a small pharmacy of drugs. Several different pill bottles could be found inside. There were over-the-counter painkillers, as well as antidepressants, Viagra, sperm boosters, and water pills to help with weight loss. There were also illicit drugs: opiates, cocaine, ketamine, psychedelic mushrooms, marijuana gummies, and Ecstasy pills in the shapes of dolphins and Obama's face. Combs would reach for this bag once, if not several times, every day.

By the early 2000s, drug use became a predominant part of Combs' everyday life. He developed a "ferocious" addiction to opiates following a surgery in 2000, popping strong painkillers throughout the day, even ahead of business meetings. At night, he'd switch to Ecstasy and MDMA, euphoric psychedelics. At times, he experimented with designer drugs, like ketamine and GHB, a powerful sedative that's also known as a "date rape" drug. It didn't matter which substance he took; Combs would be high every single day for the next twenty-five years.

A hot temper didn't mix well with drugs and high-pressure environments, and Combs was a human pressure cooker. The substances amplified all the preexisting issues Combs still hadn't addressed, like anger problems and a deep-rooted need for control. Eagle-eyed journalists and their network of sources routinely chronicled many of Combs' public spats. While renting a yacht off the elite shores of Saint-Tropez in 2003, Combs reportedly delivered a knockout blow to English actor and party boy Calum Best. "Because Calum's good-looking, and Puffy's not," a partygoer nonchalantly explained to an interloping *Vanity Fair* writer. Best was thrown off the boat, and Combs told a reporter he handled issues directly. Guests at Jermaine Dupri's Grammys after-party in 2007 overheard Combs screaming and cursing out his longtime friend Naomi Campbell. An insider dished to the *New York Post* that their flirty friendship was growing strained over Porter's jealousy and Combs' expectation that the iconic supermodel would star in his Sean John campaign for free. In spring 2007, Combs was accused of decking a Hollywood real estate broker after the man tried to tug his partner away from an overtly flirty Combs after a party. Feeling disrespected, Combs lashed out, allegedly shouting, "I'll smack [the] flames out your ass," pushing the girlfriend and attempting to spit on another woman. Months later in October, music promoter and Combs' industry acquaintance Steven Acevedo filed a report with the New York Police Department claiming Combs swung on him in the middle of a club in a dispute over a Sean John model they both had dated. Leaving Acevedo with a bloody nose and busted lip, an emboldened Combs allegedly made a chilling threat toward his love rival. "I will kill you," Combs vowed, according to a police report. "I will fucking kill you, you punk. It's nothing." The case fell apart by November, when Acevedo stopped cooperating with law enforcement and revised the statement that he had given to police. "I understand that cases involving celebrities sometimes have a life of their own, but I'd rather not be known as the person that put someone from our world behind bars," Acevedo told the press before the matter was resolved. "What goes on in our world stays in our world."

Over the years, those in his orbit have used a variety of terms to diagnose the roots of Combs' explosive conduct. "I use the term narcissist because it was all about control, and he was so good at it," said one former employee. Several called him sociopathic, based on his sheer lack of compassion for anyone but himself, and, by extension, his immediate family members. Those closer to him used a more clinical term: bipolar. One source said the terminology surfaced during therapy with Porter and two future girlfriends would also allude to it when discussing his instant flip from calm to menacing. Combs himself has brought up the condition unprompted. "I've gone to therapy for relationships I've been in, for tragedies I've been through," he told *Playboy* in 2010. "I think therapy is good. I've been called bipolar—I'm not; I just have very drastic mood swings." One Sean John staffer recalled Combs once bursting into the showroom with his newest Bad Boy signee, a young singer named Cassie, taking swigs from a red solo cup. "Today, we're going to call the collection 'Bipolar' because that's what the fuck I am," he declared.

It all fed into the chaos he seemed to delight in intentionally creating across his romantic, personal, and professional life. He needed a constant thrill to sustain himself.

---

Combs sat behind his desk on the phone negotiating an MTV appearance to coincide with the release of *Bad Boys II: The Soundtrack* in the summer of 2003. Pushing the person on the other end of the line to "bump somebody" from the show so his album could get airtime, Combs broke into a grin. He might've been accustomed to the feeling, but winning was everything to Combs. In his world, there was no such thing as a fight too small. Challenges in any form—business, low-stakes games, women—gave him an addictive rush of adrenaline. After a quick thank-you,

Combs hung up, victorious. "I'm a savage!" he shouted, throwing objects around his office in celebration. "Whatever I want, I have to get!"

Part of the reason for Combs' success was his ruthlessness. Enough was never enough, and even longtime friendships weren't safe from how Combs handled his business. It nearly cost him his friendship with Deric "D-Dot" Angelettie, who had to fight Combs over his own alter ego, the Madd Rapper, the trash-talking jester who popped up on Bad Boy artists' interludes. Combs had allegedly tried to wrestle the rights away from Angelettie, claiming the character belonged to him under Bad Boy. He only backed off when Angelettie called his bluff about taking him to court and released an album anyway.

To execute his mission of world domination, Combs ruled with an iron fist. His whims were orders, and his directives were gospel. When David James was interviewing to be Combs' personal assistant, Vashta Wilson, the human resources and operations head for Bad Boy, pointed to a framed photo of Combs hanging in her office. "She pointed at the wall, and she said, 'This is Mr. Combs' kingdom. We're all here to serve in it,'" James said. It wasn't easy to be a foot soldier. In keeping with Combs' mantra of "can't stop, won't stop," he expected his team to be devoted to his mission and to adopt his intense, borderline-obsessive work ethic.

Staffers needed to learn to work at Combs' speed or realize it was in their best interest to bow out graciously. Employees said they were all bonded through shared workplace trauma. "You feel like you were in a war zone," said one former longtime assistant. "We used to joke [that] working in Puffy's office was like working in the trenches. Once you survive that, you can survive almost anything."

Combs was always "on the edge of snapping and being scary,"

said a source who worked with Bad Boy in the early 2000s. He would frequently get into one-sided screaming matches with staffers—men and women alike, from assistants to executives—to express his displeasure. If he was particularly heated, he'd throw the nearest object at a wall or in the direction of the offending person. "It was just like yelling at everybody, chair throwing," said one Sean John employee. "One minute he wanted denim, the next minute he wanted ball gowns. There was always a fight." A former assistant said Combs would get into her face to express "how unhappy he was" when something didn't go his way. "You'd be spoken to like, 'You did this wrong. You fucked this up! How dare you? Fix it! Fix it right now!'" There were moments of physical aggression. "He put his hands on me twice, not like to fight me, but just to show me who's boss, kind of thing," said a second Sean John staffer. "I think it was just intimidation tactics."

Across the company, exposure to Combs varied by proximity. The main office braced for hurricane Combs, who could arrive at any moment and lay waste to the day. The executive suite knew how to manage Combs, dutifully absorbing his verbal lashings and temper tantrums and being the calm middleman with others. Members of his personal team—assistants, private chefs, bodyguards, and an entourage of sycophants—were exposed to the worst sides of Combs. His small army of personal assistants were at the very bottom of the totem pole and worked to the brink of exhaustion. Mia said there was a period where she worked five days straight without sleeping, taking Adderall to stay awake until she crashed. "I had a physical breakdown," she said. "I remember my hearing went. It felt like I was underwater, and my equilibrium was off, and I started [having] blurred vision. Then out of nowhere, like [I] didn't mean to, but I burst into tears, hysterical, and couldn't stop crying." Only then did Combs tell Mia she could sleep.

Combs' assistants were in charge of organizing his entire day, from the moment he woke up until he dismissed them in the early hours of the morning. When iPhones introduced group messaging, the assistants had a text thread tracking Combs' location, mood, needs, and sleep. Mia once tried to summarize her daily tasks for his chief of staff, Toni Bias Fletcher, in 2011, in a stream-of-consciousness, two-page email. She managed his schedule; served as a liaison between department heads, family members, and friends; oversaw his social media; and acted as a personal concierge. "PROTECT HIM AT ALL TIMES," she stressed. No two days were alike. "PD can ask you to do 17,000 things at one time that range from cracking his knuckles to writing his next movie to doing his taxes," she concluded. "He can also just have you standing next to him for 22 hours + not ask you one thing."

Combs' expectation of constant perfection and his moody whiplashes left employees constantly anxious that any day at Bad Boy might be their last. George Kaplan was in the first week of working as Combs' personal assistant in September 2014 when his new boss sent him to pick up a BPA-free gallon water bottle. The Whole Foods shelves had only half-gallon water bottles, so Kaplan purchased two. Combs threatened to fire him on the spot. "He told me that I did not bring him what he asked for," Kaplan said, noting Combs was "angry" and inches away from his face. It would become a monthly ritual for Combs to threaten his job. He also routinely weaponized promotions, salaries, and opportunities, reminding his subordinates that just as easily as he gave, he could take away.

While staff back in the office could sense Combs' capacity for violence, those who worked out of his personal homes experienced it firsthand. Two well-placed former staffers said they knew at least eight employees who obtained settlements from Combs after he physically assaulted or threatened to assault them. There were fights with his personal bodyguards and his personal barber. His private chef, Jourdan Cha'Taun Atkinson, secretly called the head of HR for help as Combs cursed out his house manager in Miami in 2007. "I'm the motherfucking king and you are lying to my fucking face right now?" he bellowed about a misunderstanding over whether gardening staff could eat catered meals. Months later, in March 2008, no one intervened on Atkinson's behalf when Combs began screaming at her and "used all of his might" to physically shove her out of his house, sending her tumbling down two steps.

In Capricorn Clark's first year as Combs' personal assistant, she claimed her boss had his security staff lock her inside a gutted Midtown office to take a lie detector test. Items that Combs was renting from hip-hop's go-to diamond man, Jacob the Jeweler, had gone missing, and Clark was the last person believed to have seen the jewelry. Over five consecutive days, a heavyset man who chain-smoked cigarettes and guzzled black coffee administered a polygraph test to Clark. He allegedly warned, "If you fail these tests, they're going to throw you in the East River." Repeatedly drawing inconclusive results, Clark "was petrified," she said. "I was afraid of what would happen if I didn't pass this test, and I felt the test was the only way to get through this thing." By summer 2006, Clark had developed stress-based alopecia as a result of the $65,000-a-year job. She was fed up with running on four hours of sleep and adhering to Combs' directives, like a weekend in Miami when he forbade her from leaving his house. "See, your problem is you want a life, and you can't have that here," he told her. "I hate it here," Clark sighed to the personal chef. Combs caught wind of the comment and charged at Clark, shoving her backward until she was out of the house. "You hate it here? Get the fuck out of my house," Combs yelled. Clark said, "He repeated it until we were outside." She promptly quit.

Of course, there was a tremendous upside to working for Combs. Beyond bragging rights, the semi-decent paycheck, connections to the right kind of people, and an impressive line on a résumé, Combs had the power and charm to make people feel valued and seen. He was an infectious motivator; his work ethic was unparalleled; and his business acumen was something to learn from. "I'm very grateful for having learned those lessons from him," George Kaplan said. "I keep lessons from him to this day, from a business perspective that I use in my career every day. He taught me to have the work ethic that I have, understanding that no job was too big or small, and frankly, without a bunch of these lessons, I don't believe that I would have had the jobs that I've had since then." Yet admiration could blur into allegiance. When they explain the complex dynamic Combs fostered, former employees repeatedly cite loyalty. It was almost two-pronged. They needed to demonstrate their dedication to working for Combs' companies, and they were also expected to be devoted to him. "He saw himself as Bad Boy; he was Sean John, and the loyalty was to him," mused one former Sean John staffer. "The reason why I say that is because there was no team in it. The entire team would cut each other's throats if Puff said so, and he liked that. He loved it."

Those who proved their loyalty were elevated to higher positions in his companies and adopted into the Bad Boy family. They were given a sense of purpose—a mission that not only created something great but also made them the forces of greatness. To be part of the family meant you had friends in high places for life. "Puffy exploited people's desires to be in those environments," said a freelancer who worked with Bad Boy. As a result, "people did whatever he said to stay in his good graces."

Roger Bonds worked as a security guard for Combs, and in the span of two years he went from prison to flying with the mogul on a private jet. Earning $75,000 a year for around-the-clock protection, Bonds rose through the ranks, permitted to sleep in the guest rooms of Combs' residences, to travel internationally, and to kick it socially. He was convinced that through his proximity to Combs, wealth and opportunity would eventually trickle down to him. After all, "you're family," Combs told him, Bonds wrote in his book, *Bonds: Loyalty, Lies, and the Life That Almost Killed Me.* A rude wake-up call would come in 2012. When, after a decade of being Combs' ever-present shadow, Bonds asked to take a step back and be put on the Cîroc team, Combs effectively punished him, cutting his pay and slowly diminishing his role until he was out of work.

There was no guarantee how long someone's favored status would last. If Combs turned his back on an employee, the rest of the organization followed suit. To be cast out of Bad Boy was to be shunned by their chosen family. All these dynamics created a culture of submission where employees would turn a blind eye to save themselves. "He was so untouchable," said another staffer who worked at Sean John. "Like he could literally get away with murder—that was always the air he had. Everybody would bow down to him, whatever he wanted."

---

In 2002, the modern era of reality TV was just beginning to take off, and MTV came knocking for Combs. The network had acquired the talent-competition series *Making the Band* from ABC and was in search of a charismatic personality to anchor the show. The timing couldn't have been better. MTV was dominating ratings with its reality programs, *The Real World* and *The Osbournes*, and Combs was working on his mass-market, PG-13 image overhaul. To be teleported into the homes of millions of young people of many racial backgrounds and earn a paycheck? Combs eagerly accepted. It was an obvious strategic play, one that even earned him a rare rebuke from longtime peer Russell Simmons, who labeled Combs' foray into reality TV a flagrant ploy to feed his own ego. "It is his way of saying, 'Please, please don't ignore me,'" he told *The New York Times* when the series was first floated in May 2002. (A few years later, Simmons would star in his own show, *Running Russell Simmons*, which lasted for one season.)

Combs hit the road in the first season of *Making the Band 2*, taking Bad Boy's executives across the country in search of the label's next hip-hop-based crew. The show's premise was straightforward: Combs and his all-star team of executive producers, talent managers, vocal coaches, and choreographers would weed out the contestants by putting them through a high-stakes boot camp to see if they could be molded into artists worthy of repping Bad Boy. If they earned their stripes, they were offered a record deal. The opportunity seemed like a golden ticket to one of the world's top labels. If the contestants pushed themselves to the limit, their reward was a shot at greatness.

More than forty thousand hopefuls showed up to auditions. "I didn't know it was a TV show," said rapper Freddrick "Freddy P" Watson of Da Band. "I really thought it was a competition to be a group." Brooklyn rapper Lynese "Babs Bunny" Wiley, who auditioned in the first season and became part of Da Band, still gets emotional thinking about the pride and excitement she felt when she sat in the same studio where Biggie had laid down his vocals and kicked it with his Junior M.A.F.I.A. crew. "It was so amazing, it's almost bringing me to tears," Wiley said. "Bad Boy was a big deal. P. Diddy, Puffy was a big deal. I was excited to be a part of that. I'm working with the same people that [Biggie] broke with. We all thought, I'm a part of this legacy."

For Combs, *Making the Band* was both a hefty paycheck and a free promotional vehicle for the P. Diddy brand. Combs played the part of a shrewd music executive well. He was harsh, direct, and demanding. In reality, it was just a slightly toned-down version of himself. Episodes typically revolved around the boot camp atmosphere and petty dramas between the contestants. Combs would show up, deliver feedback, bark orders, and then leave his team to handle the rest. One eliminated contestant from *Making the Band 3* described Combs as "cold" and "rude" when he interacted with the women who were vying to be part of his girl group. "He didn't seem like he cared at all," she said. "We were young women who were trying to make our dreams come true. We would be pouring our heart out, singing and dancing. Most of the time, he wouldn't even look up to acknowledge us when we were performing." Whether the artists' music could translate into a genuine, commercial hit seemed incidental—as was evident when a nonplussed Combs gave his bands an insane five to six weeks to deliver a full album. (Typically, albums take between six months and a year to complete.) The disconnect between the contestants' wide-eyed expectations and Combs' indifference didn't go unnoticed by the production team. "We saw that happening the whole time," said Kenny Hull, a show director. "He hated them."

There were moments clearly designed for humiliation, like Da Band's now-infamous cheesecake walk during season 2 of *Making the Band 2*. Standing outside the studios of Daddy's House, Wiley had cameras in her face as hot tears ran down her cheeks and she adamantly protested the idea of trekking ten miles across the Manhattan Bridge to downtown Brooklyn and back again to fetch a late-night dessert for Combs. "If I'm going to Brooklyn, I'm going the fuck home," Wiley told her bandmates. "That's where the fuck I live!"

Behind the scenes, he was just as demanding, sometimes calling the show's production team to film with him as early as 4:00 a.m. The crew sensed an unsettling undercurrent to his energy. "He always felt violent, like a coiled spring," Hull added. "Like he could just jump off at any time." Nothing was ever captured on camera, but there were flashes of violence. In April 2007, Combs ordered cameras out of the room during an escalating argument with his longtime choreographer Laurieann Gibson. Observing a dance rehearsal in *Making the Band 4*, season 1, Combs was not happy with what he saw of the contestants vying for a slot in his new all-male R&B group. He lashed out at Gibson, who ignored his order to have the men rehearse all weekend. As Gibson tried to defend her reasoning, Combs cut her off. "I'm not taking no interjection," he said. "Now I'm fucking psycho for real. Get the fuck out then. You are disrespectful." The contestants and camera crew stood in the hallway where they could still hear Combs cursing and yelling. "You don't scare me," Gibson shouted and called his show "corny."

Weeks later, she filed a report with police, claiming that behind those doors Combs grabbed a chair and threatened to hurt her with it. At the time, people in Combs' camp claimed he never picked up a chair and said if anything the argument was staged to drum up drama for the show. Nevertheless, Gibson was fired. And during a scene filmed at Sean John's offices, the crew overheard Combs speaking to his assistant. "We just hear, 'Slow your roll playboy,'" said one high-ranking production member. "We turn, and he knocks out his assistant. He knew our cameras weren't up. That's why he did it then. We were shocked. The guy got up and scurried out; [we] never saw him again."

The show was a success but it seemed like everyone was in on the joke except for the contestants. "The whole point of that show was to make a TV show, not to make a band," said one production member. For Watson, the veil finally lifted shortly before Combs disbanded Da Band. Watson was growing increasingly frustrated with his bandmates and wanted to pursue a solo career. He was annoyed that Da Band's exposure wasn't translating into tangible, financial success. Da Band members seemed to be just scraping by after receiving a $25,000 advance for signing with Bad Boy and the $5,000 they each earned when playing shows. It seemed paltry considering the level of fame they had as stars of a hit reality program, appearing on the *Bad Boys II* soundtrack, and selling six hundred thousand copies of their lone album, *Too Hot for T.V.*

Combs caught wind of Watson's griping. "One day, he just called me in the office, he was like, 'Man, take your mic off.' He was like, 'Man, you think I give a fuck about this shit?' He's like, 'I don't care nothing about this shit. This is a TV show. This is what we call free promotion.'" Combs used the *Making the Band 2* season 3 finale to break the news. Da Band members who had left their hometowns and families, who had invested two years of sweat equity to pursue their dreams, were now kicked to the curb—literally. The camera crew got their final shots of the stunned artists standing on the street outside the Bad Boy offices. Although members kicked themselves over their petty complaints and arguments, in truth, there wasn't anything they could have done to change their fate. "We all knew around the office he was gonna dismantle that band because that would make good TV," Damien Vazquez said.

He orchestrated a similar public shaming with Danity Kane, the all-girl group he formed during *Making the Band 3*. Scouting the country for talent like he did with Da Band, Combs eventually landed on powerhouse singers Aubrey O'Day, D. Woods, Dawn Richard, Shannon Bex, and Aundrea Fimbres for the R&B-leaning quintet. Unlike Da Band, Danity Kane became a legitimate mainstream act, with their 2006 single "Show Stopper" peaking at number eight on Billboard's Hot 100 chart and their self-titled album selling more than a million copies within three months. Despite their popularity, even after delivering a second top-ten hit with "Damaged" in 2008, Combs dismantled the group when he abruptly fired O'Day and Woods during the *Making the Band 4* season 3 finale. "We never knew if [the] man [who] was going to enter the room was the one that makes you feel like you're a million bucks and better than everybody out there in the world," O'Day explained. "There's two men inside of him. He's a complicated human to dissect." In the end, the groups formed on *Making the Band*, including Da Band, Danity Kane, Day 26, and solo artist Donnie Klang, would all peter out. But it was never about the bands. The show's popularity, in part, had further helped turn Combs into a household name.

---

As Combs chased after the next lucrative business venture and prioritizing his social life, he was stretching himself thin, and the Bad Boy label was at a crisis point.

One by one, his talent began to drift away. Black Rob slipped into addiction, as did G. Dep, who battled a severe PCP habit. Between 2000 and 2010, more than a dozen rappers and groups broke away from Bad Boy, including major stars Faith Evans and the LOX. "Being that [Combs] has so much going on, I didn't want to be the nagging artist," Loon said at the time of his departure in 2004. "I was happy for all his success, but I was at a crossroads as an artist. I wanted to put forth the same effort for myself that I was putting forth for Bad Boy."

Although he continued to sign new acts, like the teenage girl group Dream and a nineteen-year-old singer named Cassie, whose platinum-selling single "Me & U" was dominating the radio, Combs allowed older acts to flatline. His primary interest was how the label could serve him.

Vazquez specifically recalled interns and street team members being sent out to purchase Combs' solo projects to ensure he'd top the *Billboard* list. "It comes down to money and image with him," he said. "We used to have boxes and boxes of CDs from going to stores and buying [the albums] so it could become No. 1." Other artists? Not so much. "We didn't go as hard [for them] as we did for him. I don't ever remember going out for any other artists. We didn't buy those albums." Kevin Rogers Francis, who used to work at Justin's restaurant and other Bad Boy–related ventures, said Combs would have his entire army of employees plug his solo projects whenever they answered company phones. "Good morning, this is Kevin—Puff Daddy *Forever* in stores August 24" was the typical script staffers were made to recite, Francis said, a line he still had memorized some twenty-five years later. "And that's it. You cannot fail. If you pick up that phone, that's what better be said. He would test it out and call around and see—whoever fumbles that, they were out."

Those who remained languished as they hoped Combs' full attention would someday return. It was a frustrating waiting game for artists, some of whom spent years at the label without ever releasing a single album, although they recorded music constantly. If something did get the green light, it was often co-opted for one of Combs' solo projects or pulled in for yet another remix.

Many artists who left Bad Boy felt their careers went nowhere afterward. Some, like Mack's first wife, Roxanne Alexis Hill-Johnson, blamed Combs. She accused him of blackballing Mack and sending him on a downward spiral. Mack died of complications from HIV at age forty-seven, in 2018, while living among a religious doomsday group in South Carolina. "I do feel like Puff's the trigger—he fucked my family up," Mack's ex-wife Hill-Johnson said. "Puff kicked it off; he was the catalyst."

Francesca Spero joined Bad Boy Entertainment in 1998, rising to become senior vice president of music publishing, although her unofficial title was "Ma" to her colleagues. But, Spero said, a decade of being Combs' right-hand woman meant little when he unceremoniously fired her in 2010. A hip surgery had triggered a lapse in her sobriety, which she quickly addressed by voluntarily checking into a rehab facility before Christmas in 2008. When Spero disclosed the stay to another executive, gossip ran rampant in the office. Combs "froze" her out of her duties before he illegally fired her, she alleged in an age and disability discrimination lawsuit. Spero tried to continue working in the music industry, but despite her experience, opportunities with promising leads would suddenly go cold with no explanation, a family member said. "Once it became clear that her career was sort of over, that's quite honestly when the downward spiral really started," they explained. "It led to relapse, which led to significant health issues which brought her to her end." The family member said Combs never offered his condolences or acknowledged her death in 2014.

Although Lynese "Babs Bunny" Wiley continued as a solo act at Bad Boy after Da Band disbanded, believing she'd be Bad Boy's first female rapper, she never released any music with the label. Reluctant to directly accuse Combs of wrongdoing, she acknowledged that she felt "blackballed" after she got out of her contract. "Working with Bad Boy and Puff, as far as doing the music, was a great process for me," she said. "I learned a lot. I will say business is business, right? And there is no morals in business. My moral side would say, 'Yo Puff, you got a heart?'"

---

Asia Nitollano also felt the chilling effect of Combs' fondness for retribution. She was nineteen years old and had just secured her spot as the seventh member of the Pussycat Dolls after beating out a host of competitors on the *Making the Band* knockoff series,

*Pussycat Dolls Present: The Search for the Next Doll.* Nitollano was looking to wriggle out of the show's contract and pursue a solo career when she bumped into Combs at a party for Kanye West in 2007. Apparently, Combs was a fan and offered Nitollano a starring role in the upcoming Sean John women's clothing line campaign alongside Bad Boy artist Cassie and rising actress Lauren London. A Bronx native, Nitollano describes herself as no-nonsense and unfazed by celebrity. That's why she was unimpressed when she learned the offer came with no financial incentive. Combs wanted her to star in the campaign for free. But she was convinced by her team that the exposure and making inroads with Combs would be worth forgoing payment, and Nitollano ultimately agreed.

By the day of the shoot, Nitollano was beginning to regret the decision. The models stood around for long periods; there was no food to be seen; and the idea that this was all for free annoyed her, so she grumbled to London. "I believe someone went back and told Diddy that I wasn't happy," Nitollano said. Combs suddenly reappeared on set, making a beeline for Nitollano and whisking her off to a private room to chat. Instead of blowing up at her, Combs took a different approach, flirting in a condescending, patronizing manner. "He tried belittling me, like, 'What's the matter? You want some ice cream? Can I get you some ice cream?'" Nitollano said. "I didn't think it was funny." Seeing that his charm offensive didn't work, Combs switched tactics. He asked Nitollano about her music career and whether it was true that she was considering signing a deal with Jimmy Iovine of Interscope. "I felt he was presenting himself as an option," Nitollano said. "I don't think he liked my response. I don't think I really gave an attitude; I was just honest [about not wanting to sign to Bad Boy] and he didn't like it."

The shoot eventually wrapped, and Nitollano was iced out

from the rest of the campaign. She largely brushed it off—ignoring that she was never sent the conciliatory box of Sean John clothes and that her invite to the launch party never materialized—until she began to run into problems advancing her music career. A Jive A&R executive and Murder Inc. Records' Irv Gotti directly told Nitollano that Combs had explicitly warned them against working with her, labeling her as difficult and with an attitude problem. "That was my first hint of Diddy and what he does, and what he continued to do," she said. "All from this one little conversation. You're so mad, telling everyone not to work with me. I don't think he liked anyone going against him, not wanting to work with him, or not being on their hands and knees for him. It's really scary with these types of men and what they try to do to women. If you don't like them or [don't] want to date them, then they no longer want to work with you."

Several women felt forced to walk a delicate tightrope as Combs blurred professional lines, while colleagues watched from a safe distance. Those who didn't want to damage a working relationship played along with Combs' flirtatious banter and ignored his sexualized comments about their bodies. They needed to play nice or risk having their careers preemptively squashed. Models who were brought to Sean John casting calls and bookings were seen as potential entries in his little black book. One model recalled him continually trying to hit on her during a shoot, making her uncomfortable by pressuring her to come back home with him. Kendra Haffoney, a contestant on *I Want to Work for Diddy*, an *Apprentice*-style reality show about Combs' search for a personal assistant, claimed Combs flattered her, calling her beautiful and expressing excitement that she was participating in the competition before pursuing sexual favors from her. Haffoney was eliminated by the eighth episode.

Artists Sara Stokes, Aubrey O'Day, and Dawn Richard all

claimed Combs made repeatedly humiliating and sexually harassing comments about their bodies. During an impromptu "inspection," Combs zeroed in on Stokes in front of an entire room and asked if she had gained weight. Stokes, whose tight, low-cut jeans exposed her toned midriff, was confused. "Not really," she replied. Her stomach looked a little "loose," Combs lied. Attempting to trigger Stokes' insecurity, knowing she had left three young children back home in Detroit with her husband to be part of the group, Combs had Stokes turn around. She needed to get everything "firmed up," he said, and told her to start running. Richard claimed Combs would flip-flop between calling her too skinny and telling her she was fat, ugly, and lazy. Combs rode O'Day particularly hard, frequently criticizing her appearance, calling her "overly raunchy, promiscuous," and goading her into arguments. He once sent her out of the studio and straight to the salon because he didn't like the way her toenails were polished.

When cameras were down, a different side of Combs emerged, the women claimed. Stokes claimed Combs tried to get her alone several times, once cornering her and speaking suggestively while grazing his hand across her chest. Under the guise of overseeing Richard's wardrobe options, Combs would allegedly barge into her dressing room, grope and caress her body, and once offered to gift her with a breast augmentation for Christmas. "You're an A; I'm thinking a D," he reportedly said, cupping Richard's breasts. O'Day claimed she experienced a heightened pursuit. He called her into the studio after hours, actively pitted her against her bandmates, and sent her sexually explicit messages. "I saw a lot of things that he would email her," bandmate D. Woods said in the documentary *The Fall of Diddy*. "Very sexual in nature, overtly pornographic, like things that he wanted to do to her. She was kinda just like, 'What do I do?' I remember telling her, 'Girl put that in a folder, send it to your mama, save that.'"

Only years later would O'Day share what Combs was attempting to push her into off camera. "I don't want to just fuck you, I want to turn you out," Combs allegedly wrote to O'Day in an email dated March 23, 2008. "I can see you being with some motherfucker that you tell what to do. I make my woman do what I tell her to do, and she loves it. I just want and like to do things different. I'm-a finish watching this porn and finish masturbating. I'll think of you. If you change your mind and get ready to do what I say, hit me." The early-morning message included Combs' standard signature at the time: "God bless. Diddy. God is the Greatest." Months later, when Combs dramatically broke up his top-charting group, he fired O'Day first. She believes it was direct retaliation for refusing his advances.

By no means was Bad Boy an outlier in harboring a misogynistic environment; it was prevalent not just in the music business but across numerous industries in the aughts. Men were emboldened by their wealth, status, and clout and often treated women as sexual conquests. The perceived music culture—late studio sessions, groupies, and sex, drugs, and rock 'n' roll—led to stigmatization of those who didn't participate in that scene on the grounds that they knew what they were signing up for when they entered those spaces. A tidal wave of reckoning came for the world of entertainment in 2017, putting Hollywood producer Harvey Weinstein and child sex offender R. Kelly behind bars. However, in the early 2000s, it was still predominantly a man's world—one in which people at the Bad Boy office and Daddy's House studio gathered around the conference room to watch Kelly's leaked sex tape. "They were having a 'play it party,' and they had Ecstasy going around the studio," then-seventeen-year-old singer-songwriter Tierra Brown, who was in the girl group Four Colourz and toured with Bad Boy in Europe, recalled. "I remember asking the guys, because they were like, 'You should take some, it makes you feel really good.' . . . Even at that age, I remember thinking, 'Why would you want to go watch a sex tape with guys on drugs?'" The teenage girls of Dream awkwardly averted their eyes from a discarded purse and a pair of high heels as they waited twenty minutes for Combs at a Beverly Hills hotel bungalow. When Combs finally emerged from the bedroom in a bathrobe, it was obvious what had been keeping him occupied. "It's like, you can't even keep our innocence," member Kasey Sheridan said. "I'm fifteen, walking into this situation knowing exactly what he was doing next door."

Shielded by a culture of silence and complicity, Combs acted with impunity. In the early 2000s, Combs did a poor job of hiding his office dalliance with Erica Kue, a junior account executive he had hired away from Hugo Boss to serve as the new creative director of Sean John's women's division. Occupying a Hello Kitty–themed office, Kue "would put makeup on, then wait for [Combs] to get there to walk down the hall to see him," said one colleague. Those close to Combs often looked the other way. His head security guard, Roger Bonds, recalled to hip-hop interviewer DJ Vlad that he witnessed Combs get into an argument with Kue at his residence, smacking her across her face. "It didn't escalate," he said of why he didn't intervene. Though he reasoned, "She was timid. So, being that she worked at [Sean John,] there was only so much that she could do."

In many cases, people on his payroll were complicit with, enabled, or mirrored his behavior, taking their cues from him. It was no secret around the office that some Bad Boy A&R executives expected sexual favors from female artists in exchange for professional attention. "I would hear about [female artists] being asked to do stuff with some of the other male executives," said one former Bad Boy staffer. "Like, 'We can make or break your career, what are you gonna do about it?'" Women were hired for specific shoots explicitly because certain producers and executives thought they were hot. "They would rate the women based on their physical appearance, and that's who they would reach out to be in the shoots," said another ex-employee. "Now what happened there? I'll be honest, I don't know because I didn't go to those shoots. But you hear stuff, and it comes back—locker room talk."

The objectification and harassment were rampant, but going to HR, several said, was useless. Its primary function was to serve and protect Combs. Raising alarms outside the company could trigger litigation as well; employees were routinely required to sign nondisclosure agreements, or NDAs. "There was definitely a culture of: Whatever happens here stays here. Don't ever talk about it. Not the press, not to anybody," said one former staffer. "Even when people were being harassed, if altercations happened or arguments that got out of control, nobody could complain."

That permissive environment, according to several women, became the backdrop for repeated acts of sexual violence in Combs' place of work. His longtime personal assistant Mia said Combs sporadically sexually assaulted her throughout her employment; she never knew when it would happen next. She claimed that he climbed into the staff bunk bed with her at his home in Los Angeles; that he assaulted her after his fortieth birthday party at the Plaza Hotel in November 2009; that he grabbed her inside his closet while she packed his clothes; and that he pushed her into a bathroom on a private plane. There was no romantic relationship between them, Mia said, and his girlfriends weren't around when these assaults occurred. She couldn't process what happened, only that she was expected to "keep it moving." Mia said she didn't even think about reporting anything to HR. Instead, she buried the memories, unsure of how many times exactly she was assaulted, getting "a specific horrible dark feeling in my stomach" when trying to recall specifics around certain events.

Sexual abuse was also playing out at Daddy's House, according to three women who claimed Combs brazenly sexually assaulted them at his recording studio in the presence of his entourage in the early 2000s. In two of those alleged instances, men on Combs' payroll were accused of participating in the abuse. Thalia Graves had been to Daddy's House before. She was dating one of Bad Boy's executives and sometimes stopped by the studio, where she casually met Combs. It didn't strike her as odd when Combs called her one day in summer 2001, saying he was concerned her boyfriend was slipping up at work and wanted some advice. Graves accepted his offer to pick her up, as well as the glass of wine he handed her when she got in the car. She claimed that after being taken to Daddy's House, feeling lightheaded and dizzy, she was stripped naked and raped by Combs and his bodyguard over a pool table. Later, a driver tried to take her to the hospital, but Graves said she refused out of fear.

Anna Kane couldn't believe that she ended up inside Daddy's House in 2003. The seventeen-year-old high school student wanted to remember everything about the night and had an impromptu photo shoot around the recording studio. Wearing a belted denim miniskirt and a low-cut D&G shirt, she pointed to *PD* on the wall and mimicked singing into a microphone in a recording booth. And to get proof for friends back home in Detroit that she really did hang out with P. Diddy in New York, she scootched herself into his lap and the two posed for a photo. Two decades later, Kane would use the photos as evidence of something else: that she was gang-raped by Combs and two other Bad Boy affiliates that night.

Hours earlier, Kane had been in Detroit, where Bad Boy executive Harve Pierre approached her while she was with friends at a local lounge bar. He started hitting on her, telling her she was "hot," and bragged about his friendship with Combs, at one point calling Combs, who invited Kane to fly back to New York with

Pierre to meet him. She readily accepted. Before taking off for the airport, Pierre pulled Kane inside the bar's bathroom. He took a hit of crack cocaine and allegedly forced the teen to perform oral sex on him. Then Pierre and two other suited men, presumed to be with Bad Boy, flew with her in a private jet back to New York City, where she was hand-delivered to Combs. The rest of the night passed with the men complimenting Kane's body, remarking how "sexy" she was, and begging to see her "ass," while supplying her with drugs and alcohol. There came a point where Kane was extremely inebriated, going in and out of consciousness. That's when Combs brought her to the bathroom, bent her over the sink, and began having sex with her, she alleged in a fourteen-page lawsuit. When Combs was done, she claimed, he watched as Pierre and a third man took their turns raping her. When they were done, she fell in a fetal position on the floor. Someone had to help walk an off-balance Kane to a waiting car, which then dropped her off at an airport. She remembered little of the trip back to Michigan, knowing only that she was missing her underwear.

Model Crystal McKinney claimed that, also in 2003, she was drugged and forced to perform oral sex on Combs in the studio's bathroom. The lanky twenty-two-year-old had met Combs for the first time earlier in the evening after attending his Sean John fashion show. She came as a guest of Italian fashion designer Roberto Cavalli, who went to great lengths to dress and style her for the event to introduce her to Combs. Later that evening at a dinner hosted at Cipriani Downtown, McKinney felt she was being put on display by Cavalli, who sat her directly across from Combs. The womanizer instantly took the bait and began showering her with compliments, then slipped her his number, promising to help with her modeling career. Later that night, Combs summoned her to the studio where he was smoking and drinking with friends. He passed her a hit of his joint. "You've never had weed like this before," she was told. McKinney understood only later what that meant. Combs continued to push her to drink and smoke more, teasing her that she was too uptight. By that point, McKinney felt like she was floating. Combs soon led her into the bathroom, where he forced himself on her, McKinney alleged. She lost consciousness once she was back in the studio's lounge; her next memory was of being alone in a moving taxicab that was taking her back to Cavalli's apartment. She kept a bundle of her unwashed clothing, safely stored in plastic wrap in her closet.

---

In summer 2007, Kim Porter locked the door of her suite at the Beverly Hills Hotel and braced herself for Combs' wrath. More than a decade into their on-off relationship, Porter wasn't afraid of Combs; she was more concerned about the consequences of his rage. She anticipated that Combs would track her down and bang on her door, demanding that she speak to him. Next would come a series of threats, like taking back the Bentley convertible he had gifted her on Mother's Day. With her usual steely cool-girl reserve, Porter had known what awaited her when she had begun leaking the news of their breakup. She didn't care. Porter was finally putting her foot down and doing it publicly.

She had tried to exert control before. During the two-year back-and-forth period with Lopez, Porter had tried to end things numerous times. The day after Combs was acquitted in the nightclub shooting in 2001, Porter had dropped the bomb that she'd be taking him to court for child support. Up until then, she'd lived rent-free in one of Combs' properties, and they had no formal agreement in place regarding the care of their three-year-old, Christian. But the Lopez situation squashed their domestic bliss, and Porter moved into a swanky $6,800-a-month apartment on the Upper West Side, for which Combs footed the bill. Once Combs' criminal trial was out of the way, Porter wanted security for their son. Although they spent the duration of the year hammering out the specifics of the agreement, the two reconciled, turning up to court hand in hand and letting their attorneys duke it out while they went out for dinner. In the end, Porter won support for Christian until he turned twenty-one. Specifics of the financials weren't disclosed, but the monthly figure was estimated to be between $12,000 and $20,000 per month, and Combs would cover all medical and educational costs.

Despite Combs' waxing poetic about his deep love and respect for women, there was a clear disconnect between what he professed publicly and how he behaved privately. He tended to see the women in his life not as individuals but as extensions of his own image and ego. He steamrolled their choices; *no* wasn't a word he accepted readily. The desire to control was present in almost all his romantic relationships, but with Porter, it was heightened. He wanted a say in how she looked, hiring a glam team for small and big occasions alike to ensure she was always well-groomed and immaculate. "We made her a star," celebrity makeup artist Mylah Morales said. One associate who vacationed with the couple in the early 2000s found it unusual how involved Combs was in Porter's wardrobe choices and thought it was odd that he snapped Polaroids of her before she left the house.

This fixation on managing every detail of Porter's outward appearance only scratched the surface of Combs' deeper desire to control her completely. He was extremely jealous and possessive, going so far as to keep "tabs" on her by hiring private investigators to trail her, two sources said. "He'd know exactly who she was with," Porter's former attorney Suzanne Bracker said. "He was so crazy about her that he had her followed. Why? He didn't want her to be with anybody. He was going to intimidate anybody that she was with." There was a point, former Bad Boy rapper Mark Curry said, when he believed Combs had somehow bugged Porter's phone during the height of his romance with Lopez. While Combs was gallivanting around the world with his girlfriend, he expected Porter to remain single. Curry recalled Combs listening to a message that top Atlanta music executive Shakir Stewart had left for Porter, indicating a blossoming relationship between the pair. Seething, Combs confronted Stewart at L.A. Reid's Italy wedding in 2000. Flanked by his lackeys, he barged into his peer's room and broke a chair over his head, the late executive's mother and two of his close friends said. "He left him bleeding on a hotel floor in Italy," Stewart's mother, Portia, said. "He had to have stitches and then [Combs] threatened him. . . . 'I'm going to kill you.' . . . That's when I said you need to get out of this business. This man is crazy."

Their turbulent relationship, though, never seemed marred by hatred. Porter never once uttered a spiteful word toward Combs in the press, even though she had good reason to. They had their issues, disagreements, and fights, but they always managed to find their way back together. By 2006, the lothario seemed intent on settling down when he and Porter announced they were expecting twin girls. Speaking with a *Vibe* reporter that year, Combs looked as if he was going to cry tears of happiness thinking about his daughters. "People say, to a so-called ladies' man or whatever, that when you have girls, it changes you," Combs said. "So, I was like, 'What's God trying to tell me by giving me two girls?'" Combs and Porter seemed to be finally in harmony. "No Ordinary Love," *Essence* declared in a multipage spread of the happy couple. Combs cradled Porter's swelling belly, and the on-off couple, who seemed back on for good, discussed plans for their growing family's future. Combs gushed about his admiration for Porter, copping to his own hubris that had led him astray in the past. "With Jennifer, I was attracted to someone who had the same energy as me, but that isn't necessarily the best," Combs admitted. "Because I'm so aggressive, the best energy for me is someone who slows me down and makes me feel like I can breathe. It's hard for me to breathe. When I'm around Kim, I feel like I can do that." Days before Christmas, they welcomed twin girls Jessie and D'Lila, named after Combs' and Porters' respective maternal grandmothers.

The newborn bliss would be short-lived. Combs' professions of devotion to Porter turned out to be all lip service. Barely a month after Porter gave birth, Combs was photographed partying until daylight with British actress Sienna Miller. Combs looked sheepish when he was caught accompanying the pretty blonde back to her hotel room at 9:00 a.m. and tried his best to persuade a snapper not to use the compromising pictures of them. But that was minor compared to the real transgression. Porter caught wind of swirling gossip that Combs had fathered another child, a daughter named Chance, with his on-off fling Sarah Chapman—an Atlanta woman who had briefly dated Tupac Shakur and whom Combs had been casually seeing since the 1990s—just a few months before the twins arrived.

His camp adamantly denied the rumor. But it was very much true. He came clean only after the little girl was born. It wasn't necessarily the cheating that bothered Porter as it was the realization that Combs would never change. She had been holding out hope for marriage and for their relationship to evolve into a stable family life. A decade in, that still wasn't happening. Porter felt she had to finally draw a boundary and plot her exit. Secrecy was paramount; she knew Combs would not let her "walk out the door" if he caught wind of her plan. And so, while he was out of town, Porter called over her girlfriends one night and together they helped pack up her entire life to move to Los Angeles. "I wanted to be dramatic," Porter later told *Essence*. "I wanted him to know I wasn't breaking up with him for two weeks—or maybe leaving for two days. If I pack up everything—twins and all—it means I'm out! Puffy's an action person, not a talk person. So, I had to have an action. Telling him, 'Babe, I'm leaving,' was not gonna do it."

Combs couldn't stay away. "He somehow tracked her down," said an associate of Porter's. "He followed, and that's how he ended up in California." He turned up at her new house one night, convinced a new boyfriend was staying over, and started banging on the door and trying every lower-level window to get inside. "We aren't leaving until I get in this house," he reportedly told his security head, Roger Bonds.

It was an eerie callback to Combs' song from around that time: "Last Night" with Keyshia Cole. The ballad is a cross between a man's desperate reunification plea and a tormented woman's warning to stay away, and Combs seemed to inject himself into some of the lyrics, particularly the outro, which was cut from the radio version. A rueful Combs can be heard sweet-talking the woman, explaining how he has been trying to reach her "all night," before his mood darkens and he curses her out, makes a series of threats, and warns that she "better stop fucking playing with a nigga's feelings." After a few seconds of the tirade, Combs breaks his assumed character, laughing and telling the room, "That's really how it goes down, right?"

"If you ever really want to know the truth [of how Combs is feeling]," said Tierra Brown of Four Colourz, "listen to the music."

Inside the Beverly Hills Hotel room, Porter was steeling herself for how Combs might react to her detonating the breakup news. Her apprehension reflected an unspoken uncertainty surrounding their relationship, an underlying tension that insiders noticed but were reluctant to discuss openly: domestic violence. Sources close to Porter often danced around whether Combs was ever physically abusive to her, feeling it wasn't their place to make definitive statements about her experiences either way. One associate was adamant that Combs would never lay a hand on Porter, whom they described as no-nonsense and able to hold her own in any situation. "She would have beaten him back twice as hard," they said. "She was very scrappy." Others demurred. "I remember Kim used to go through a lot of stuff," was all former Bad Boy artist Mark Curry would offer. "If you live around them, you get to see the toxic relationship. I think every relationship he may have had that I experienced around him was like that."

Still, there was a prevalent whisper network. Combs blamed a jagged scar that cut across his wrist and sliced up his forearm on an unfortunate accident involving a champagne glass catching on his bracelet in 1996. "A freak accident," a spokesperson described it. A security guard claimed it was a lasting reminder of a nasty fight with Porter. In 2005, a Band-Aid on her nose following a Saint-Tropez yacht trip was blamed on falling into a table. Online forums were more direct. Two anonymous users who purported to be close to Porter posted about a series of clashes between the pair. At the time, their stories were dismissed as unfounded and unverifiable rumors. But the specificity of at least one event was shockingly similar to what another woman and her friends would publicly testify to two decades later. "I remember one time when [Porter] had an apt in Harlem (near Central Park)," the user wrote in August 2005. "He came up there and tried to kick her door in for something so stupid we hoped she wouldn't open the door, but she did, and he dragged her out the apt by her hair." It was the same year Danity Kane and Diddy-Dirty Money member Dawn Richard saw Porter slip out from a recording studio in tears, with visible facial injuries and a busted lip. She had been in the room with Combs.

Bonds, who worked as Combs' security head between 2003

and 2012, claimed in an interview with DJ Vlad that Combs once ordered him out of the car during a tense argument he was having with Porter. When the vehicle started shaking, Bonds intervened, warning that they were outside the Beverly Hills Hotel. "Kim got out of the car, she fixed her hair, and she said, 'Put your hands on me again, and you are gonna have to explain this scratch I'm about to put on your face,'" Bonds recalled. "She knew that if she at least fought back, then there was a chance that she could leave a mark on him. And if she left a mark on him, he had a lot of explaining to do of what that mark was about. It would check him and put him back into his place of, 'Yeah, I can't do that to her.'"

Porter went through with leaking the breakup news, although Combs' team continued to deny the split, right up until Porter released a personal statement in July. "In ending this relationship, I made a decision that was in the best interest of myself, Sean, and our family," she said, making clear she was the one who walked away. "I look forward to moving on with my life and my career, and wish him prosperity, health, and happiness in life and in love. We will remain friends and committed parents to our children." *Essence* then dropped a tell-all two-part interview that laid bare some of what was happening behind closed doors.

Porter wouldn't disclose everything, though. As she holed up in the hotel room, she placed a phone call to a longtime friend, lamenting about what she had been putting up with for the past decade, the breaches of trust, his refusal to allow her to move on, and, yes, physical violence.

Eventually, tensions simmered down between the couple, and they navigated what many understood to be an open relationship, at least on Combs' end. "She was a special figure to him," said George Kaplan. "I didn't see her as being a girlfriend. She was vaunted above it." Amid all the turbulence, they also shared a deep love and understanding. Some mused that Porter's manner with

Combs sometimes veered toward motherly. They were best friends and confidants. They shared a bond that had been tested repeatedly but was ultimately unbreakable. There was one small change. In 2012, the same year Combs went public with a new girlfriend, his artist Casandra "Cassie" Ventura, Porter decided to switch up her usual manicure. Although she had been photographed for the past decade with consistently white or French tip nails, she started wearing bright, bold colors.

# CHAPTER 6 | CASANDRA VENTURA

**"I HOPE TO JUST BE ABLE** to learn what it is you want in a woman and give it to you," a pleading Casandra "Cassie" Ventura wrote to Combs in October 2007.

The twenty-one-year-old singer was torn, feeling overwhelmed by the thrill of her new, high-stakes romance with Combs and drained by the emotional whiplash she experienced in his presence. In recent weeks, Combs had gone from playfully flirting with Ventura to fully pursuing her, ignoring whatever boundaries that exist between a label boss and their artist. Fresh off a weekend of intimacy in Miami—the first time the pair had spent extensive time alone together—Ventura found herself on unsure footing.

Seventeen years her senior, Combs had signed the model-turned-singer to what seemed like a lucrative ten album deal when she was just nineteen years old in 2006, with only the seductive, electro-R&B club hit "Me & U" under her belt. But Ventura had all the makings of a star. Strikingly beautiful, she had an airy, sweet voice and a girlish disposition that could be crafted into a femme fatale archetype. Combs signed her on the spot after hearing her sing over a business dinner at Cipriani. Her self-titled album was released in August 2006, selling more than six hundred thousand copies worldwide, and an eager Ventura went back into the booth to get started on her second album. Combs seemed intent on making Ventura the lead female act on the label's dwindling roster, directing ample resources into her blooming career. When Ventura had a series of rocky performances, Combs stepped in as her protector, going out of his way to publicly back her. Still, outside of work, the two were more acquaintances than friends, occasionally bumping into each other at industry events in New York.

Things changed in early September 2007. Ventura flew to Las Vegas to attend the MTV Video Music Awards and celebrate her late-August birthday. Combs crashed the star-studded event for his young artist, photographed draping a diamond-encrusted wrist across her bare shoulder and raising a nearly empty rocks glass, as a shy Ventura giggled into her glass of champagne. She posed for pictures with her then boyfriend, producer and songwriter Ryan Leslie, and a partying, fedora-sporting Britney Spears. As the night stretched into the early hours of the morning, Ventura and her friends continued the party back at Combs' hotel suite, piling onto a patio couch as they drunkenly posed for more photos. Ventura gave a bright smile as she snuggled into a reclining Combs. The night would end in tears for Ventura, who said Combs later followed her into a bathroom and unexpectedly kissed her. Confused by the sudden shift in their dynamic, Ventura cried as she hurriedly headed back to her own hotel room.

Combs' lifestyle was a fantasy compared to Ventura's modest upbringing in New London, Connecticut, a coastal, working-class city. Her mother, Regina, worked as an administrative assistant at Pfizer, and her father, Rodrick, was a respected local EMT and firefighter for over twenty years. Her parents enrolled her in typical childhood after-school activities—karate, ballet, and piano—but it was performing that Ventura instinctively felt called to, specifically singing and dancing. Yet, discouraged by feedback about the strength of her vocals, Ventura pivoted to modeling. She signed with premier agency Wilhelmina, landing an Abercrombie & Fitch campaign and booking catalog shoots with clothing retailers JCPenney and dELiA*s. For a while, she commuted back and forth to New York, and after graduating from high school, she decided to use her savings to move to Manhattan with her best friend, Kerry Morgan, whom she met through modeling, in 2004. The two did everything together. "She was very confident," Morgan would testify of her impression of Ventura when they first met. "[She was] young, fun; she worked really hard." They followed in the footsteps of many new arrivals to the city, sharing an apartment space in the Financial District and learning how to navigate the streets on their own. Teenage Ventura wasn't much of a drinker, Morgan said, and if she did sneak a cocktail or two, she was a total lightweight. Now, Ventura was being thrown off into the deep end.

In the weeks that followed Ventura's birthday in Vegas, Combs aggressively pursued her back home in New York, at first under the guise of work. He'd beckon Ventura to his suite at the Trump Hotel in Columbus Circle—where he was staying while his Midtown residence was being renovated—for what she believed were discussions about the direction for her sophomore album. Yet the conversation would veer into personal, sexual territory. At one meetup, Combs performed oral sex on Ventura. After she left without returning the favor, Combs gave her an earful. "He made me feel crazy for not reciprocating," Ventura later said.

Although Ventura was still in a relationship with Leslie, Combs' attention was intoxicating. To be around him was to be dazzled. Combs was worldly and engaging, and yet he still retained a playful, boyish charm. Eager to whisk Ventura away from her boyfriend, Combs concocted a scheme to bring her to Miami. Emerging and longtime artists can make a quick buck by appearing at nightclubs, needing only to show up long enough to collect their check. It was the perfect cover that wouldn't raise too much suspicion from Leslie. Days later, a fake flyer was drawn up, and Ventura boarded a Florida-bound flight.

Combs wanted to pull out all the stops for his new, young romantic interest, wooing her with showy gestures. His personal assistant David James recalled that Combs seemed hell-bent on impressing Ventura for the getaway, renting a private boat to take the pair out on the sparkling waterfront. Combs had clear expectations for how the trip would go, cursing out James for forgetting to pack condoms.

The weekend would be a series of firsts for Ventura—among them, having sex with Combs and accepting from him a blue Ecstasy pill in the shape of a dolphin. The euphoric, sense-heightening drug would later become a staple of their sex lives. Ventura reclined on the boat in a blissful daze. She paid no mind to a friend snapping her photo, her eyes shielded by dark, oversize sunglasses, despite the sky being pitch-black, and her legs haphazardly splayed apart, her lower body barely covered by a waffle-knit bathrobe. Dressed in just a white undershirt and boxer briefs, Combs hovered nearby, looking directly into the camera with a deadpan stare. "Everything kind of happened that weekend," Ventura said.

The rest of the trip flew by in a drug-and-booze-fueled haze. "They partied all weekend," James said. Combs' personal chef, Jourdan Cha'Taun Atkinson, said she offered to make Ventura food when seeing her "high out of her mind," hoping a meal would help with her comedown. It stuck out in her mind, Atkinson said, because "that's when I knew this was no longer a working relationship." Instead, Combs was "in the grooming phase. . . . He was working her down, like men with money do." That trip was the culmination of Combs' pursuit of Ventura. "We spent a lot of time with each other after that," she said. "Now I know in hindsight, but I had become one of his girlfriends after that trip."

The warning signs of the impending tumult came quickly. Only a few weeks in, Combs began scolding Ventura for what he labeled childish behavior, causing Ventura to email him trying to articulate her confusion over what felt like a yo-yo dynamic. A self-described naive and sexually inexperienced young woman, Ventura felt out of her depth in the escalating romance. And at the same time, she felt immense pressure to hold Combs' interest, often measuring herself against Porter and even her best friend, Morgan.

"We've only really had one week of each other just together, and I can say that it's been the best and worst," Ventura wrote in the email to Combs. "I've never felt so loved, safe, and empowered since we've come together. When I'm with you, I feel like I'm your woman and no one else's. I feel protected when I'm in your arms and so comfortable that I can sleep and not worry about anything. You are one of the sweetest, most sincere people I've met in a long time, and I cannot express enough how grateful I am that you've chosen to be a part of my life. I don't want to rush things, but I can't help but sit with you and dream up a beautiful future together. Who knew I'd fall so fast? You make me feel like I can do anything . . . and that's real."

But on the other hand, she ventured, "You're constantly weary of me. . . . I'm sneaky, I never seem to make the right decisions to you, I'm a spoiled brat, I'm dramatic, disrespectful, and for some reason, you just don't trust me. It always goes back to, well, maybe Kerry would have been the better one to go after, since I've witnessed (more than once) you realizing that she is way better fitting for you than I am. It's hard for me to handle that as I feel like I have given so much of myself in this short time, but whatever, I can take it—I'm guessing there will always be something negative. I don't know, I really don't. I'm hurt that you think that I'm a malicious person. The dinner I went to last night was definitely bad timing, but it had been planned before all of the drama and things had to be handled, just like you have to handle your business. I never step on your toes when it comes to handling yours. I'm about to get on this plane and I'm sad, mad, frustrated, and hurt that you just don't feel like I'm the right one. I really do love you, and I hope to just be able to learn what it is you want in a woman and give it to you. You're very important to me, I hope you know that. X Ca$."

That early message foreshadowed the couple's doomed relationship. In almost every major romance Combs had—Ventura, Porter, Misa Hylton, Jennifer Lopez, and his girlfriend at Howard, among many others—there were whispers about how he treated the women he professed to love. He'd refer to his partners as "queens," speaking in lofty terms about his deep love and respect for women, yet when a journalist wasn't taking quotes, the adoration seemed to fly out the window. In Combs' view, if he was going to treat his girlfriend like royalty—lavishing her with gifts and giving her the honor of hanging off his arm at events—he expected to be the king. Women were beautiful playthings, existing to fulfill his sexual desires and to give him emotional support. A woman worthy of Combs needed to be submissive to him in all things. To upset Combs on this particular view of his world brought extreme consequences.

Combs' relationship with Ventura would lay bare the full scope of his masterful level of mind games, jealousy, and all-consuming need for control. His old girlfriends might have confided in close friends about his temper, and those around him might have seen bursts of violence, but what Ventura—and the group that orbited the toxic couple in the 2010s—saw was unparalleled and distressingly dark. At the beginning, Ventura felt she needed to grovel for Combs' approval and to prove herself to him, over and over again. Combs had designed it that way. "'I got her right where I want her. She's young,'" James recalled Combs telling a friend about Ventura in those early days. "He said that she was very moldable."

---

In the early to mid-2010s, Combs was culturally omnipresent. In 2010, he played a manic record executive in *Get Him to the Greek*, a telling caricature of himself. In 2014, he appeared in a *Muppets* film. He launched *I Want to Work for Diddy*, a reality spin-off of *Making the Band* (and a knockoff of his old pal Donald Trump's *The Apprentice*). Now in his forties, Combs began cultivating ties with the next generation of rap's elite: French Montana, Kanye West, Future, Machine Gun Kelly, Meek Mill, and Trey Songz. After successfully capturing a pop audience with *Making the Band*, he introduced Diddy-Dirty Money, his trio group with Kalenna Harper and Danity Kane's Dawn Richard, with an experimental album, *Last Train to Paris*, in December 2010. At a time when anyone in Combs' position might have pulled their foot off the gas and taken time to enjoy the world they'd created, Combs smashed his foot on the pedal.

His wealth was also growing at an expeditious rate, thanks to his Cîroc ambassadorship. The evenly split profit-sharing deal ended up being a perfect pairing. Combs aggressively promoted the brand. In his ten commandments for throwing a great party, Cîroc ranked number two for "essential party ingredients" on a list dominated by the word *sexy*.

There wasn't a Combs-affiliated business event that didn't have a few of the sleek clear bottles on display. At his recording studio Daddy's House, Combs expected several bottles to be waiting on ice for him when he entered with his entourage of producers and assistants. Commercials helped make Cîroc—and Combs himself—synonymous with the nightlife and club scene. A tagline declared, "Cîroc is for the culture," a not-so-subtle signal that the ultra-premium vodka was for those who reflected the community of Black and racially diverse men and women in Combs' world, those with their fingers on the pulse of entertainment. It was more than a partnership: Combs made Cîroc an extension of himself, and within two years of inking the deal, annual sales for Cîroc jumped from 75,000 cases a year to 400,000. By 2014, that number skyrocketed to 2.6 million.

Encouraged by the obscene amount of money he was raking in from Cîroc, Combs eyed another opportunity to make even more cash in 2013. While vodka had long been the United States' top-selling spirit, tequila had steadily gained momentum, becoming the fastest-growing liquor for years on end. Always ahead of the curve, Combs acquired the award-winning brand DeLeón, splitting ownership with Diageo. He hoped to replicate his success with Cîroc, only this time with an ownership stake. That same year, Combs launched Revolt, a Black-owned media company and television network, solidifying him as a multi-hyphenate mogul.

In many ways, Combs was one of the original influencers, creating what would become the standardized hip-hop mogul and even celebrity playbook. He leveraged his initial platform and well-earned social currency to launch restaurants and a clothing line; secure gigs on Broadway, television, and films; and establish himself as a cultural steward. Combs envisioned himself as larger than a brand; he was a lifestyle. In his ideal world, fans and consumers alike would live in a Diddy-fied universe. Combs said of his ideal world, "You wake up in the morning, you turn on the radio, you get in the shower, [you] listen to one of my records. Get out the shower, put on some Sean John clothes. Finish it off with Sean John Unforgivable fragrance. You may come to work for one of my many companies, you'll leave and go have dinner at my restaurant. After dinner, you turn on the television, watch one of my television shows. You'll put on some more Sean John, go out to a nightclub, hear some more records, and possibly have some Cîroc."

Thanks to his partnership with Cîroc, Combs further leaned into party culture, going back to his love of underground house music that he grew up dancing to in Washington, DC, and at clubs like Tunnel in New York to create the 2014 album *11 11* with Israeli DJ Guy Gerber. He wanted to name it "Ketamine," for the "demented, after-hours minds," but label heads advised against it. At this professional peak, his drug use was also at an all-time high. Several who saw Combs over the course of many years—at work, industry events, and parties alike—stressed that he always seemed to be coherent and in control of himself. Combs became a master of hiding his substance usage, even something as relatively innocuous as smoking weed, from those not in his inner sanctum. "He had an intern that was assigned to him that would take marijuana and put it into cigarettes because he didn't want people seeing [him] smoking marijuana," said former intern Damien Vazquez. His team acted as a logistics network: refilling prescriptions under his aliases and sometimes under their own names, coordinating with local dealers kept on speed dial, and arranging cash handoffs.

There were at least two instances in which he overdosed: once between 2008 and 2009 and the second while at an event at the Playboy mansion in February 2012. One staffer recalled rushing to call 911 after seeing Combs on the ground in his underwear, foam coming out of his mouth. His executive team advised against it, instead calling a personal doctor. The staffer said she was gaslit about the situation: She was told Combs hadn't overdosed but had just had a bad reaction to his medication. He sought out rehab and treatment several times, but nothing stuck for long. Instead, he began drifting toward a different outlet, something he'd equate to true release.

---

Even disguised in a red wig and dark sunglasses, the woman peeking through a hotel room door at the Gramercy Park Hotel in 2012 was the most beautiful woman Daniel Phillip had ever laid eyes on. Although a welcome surprise, this was not what Phillip was expecting when he agreed to take on a last-minute booking for a bachelorette party.

Phillip didn't typically make house calls. He worked as a manager for a male revue show—a buttoned-up term for what's typically a rowdy, *Magic Mike*–esque spectacle in New York. Phillip oversaw the nightly operation where shrieking women eagerly stuffed dollar bills in beefy male strippers' pants as they thrusted and gyrated onstage. But earlier that evening, Phillip's boss had called, saying a group of women had specifically requested a Black male dancer to perform a striptease for their bachelorette shenanigans. No other dancers who fit that description were available on such short notice, so Phillip agreed to go himself.

He was given an address and instructions to come dressed as a New York City policeman. On such a tight turnaround, Phillip was only able to scrounge up an NYPD shirt—something easily found at any generic souvenir shop near Times Square. He arrived at the luxury hotel after midnight and headed up to the room, where he was greeted by the mystery woman dressed in racy red lingerie and dangerously tall heels.

She brought Phillip into the foyer of the suite before coming clean about the true purpose of his visit that night. There was no bachelorette party. Instead, she explained, it was her birthday and her husband wanted to treat her to a sensual experience. If Phillip was open to it, he would give her a massage, rub her down with baby oil, and see where things led. The woman pushed a few thousand dollars in cash into Phillip's hands, promising him a significant tip at the end of the night. As if she sensed Phillip's nerves, the woman assured him there'd be no physical contact between the two men. Her husband, she stressed, only wanted to watch.

Entering a dimly lit space, set aglow by flickering candles, Phillip took in his surroundings. The space opened up to a living room area with velvet couches, and a large center table was set up with bottles of baby oil and Astroglide, a clear indication of the couple's hopes of where the night would lead. Phillip's eyes landed on another disguised figure sitting silently in the corner of the room: a man wearing a bathrobe, a hat slung low over his forehead and a bandanna covering the lower half of his face. Phillip greeted the man and, in a weak attempt at small talk, asked what he did for a living. "Importing and exporting" was the short reply. Although the man clearly took measures to conceal his identity, Phillip recognized the voice instantly: It was Sean Combs.

The sexual encounter between Phillip and the gorgeous stranger didn't last long. A few moments of rubbing baby oil on each other's stripped-down bodies and erotic touching quickly escalated into sexual intercourse. Phillip forwent a condom as Combs remained in the corner, masturbating silently as he watched the activity unfold. Afterward, the woman handed Phillip another few thousand dollars. Before he left, Combs told Phillip that his boss had created a bit of a headache for them when booking, suggesting it might be easier if they could just contact Phillip directly if he'd be willing to see them again. Phillip agreed, giving his number to the woman and leaving the hotel. Not even five minutes later, Phillip received a message from the woman, asking for a photo of his penis, which he obliged. The following message was a request for Phillip to come back to the room. He wouldn't leave the hotel until the early hours of the morning, going through the same sequence of events all over again, this time more prolonged.

Phillip later came to know the woman as Ventura and saw her and Combs several more times over the next two years when they were in New York. He didn't know the term at the time, but that night, Phillip had been hired for his first freak-off. "I was in complete shock and just was, like, 'Did that just happen?'" Phillip said.

By the mid-2010s, Combs had successfully molded Ventura into his ultimate fantasy girl, a far cry from the twentysomething who sheepishly admitted she didn't fully understand the concept of oral sex when they first started dating. "I didn't have the vocabulary for some of the things that we talked about," Ventura said. "At that time, [I] didn't understand that kind of a sexual relationship." When Phillip found himself summoned to the Gramercy Park Hotel, Ventura seemed like she could match Combs' insatiable stamina, almost always agreeable to having sex when and how he wanted. "When do you want to freak-off?" Combs messaged Ventura in August 2009. "I'm always ready to freak-off," she replied.

It was within the first year of their relationship that Combs introduced the idea of freak-offs to Ventura. Although Combs didn't always use the term to describe the sexual sessions that often stretched days, it's what Ventura began to know the nights as. "Sean proposed to me this idea, this sexual encounter that he called voyeurism, where he would watch me have intercourse and sexual activity with a third party, specifically another man," she said. "I just remember, like, my stomach falling to my butt. The nervousness and the confusion in that moment. I had just turned twenty-two. I didn't have a concept of how that would be a turn-on, but I also felt a sense of responsibility with him sharing something like that with me."

Hesitant but also willing to do anything to make Combs happy, Ventura agreed. For that first time, Combs took charge of the entire arrangement. He handpicked and booked the male escort for the night and secured a supply of illicit substances for them to take—the same blue dolphin-shaped Ecstasy pills Ventura first tried during her secret Miami trip. The duo wore masks to conceal their identities, and Combs walked Ventura through every aspect of what he wanted to see. Afterward, Ventura was left with a flood of mixed emotions, as well as a harsh comedown from the party drugs. "I think it was a mixture of dirty and confusion with, like, 'OK, he's really happy with me and I did something right,'" she explained. "I didn't know what was going to happen after that." Within weeks, Combs was pushing for another freak-off. It would become the dominant aspect of their relationship, lasting until Ventura broke up with Combs in 2018. Over the decade the couple was together, Ventura had hundreds of freak-offs with dozens of strange, unvetted men around the world.

Although the nights were supposed to be spontaneous—something the self-described freaky Combs wanted in the heat of the moment—they were anything but. Freak-offs were highly organized with several moving parts, and Combs relied on his personal staff to help pull them off. It began with Combs or Ventura hiring the men, usually through online back pages and service agencies like Cowboys4Angels, which had hunky guys on call in every major city in the country. Once someone was lined up, Combs sent his security staff to retrieve between $5,000 and $10,000 in cash to pay the men. His chief of staff and company travel agent helped book last-minute hotels, typically a one-bedroom suite at a five-star hotel. And his most trusted personal assistants were in charge of preparing Combs' hotel room, arriving early to ensure the room was stocked with anything Combs might want for an indefinite period.

There were specific requirements for how the hotel rooms were set up. Some aspects were mundane, like Combs' personal toiletries arranged just so, an extra change of clothes, a portable sound system, and his laptop or iPad. Others raised eyebrows. It was crucial that there be a double-digit supply of Astroglide and Johnson's baby oil, as well as extra towels and bed linens to drape over furniture in an attempt to avoid room damage fees from the baby oil. There was also mood lighting. Combs wanted the suite filled with cheap Glade candles in the scent Clean Linen or Angel Whispers, with the labels peeled off, rounded out by a smattering of expensive Diptyque candles. An assistant once had to pick up nearly $800 worth of the designer candles in a single trip, documenting the receipt so Bad Boy could reimburse them. The cloying scent hanging in the dark, seventy-five-degree room, tinged with body odor, was overpowering. "It was super pungent and strong mixed with oil and just all of the other scents," Ventura said.

Once inside the room, the real choreography began. The sessions would always follow a specific pattern. Ventura would greet the man and bring him deeper into the dimly lit space. After making small talk, they'd reach for one of the many bottles of warm baby oil, dousing their bodies in the slick, slippery substance. The oil was a key component of the night. It was "just as important as everything else, as being there," Ventura said. Both her and the man's skin were expected "to be glistening," meaning they could easily go through a dozen bottles during an entire freak-off. Then would come the touching, before Ventura and the man performed oral sex on each other, followed by sexual intercourse. Combs would always watch. Sometimes, he'd make a show of leaving the room, so that he could creep back in, crawling on the ground to look on. The freak-offs were suspended in time, sometimes taking several days as the sexual activity continued over multiple "rounds" or "sessions."

Afterward, Combs would bring Ventura into their private adjoining bedroom to have intercourse privately as the man waited outside. The particularness of where the man should finish was clear once Combs and Ventura were alone. "He would want me to put the semen on his body," Ventura said. "Usually on his chest, on his nipples." Phillip said Combs once directed him to ejaculate inside Ventura, but he was unable to reach an orgasm. "I was in my head or whatever the problem was, but I couldn't ejaculate, and so I just pretended to do it," Phillip said. "They got up, they went into the room. And then Sean Combs came out of the room, and he asked me, he said, 'Yo, are you sure you came?' And I said, 'Yeah, I'm positive.' And he was like, 'You sure?' And I said yes. So they went back into the room. They definitely knew I pretended."

After her private time with Combs, Ventura would rinse off, put on a new outfit, and go again—sometimes with the same escort waiting in the living room, other times with an entirely new man who had just arrived at the hotel. The longest freak-off lasted for four days straight, Ventura said. There was no sleep; Ventura and Combs used drugs to keep themselves awake, alert, and high. It wasn't until Combs decided he'd seen enough that they'd finally go to sleep, sending the final man on his way with a fistful of cash, ranging between $1,500 and $6,000, depending on his performance. The day after, Combs and Ventura would crash and order liquid IV drips to help with the brutal comedowns. Then, Combs was off to work. Ventura did her best to tidy up the destroyed rooms, but it wasn't always enough. Combs was charged thousands of dollars in deep cleaning and damage fees when the oil and spilled candle wax ruined the rooms' carpets and drapes, various hotel records show. Hotels kept internal records about the damages and the strong odor emitting from Combs' boiling-hot room. In October 2012, the InterContinental in New York charged Combs nearly $50,000 in damages to the penthouse suite.

Sharay Hayes, a New York City male exotic dancer known by his stage name, the Punisher, said his understanding was that his role was to create a sexy, erotic scene for Combs' enjoyment. His first encounter with the couple was similar to Phillip's: He was contacted by a woman who said she wanted to hire a dancer to perform a striptease for a group of women at a party. But upon arrival, the plans changed—the woman disclosed the booking's true intention. Hayes said the first time he met Combs, he was completely nude apart from a burqa-style veil that showed only his eyes. "I could not see his face," Hayes said. "I could see he had what I saw as a bottle of Astroglide he was carrying."

Combs wasn't just playing the role of a voyeur silently watching his girlfriend and the man engage in the activity. Rather, he was the one in charge. In these dark hotel suites, Combs liked to think of himself as an amateur pornographer on a closed film set, and Ventura and the escort of the night as his lead stars. He'd frequently record the freak-offs, giving directions to Ventura, telling her how to position her body and tinkering with the candle lighting to get a better view. He'd instruct Ventura and the man on when they should proceed to the next stage of activity and give permission for when and where the man could finish. If Ventura tried to move to another stage too quickly, Combs would interject, telling the pair to slow it down. Sometimes they'd have to restart the entire scene, having to "go back to square one," Ventura said. She was always attuned to Combs' preferences. "She was definitely seeking cues," said Hayes. Combs' pervasive presence threw several men off, and it wasn't uncommon for them to have trouble gaining and maintaining an erection during freak-offs. "It was actually pretty frequent with people that we didn't know well," Ventura said. "They would express it. Every time Sean would talk, it would throw them off, or if he moved a candle or, you know, just was distracting, I guess. . . . Some of the men would actually say that—having someone else in the room was disturbing for them. It made them uncomfortable." Hayes was one such man who struggled with erectile dysfunction in front of Combs. Although he tried Viagra and other methods to sustain himself, Hayes said he felt enormous pressure to perform. It was specifically Combs giving directions and breaking the fourth wall that distracted Hayes. During a freak-off around 2015, an "assertive" and "aggressive" Combs threw a packet of condoms on the couch where Hayes was tangled with Ventura. "As he presented the condoms, he said, 'I'm ready to see you fuck her,'" Hayes said. He was too thrown off to finish having intercourse with Ventura. It was the last time he was hired for a freak-off.

For Phillip, the first time he was unable to maintain an erection during a freak-off was after he saw Combs attack Ventura. He had been invited to her West Side apartment for what he'd come to know as a typical encounter. They were in between sessions when Ventura was on her computer, while Combs stayed in her bedroom. Phillip was waiting on the couch, sitting directly behind Ventura. "I heard him yell out, 'Babe, come here,'" Phillip recalled, then Ventura told Combs to give her a moment. Things escalated in a flash. "Mr. Combs came out of the room, and I just saw a [liquor] bottle fly past her and hit the wall," he said. "Mr. Combs walked over to her, to Cassie. He grabbed her by her hair, and started dragging her by her hair into her bedroom. I could hear what sounded like him slapping her. She was screaming, 'I'm sorry, I'm sorry.' He was saying, 'Bitch, when I tell you to come here, you come now, not later.'"

It wasn't an anomaly for Combs to explode on Ventura during the middle of a freak-off. Drugs heightened the tenor of the night, and Combs' unpredictability went into overdrive. In those rooms, he expected total compliance from a high, naked, and vulnerable Ventura, and his satisfaction came above all. The chaos that Phillip overheard lasted briefly before the pair emerged. Ventura looked rattled and Combs defiant. "Cassie was visibly very upset, [she] did not look like she wanted to continue doing anything," Phillip said. "But Mr. Combs asked, 'Are y'all ready to continue now?' I couldn't do anything after that."

---

Outside the bedroom, Combs began to insert himself into every aspect of Ventura's life. It was both flattering and overwhelming when he heaped the full weight of his attention onto her. There were lavish dinners, shopping trips, and beach vacations. In the throes of passion, Combs wanted his girlfriend to be constantly available to him. As a birthday gift, Combs made a show of upgrading her apartment to a modern two-bedroom, two-bathroom unit on the West Side, giving Ventura's parents a tour of the pad. The high-end building was conveniently situated a few avenues away from the Bad Boy Midtown offices and Daddy's House recording studio—cutting her commute down to a tight five minutes. It also meant she was closer to Combs, whose residence was right off Broadway, too.

But with Combs, extravagant gifts and grand gestures always had strings attached. The presents were more akin to handcuffs, keeping Ventura financially dependent and at the mercy of his mood swings. Before dating Combs, she had mainly been financially independent, earning around $250,000 a year from modeling gigs. Once they were together, Combs began weighing in on what jobs Ventura could and couldn't take, and he kept delaying her second album. Keeping a tight grip on her incoming finances, Ventura relied on Combs' monthly rent payments and his financial generosity in part to help keep her afloat. His control ran deeper than just money; he also had a specific vision of how she should look. When it came to her nails, Combs preferred bright white polish or a French manicure, exactly the styles Porter had worn before her public split from Combs. He gave significant input on how she should dress, sometimes wanting her to be overtly sexy and "his woman." Other times, he encouraged Ventura to lean into a tomboy, punky look. "He was just very involved," Ventura said. "Appearance was very important to him, my appearance." The critiques came daily, but it seemed natural for Combs to want to have a say over Ventura's image. He was just looking out for her, Ventura reasoned. He was the veteran music executive, and she was a newcomer. "After a while, that wears down on you," Ventura said. "Definitely my self-worth took a hit for the entirety of the relationship, just trying to establish who I was, who I wanted to be, and who I was allowed to be."

This need for control would often turn violent. In January 2009, Combs didn't like what he saw when he observed a drunk Ventura chatting with a music producer during Combs' event at the Ace of Diamonds strip club in West Hollywood. Nearly three years after Ventura released her first album, she was still in a standoff with Combs over finalizing a release date for her sophomore album. It wasn't for lack of work; rather, Ventura had no one to advocate on her behalf. Combs had already blurred professional lines. At his urging, Ventura parted ways with her manager, industry power player and former CEO of Sony Music Tommy Mottola. It was a "major conflict of interest," Combs insisted, because Mottola's team also managed her ex-boyfriend Ryan Leslie. Combs installed himself and his team as Ventura's new management.

What was intended as her follow-up project, "Connecticut Fever," had been teased to the press since 2007, and two singles followed, the synthy R&B "Is It You" from the *Step Up 2: The Streets* soundtrack, in which Ventura had a small role, and the fan-favorite plea of a song "Official Girl" (featuring Lil Wayne). As 2008 came to a close with no album from Ventura, a music writer from *The Guardian* praised the unreleased "Connecticut Fever" as "magnificent" and hailed the leaked track "Turn the Lights Off" as their favorite song of the year. "Had *Connecticut Fever* existed," they added, "it would be an easy contender for album of the year." The glowing piece was published a few days before Ventura found herself discussing work with the producer at Ace of Diamonds.

Whether the ever-watchful Combs took offense at just the conversation or believed Ventura was blatantly flirting was unclear. But he made his distaste known when he spat the word *slut* at Ventura. She was humiliated. As the entourage piled back into an Escalade, an intoxicated Ventura unloaded on Combs, swinging on him as hard as she could. It was the first time she could recall hitting Combs, though it was not the first time violence had surfaced in the couple's relationship.

In the midst of their head-over-heels honeymoon period, Combs had started to become physical with Ventura, slapping and hitting her, and the frequency was escalating. Something as small as a sly comment could set Combs off, and he would lash out at her both verbally and physically. But the ride following the Ace of Diamonds club appearance was different. Combs' eyes darkened and his energy shifted, as he turned into a man Ventura would come to fear. In a flash, Ventura found herself on the floor of the

SUV with Combs' heavy foot crushing down on her face. "I was basically underneath the backseat in the Escalade, just trying to cover my face," Ventura said. "Because Sean was stomping on it with his foot."

At least two members of Combs' personal team were in the car with them, but no one intervened during the entirety of Ventura's nightmare journey back to Combs' rental. "I just never experienced anything like that before, where I just was getting really, really badly beaten," she said. As the car pulled up to the house, roughly ten minutes later, Ventura went into flight mode, bursting from the vehicle and running away. She didn't make it far, caught by Combs' head of security, Roger Bonds. Inside the house, a disheveled Ventura examined her face. She was bloodied, and golf-ball-sized knots were already forming on her head. When Combs saw her, he sent her away to The London hotel in West Hollywood, instructing her to stay put until her injuries healed.

Hours later, a blind item appeared on Lipstick Alley, an anonymous blog forum that kept extensive tabs on Combs. An incognito user posted a thread that would take another fifteen years to be publicly corroborated. Under the title "Diddy Opens up a can of WHOOP *** on Cassie," the user wrote, "According to a reliable source, Diddy beat the shit out of Cassie for talking to another guy. He pushed her to the ground and kicked her in the face, and this is not the first time he has hit her." The board quickly filled with commentary. Some expressed shock, while others quipped that Ventura should have known better considering the rampant whispers about Combs allegedly being violent with Porter and his other ex-girlfriends. They also had more questions for the poster, who returned with what would be an alarmingly accurate play-by-play of the night.

"Last night Diddy and Cassie were out at a club in Los Angeles," the anonymous user informed the forum readers. "Cassie was chopping it up with some producer a bit too long for Diddy's taste. Diddy goes over to her, grabs her arm and starts going off on her in front of the dude. At this point they proceed to leave the club. They get mouthing off and [Cassie] bops Diddy upside the back of the head. Of course, all hell breaks loose. Diddy smacks her in the face and is shaking her and shit. His bodyguard tries to intervene, telling Diddy to chill. They continue arguing all the way to the house in the limo. Once they get there Cassie runs and grabs her shit like she is leaving and goes walking off down the street. Diddy goes after her and proceeds to knock her to the ground at which point he kicks her a few times in the face. The bodyguard pulls him off of her. Cassie, crying and bleeding, is then taken to her hotel by one of the assistants."

That night was just one of many physical beatings Ventura withstood during her relationship with Combs. "He would mash me in my head, knock me over, drag me, kick me, stomp me in the head if I was down," she said. The attacks could be random: Once, he hurled a kitchen knife at her out of nowhere. Another time, Ventura's friend Kerry Morgan was on vacation with the couple in Jamaica in January 2013; hearing Ventura let out a "guttural" and "terrifying" scream, Morgan rounded a corner in the direction of the sound to see Combs dragging Ventura by her hair down a long hallway. Once they were outside, Combs shoved Ventura to the ground, her head smacking against the brick pavement. She lay there, still. Her perceived offense? Taking too long in the bathroom. Combs liked keeping Ventura in a perpetual state of fear and submissiveness. The unpredictable and ever-present threat of violence kept Ventura meek and compliant. The beatings were frequent, and over time, Combs' abuse became an open secret within his close-knit Bad Boy circle, particularly those who worked on his personal team and out of his homes. But the turnover in those roles was high, reinforcing a self-contained culture of silence.

Fellow Bad Boy artist Dawn Richard's one-on-one exposure to Combs was minimal during the filming of *Making the Band*, but after Danity Kane dissolved, Combs brought her into his new side project, Diddy-Dirty Money, with singer Kalenna Harper. Combs began working on their album, *Last Train to Paris*, from his rented Beverly Hills home in 2009. What was supposed to be an exciting first day of work was marred when Richard saw Combs explode at Ventura over how she was cooking his eggs. He screamed insults at his girlfriend and picked up the hot frying pan as if he were about to bash it over her head. Ventura instinctively dropped into a fetal position, bracing herself for what might come next. "He proceeded to take his arm around her neck and put his hand in her hair and dragged her upstairs to the first floor," Richard said. She stood frozen in fear in the kitchen, as sounds of glass breaking and screaming came from above.

Deonte Nash, a Bad Boy stylist who became a close friend to Ventura while they worked together, jumped on Combs' back in a failed effort to slow him down as he lunged at Ventura in her apartment in summer 2013. After tossing Nash to the floor, Combs bashed Ventura's head into her bed frame corner. Blood started gushing from a large, deep gash on her eyebrow, but Combs was in a blind rage. "He still continued to hit her for a short time," Nash said. Finally, "when he noticed the blood, he just panicked." A new assistant, Kala Faulkner, was instructed to call a plastic surgeon to stitch together Ventura's face. Some time later, Faulkner confided to Combs' chief of staff that she feared Combs was physically abusing Ventura. She was then fired. The decision to terminate the recent college graduate was made during a conference call with the head of HR and other Bad Boy executives, according to the former assistant Mia. Later, Combs warned Mia that if Faulkner filed a lawsuit over her dismissal, she would "have to get up on the stand and testify everything that he told me to say," Mia claimed.

In another incident, the sound of shattering glass caught Combs' personal assistant George Kaplan off guard in 2015. Team Combs was on a private plane bound for Las Vegas, and the music mogul and Ventura were in the back of the aircraft, hidden by a partition. Still, a "tremendous commotion" could be heard. Turning his head, Kaplan saw Combs with a rocks glass in his hand, standing over a cowering Ventura. He averted his gaze as more glass crashed against a wall. "Cassie screamed, 'Isn't anybody seeing this?'" Kaplan said. No one responded. "I was twenty-three years old," Kaplan said, trying to explain why he turned away from Ventura even as she begged for help. "All I wanted to do was to have a great job in the entertainment industry. I could not believe my good fortune would be working for such an icon. And the last way that I thought that I would be successful in that career would be to compromise his well-being in any way."

Even people on the periphery caught glimpses of Combs' abuse and its aftermath. Prince's security intervened when Combs chased a fleeing Ventura through the grounds of the "Purple Rain" singer's estate, Combs knocking her to the ground when he caught up to her. He had instructed Ventura not to leave her hotel that night and was furious when he spied her at a Grammys event. And a fashion stylist who dropped by an intimate get-together at Combs' Los Angeles home in the 2010s was unnerved when Combs spent the entirety of the night barking at a vacant-looking Ventura. The stylist said they were so uncomfortable with the constant verbal denigration that they dipped out of the party early.

Employees were often caught in the middle of Combs' abuse of Ventura. Some tried to intervene, helplessly yelling at Combs to stop or physically trying to break them apart, despite the potential repercussions. Others were shell-shocked, rendered frozen while they worried about losing their jobs and their own personal safety. They were right to fear both. Feeling powerless against Combs was common among employees who witnessed his abuse but felt they had no one to report what they witnessed to. In their view, the HR department and higher-ups at Bad Boy existed to shield Combs and that reporting his behavior would serve only to jeopardize their own careers. Staffers who excelled in lower-level positions could rise through the ranks, awarded with high-ranking positions at ancillary Bad Boy companies or within Combs' wider network. Several had already achieved this upward mobility. Combs' Howard classmate Harve Pierre went from intern, to Hitmen producer, to Bad Boy general manager, before earning the title of Bad Boy president in 2008. Dia Simms was promoted from assistant to the tippy-top C-level roles at Combs' marketing firm Blue Flame and Combs Wines and Spirits, the company that oversaw the Cîroc and DeLeón deals, and then was named as president of Combs Enterprises in 2017. The latest example was Kristina Khorram, who joined Combs' personal assistant team in 2013. She fit the stereotype of Combs' typical chief of staff: a career-driven woman with a no-nonsense personality. The chiefs of staff had intensive positions, responsible for managing the world that orbited Combs. Khorram—whom everyone called "KK"—came from a middle-class background and graduated from North Carolina State University in 2009 with a business administration degree. She had bounced between low- and mid-level jobs at AOL, Paramount Pictures, and Burberry before arriving at Combs' doorstep. The twenty-something saw a pathway for herself and was intent on proving her loyalty to Combs in ways that others would later fault her for.

The only ones who could physically stop Combs were his buddies on the security team, but they largely stood idly by as the violence unfolded. Some, like Roger Bonds and D-Roc, would try to mitigate the assaults in their own way, intervening when the situation was on the brink of escalating further than it already had. D-Roc once cried at the sight of Ventura's black eye and busted lip after Combs repeatedly kicked her for chatting with another manager during an after-party in Las Vegas in September 2015. But it was clear where their allegiances ultimately lay. They'd whisk Ventura off to recover at guarded hotel rooms and knew to grab ice packs to curb swelling bumps on her head. They played double agent, comforting Ventura before sweet-talking her into forgiving Combs.

The cycle of domestic violence repeated itself for more than a decade. Ventura couldn't possibly estimate how many times she was beaten, only knowing it was too often. She grew so accustomed to the violence that she carried arnica gel in her cosmetic bag, using the over-the-counter natural remedy to help prevent bruising and reduce swelling. As early as 2009, following the events at Ace of Diamonds, when the extreme physical violence with Combs had only just started, Lipstick Alley users wondered how Ventura could possibly stick around.

The anonymous thread poster had one more thought to share. "Cassie is very submissive," they explained. "She's pretty much given up her family and friends to be around Puff. He has cut her off from everybody."

---

Combs was whittling down Ventura's independence until she was completely under his thumb. He assigned his personal assistants to accompany her when she wanted to run simple errands. Her luxury Jaguar belonged to him. His name was on the paperwork of her luxury condo and her credit cards. Even her medical records were being sent directly to his email, and he kept track of her menstrual cycle. In heated fights, like a parent dealing with a petulant teenager, he'd repossess the car he'd gifted her, kick her out of the apartment he insisted on paying for, take back jewelry, and snatch her phone away. He frequently grounded Ventura, forbidding her from going out. He weaponized her stalled music career against her and threatened to leak her freak-off tapes, once forcing her to watch what she thought were deleted videos on repeat on a commercial flight from France to New York after an argument. If Ventura tried to run, which she did numerous times, lackeys on his payroll tracked her down and dragged her back before him again. And finally, when Combs believed Ventura had pushed him too far, his eyes would go dark and the beatings would rain down.

Combs had no problem involving Ventura's close friends when he was arguing with her, pulling them into the mayhem of his rage. Kerry Morgan alleged that Combs threw a wooden hanger at her head in 2018. Ventura's friend Bana Bongolan alleged that in a fit of inexplicable rage, Combs dangled her from Ventura's seventeenth-floor balcony before hurling her into nearby furniture in 2016. Ventura kept her circle extremely small, and many of her confidants became those on Combs' payroll, including Nash and his personal assistant Mia. Nash said he was once taking a quick smoke break on the set of one of Ventura's music videos when Combs appeared out of nowhere, threw him onto the hood of a car, and began to strangle him. "I thought I told y'all about going out, y'all wildin'!" Nash recalled Combs screaming at him over going out to parties with Ventura. Nash always kept a go bag, with $1,000 in cash, tucked away for times when Combs was out looking for the friends, so he could safely book a hotel that Combs' team couldn't trace. Many times they tried to run away and hide from Combs, but he'd find them or force them to come back by threatening their safety. Moments like this felt both suspended from reality and like life-or-death at the same time. While on vacation with the couple in Turks and Caicos in 2012, Mia said she was startled awake by a terrified Ventura, who tore into her room "screaming for help and saying, 'You got to help me. He is going to kill me!'" The two barricaded the door with furniture and, when Combs started banging on the door, they escaped outside. "We were running so fast down the beach," Mia said. "I remember being shocked at the fact that we could still be attacked by mosquitoes as we were running." During another trip to the island, the women escaped to the beach again, taking paddleboards far out into the waters as Combs paced and hollered on the shore. A storm came from out of nowhere. "I was trying to weigh if it was scarier to face Mother Nature or to go back to Puff," Mia said. They slowly paddled back to shore.

With a billion dollars at his fingertips, a wealth of connections, and dogged determination, Combs could not be evaded; Ventura was resigned to believing there was nowhere safe from him, especially after the events of December 2011.

Shortly before Christmas that year, the couple "were not in the greatest place" and on one of their many breaks. A few months earlier, Combs had introduced Ventura to the musician Scott "Kid Cudi" Mescudi as a potential collaborator. A platonic friendship turned romantic, and Ventura confided in Mescudi about the beatings. Still, Ventura wasn't entirely done with Combs. In her mind, they might have been broken up, but they were still together sexually. "That was a job," she explained.

Knowing how jealous and possessive Combs was, Ventura went to great lengths to hide that she was dating Mescudi, like using a burner phone to communicate with him. The secret was exposed during a freak-off in late December 2011, when a suspicious Combs went through Ventura's phone and discovered the dalliance. Combs saw red and charged at Ventura with a corkscrew. Ventura fled the hotel and had Mescudi pick her up in the early hours of the morning. As she weighed her options, Combs went on the warpath.

Around dawn, Combs' former assistant Capricorn Clark heard "metal on metal" on her front door. Clark had since returned to

Bad Boy as the company's global brand director and was also working closely with Ventura as her manager. And when Combs went through Ventura's phone, he learned Clark was aware of the budding romance. From the peephole, Clark observed "a very upset Puff" pacing outside, demanding that she open. "He was furious," Clark said. "That was evident." When she opened the door, Combs was holding a gun. Disheveled, with his pants split from the crotch to the knee, exposing his underwear, Combs didn't care about his appearance. Revenge was the only thing on his mind. "He said, 'Get dressed. We're going to go kill this nigga,'" Clark recalled. "I had never seen anything like this before. He had never come to my house in the entire time I'd known him. I've never seen him with a weapon. I've never seen him making me do something like this."

Under the threat of the gun, Clark said she complied and got in Combs' SUV. Rube, his longtime security member and driver, who carried over from the Junior M.A.F.I.A. days, booked it to Mescudi's mansion in the Hollywood Hills. Leaving Clark in the car, Combs and Rube waltzed into Mescudi's home through an unlocked front door. Upon finding no one at home, Combs tore through the Chanel Christmas gifts that Mescudi had bought for his family members and terrorized his dog.

From the car, a terrified Clark called Ventura, alerting her and Mescudi that Combs was roaming his house, looking for a fight. Mescudi immediately jumped in his car and dialed Combs, demanding to know if he was in his home. Combs insisted he just wanted to talk. Mescudi phoned the police, reporting a break-in, and when Combs saw a patrol car roll up toward the house, he instructed Rube to take off. When they were a comfortable distance away, Combs demanded that Clark call Ventura. "He told me to tell Cassie that he has me and he's not going to let me go until I come get her," Clark said.

Ventura gave in, ultimately going with Clark back to Combs'

house to face his fury. "Puff was standing there in a robe and his underwear and he immediately began kicking Cassie," Clark said. "[He was using] 100 percent full force, [kicking her] in her legs to begin with. She was facing him to start, and he kicked her in, like, the thigh and her leg. He kept kicking her. He never used his hands." Clark said she pleaded with her boss to stop, but he said that if she dared to intervene, "he was going to fuck me up too." Clark felt helpless. "I had never seen him do that, and I was in shock," she explained. "My heart was breaking, seeing her get hit like that." Combs was also making threats toward Ventura. "He was just so angry," Ventura said. "He told me about videos that he had that he was going to release, and how he was going to hurt Scott and I."

With Christmas around the corner, Ventura left Los Angeles and headed home to Connecticut. On the flight, trying to protect herself, Ventura sent an email to her mother and Clark memorializing the threats, writing that Combs was "going to release two explicit sex tapes of me. One on Christmas Day, maybe before or right after, and another one sometime soon after that. He has also said that he will be having someone hurt me and Scott Mescudi physically (he made a point that it wouldn't be by his hands, he actually said he'd be out of the country when it happened)."

It was a humiliating message to send to a family member. "I was physically sick," Ventura's mother, Regina, said. "I did not understand a lot of it. The sex tapes threw me. I did not know the other person in it, but I knew that he was going to try to hurt my daughter." Around that same time, Regina received another message, this time from Combs, demanding a chunk of money as reimbursement for funds he had invested into Ventura's career. "It was understood that he was going to need $20,000 to recoup money that he had spent on her because he was angry that she had a relationship with Scott Mescudi," Regina said. The elder

Venturas didn't have the money on hand, but they were panicked by the email they had just received from Ventura. They took out a home equity loan days before Christmas to secure the funds and wired the money into one of Combs' many personal accounts. It wasn't about the money for Combs; his sole purpose was to inflict as much pain on Ventura as possible. While he was pressuring the Venturas to repay him, more than $3 million in liquid funds was moving in and out of just one of his personal accounts registered under an LLC with the address of his New Jersey house, bank records show. The $20,000 Regina Ventura had wired over was minuscule in comparison to Combs spending $500,000 during that same period at a New York art gallery.

Back with her family in Connecticut, Ventura was worried that Combs would follow through on his threat to hurt both Ventura and Mescudi for their betrayals. "I took that in my mind, if I stay in this situation, we both will be hurt. If I don't, then no one will be," Ventura reasoned. She lied to her parents, saying she was going back to Los Angeles. Instead, she went to reconcile with Combs in Arizona. Around the same time, without further explanation, the Venturas saw that $20,000 had been returned to their account.

But Combs' feud with Mescudi wasn't over yet. Mescudi had ignored Combs' repeated attempts to clear the air—until January 9, 2012, when his Porsche 911 Turbo S Cabriolet was firebombed in his driveway. Lance Jimenez, an investigator with the Los Angeles Fire Department, determined that an arsonist had cut a hole in the car's sunroof and dropped a Molotov cocktail inside. The incendiary device—made from an Olde English malt liquor bottle and a white handkerchief—failed to explode properly, but enough damage was done. The front seat's buttery red leather was melted, and the interior was darkened and charred by smoke. The vehicle was totaled. Jimenez collected fingerprints from the scene, including the car and the bottle. When he learned that fingerprints had been collected from Mescudi's front door after the rapper reported the December break-in, he requested that the Los Angeles Police Department compare the fingerprints from both incidents.

Although the results from the firebombing investigation were pending, Mescudi had his own suspicions about a possible suspect. He returned Combs' calls and agreed to talk. They met at the members-only club Soho House in Los Angeles, where they called a truce over Ventura. As Mescudi was leaving, he shook Combs' hand and asked about his car. "I said, 'What are we going to do about my car?'" Mescudi recalled. "I made sure to ask him right when our hands were clasped together, where he couldn't run away, and I could look at him square in his eyes, and he looked right back at me, with a very cold stare, and said: 'I don't know what you're talking about.' I said: 'OK.' I took my hand from his. And he said, 'Wait. I thought we were cool. Is there a problem?' I was like, 'You said you didn't burn my car, right? You said that's your word.' He said, 'Yeah.' I was like, 'That's it.'" Mescudi left the meeting thinking: That man is "lying."

Combs and Ventura were back together, but Mescudi was still pushing the fire department for answers about his car—evidence from the liquor bottle had indicated the presence of female DNA. Throughout the spring and summer, Jimenez worked his leads, chasing Ventura and Clark, who wouldn't return his calls, for his report. By then, Combs had fired Clark. The explanation she was given was a cover for what Clark believed was happening: She had betrayed Combs' trust by not telling him about Ventura's affair with Mescudi. Clark hired an employment attorney to build a case of wrongful termination and secured a $500,000 settlement from Combs in October 2012. It came with the stipulation she could never publicly disparage Combs. Per the agreement, Combs was also required to write Clark a letter of recommendation. It never came.

Jimenez continued to try to contact Clark and Ventura, but unbeknownst to him, in the same month that Clark was fired, someone in the Los Angeles Police Department took the unusual step of ordering that the fingerprint cards from the break-in be destroyed. Jimenez reached a dead end and the case would remain unsolved.

---

Combs was a master of covering his tracks. Like the document Clark signed, settlements often came with non-disparagement clauses, leaving signees on the hook for $1 million if they broke the terms. And he wasn't afraid to weaponize law enforcement. In 2008, after his private chef, Jourdan Cha'Taun Atkinson, went to HR threatening legal action over Combs having violently shoved her out of his New Jersey house during a dispute, Combs sent his personal assistant David James down to the local police station thirty minutes later to file a police report against Atkinson.

There wasn't much that police could do, but Combs established a paper trail with his version of events. "Mr. Combs was satisfied," a police incident report reads after Combs gave his statement. "[He] wanted to make this a matter of record due to his celebrity status."

Then, in March 2016, a drug-fueled freak-off threatened to destroy Combs' life. The weekend was supposed to be a milestone for Ventura, whose new movie, *The Perfect Match*, in which she costarred opposite Terrence Jenkins, was premiering. Combs was pushing for a freak-off, and Ventura hesitated, not wanting to deal with a comedown shortly before what was supposed to be one of the proudest moments in her career. But saying no outright to Combs would spark a massive fight and risk ruining the premiere so Ventura tried to temper his request. "Baby, I want to FO so bad, but I don't want to fuck myself up. What am I to do," Ventura texted Combs.

"There's a lot in that little line," Ventura explained. "But I was telling him that I wanted to have a freak-off with him. Honestly, it was a bit of damage control. If I pleased him with a freak-off, then my premiere would run smoothly. That's how I looked at it."

On March 4, they had a freak-off at the InterContinental Hotel in Century City, hiring one of their frequent male escorts, Jules. Sometime the next morning, in between sex sessions, Combs struck Ventura across the face, giving her a black eye. It was everything she had been trying to avoid. "I knew I had to get out," she said. "So, when he was distracted, I don't know exactly what he was doing; he was either in the shower or on the phone. I just grabbed my stuff and ran out as fast as I could."

Hotel security footage captured Ventura clutching her bags as she speed-walked toward an elevator bank barefoot, with an oversize hoodie partially shielding her face. As she slipped on tennis shoes while waiting for the lift, Combs burst from the suite, with only a towel wrapped around his waist. He sprinted down the hallway, rounding the corner and yanking Ventura to the ground, delivering a hard kick to an unmoving Ventura. Her helplessness somehow provoked Combs further, and he stomped on her, beginning to drag her back toward the suite where the male escort was waiting. When Combs' grip suddenly snapped, Ventura hopped up and phoned down for security. Undeterred, Combs scooped up her belongings and dropped them off in the room before returning for Ventura.

The two argued in front of the elevator banks, and Ventura backed away in fear as Combs angrily approached her and hurled a flower vase in her direction. Before the situation escalated further, they were interrupted by a security guard. Ventura was able to leave safely, taking an Uber back to her apartment while Combs jumped into damage-control mode, realizing the incident had spilled out of his safeguarded bubble. Still on camera, he made his first call. His then-right-hand woman, Kristina Khorram, who had proven herself a bulldog, would launch his team into motion. She called Ventura and instructed one of Combs' personal assistants, Elie Maroun, to get answers from the hotel to assess the extent of the looming publicity disaster. "Say they had a fun drunk night to try and get more info," she instructed. "Lol no shot," Maroun replied. "They aren't playing nice."

Meanwhile, Combs relentlessly attempted to reach Ventura, calling her more than thirty times in the space of an hour. Over text, he tried a range of approaches to get her on the phone: demanding that she call him back, lying that he was about to be arrested, weaponizing the possibility that he could be taken away from his young children, accusing Ventura of abandoning him, and threatening never to speak to her again. He turned up at her apartment, manically banging on her door with a hammer, until neighbors called the police, and Khorram brought him home. Ventura responded sparingly. "I have a premiere Monday," she said. "For the biggest thing I've ever done in my life. I have a black eye and a fat lip. It was time for me to go. You are sick for thinking it's okay to do what you've done." She added, "Please stay far away from me."

As Combs hounded Ventura and had D-Roc secretly feed him updates on what she was doing, Khorram worked on cracking Eddy Garcia, one of the hotel security guards. After turning up at the hotel in hopes of at least seeing the security tape, Khorram managed to get Garcia's personal number. She called him at home and put Combs on the line. A deal was struck: $100,000 to be split among three security guards in exchange for the footage. Garcia showed up at a West Los Angeles high-rise building, where he handed over a USB drive containing the security footage and waited as Combs fed stacks of bills through a cash counter. Garcia signed a nondisclosure agreement; nestled in the fine print of the legal document was language that seemed to limit Garcia's freedom to speak to law enforcement. If he broke the agreement, he unknowingly agreed to be on the hook to Combs Enterprises for $1 million. In a back room, Khorram made a record of Garcia's and the other guard's driver's licenses. As he walked Garcia out, Combs gave him a final warning. "He said not to make any big purchases," Garcia recalled. (Weeks later, right around Easter, Combs reached out to Garcia, wanting to double-check he was still in the clear. "Eddy, my angel!" Combs greeted him. "God is good, God put you in my way for a reason.")

Tape in hand, Combs headed back home to get ready with Ventura for her big movie premiere. The two were all smiles as they posed together on the red carpet, Ventura's face and body heavy with bronzy makeup to cover up her fading black eye and body bruises. Under the bright camera flashes, a quarter-size welt was still faintly visible on her upper arm. Ventura's jitters were obvious as she exchanged hugs and kisses with Russell Simmons and other industry friends who interrupted her press interviews to congratulate her. She fielded softball questions about the movie and her own love life. "I'm just all about polite, you know pull out the chair, just like chivalry," Ventura said when asked about her dating preferences. "Guys aren't really like that nowadays. It's a dying thing. You're in a relationship and all of a sudden, you don't pull out my chair."

Five days after the assault, Combs continued to apologize to Ventura, wanting to put the incident in the past. "I'll never forget it," he vowed. It took less than two hours for Combs to suggest another freak-off. "You're being so wack," he texted Ventura, who in a rare instance turned him down. "Man you really don't know how you acting. 4 real. I don't want no beef. You're just killing me." Ventura held firm. "I still have crazy bruising from Friday," she responded. "I would be a dummy to subject myself to that possibility happening again. How would I know if the drugs are gna be bad or that you won't drink too much. When you get fucked up the wrong way, you always want to show me that you have the power and you knock me around. I'm not a rag doll. I'm someone's child. People love me and I can't keep hiding from them bc of your mistakes."

# CHAPTER 7 | THE KING

**"IF ANYONE CALLED THE** police, the police [are] a hundred percent going to lock you," Combs' longtime head of security Paul "Uncle Paulie" Offord warned Combs over text in October 2015. "Even if she begs them not to, it's the law."

Offord wasn't referring to Ventura but to Gina Huynh, a pretty single mother from Las Vegas whom Combs was dating behind Ventura's back. The two had been sneaking around for over a year after the twenty-two-year-old had stopped by his Miami house for an after-party in February 2014 and Combs had smoothly asked for her number. At first, Huynh wasn't into Combs, who dropped the love bomb on her only a month into their secret rendezvous. But eventually, she admitted, Combs' charm and persistence "grew on me." Things took a sharp turn south soon after that. "He started being an asshole," Huynh told gossip blogger Tasha K in a tearful sit-down interview in 2019. "He was always belittling me. He was mentally, emotionally, and physically abusing me."

He gave unsolicited commentary about her skin, advising Huynh to go see a dermatologist because he didn't date "women with bumps on their face." He constantly compared her to Ventura, calling Huynh the "bad one" while Ventura was the "good one." The intention, Huynh said, was to make her feel "low" about herself. She said she had two abortions over the course of four years, turning down Combs' offer of $50,000 in exchange for terminating the first pregnancy, wanting to prove her love wasn't tied to his finances. Instead of appreciating the show of good faith, Combs turned colder.

By May 2014, the physical abuse started. Huynh was Combs' date to the blowout twenty-seventh birthday party he threw for his new friend, rising Philly rapper Meek Mill, whose upcoming sophomore album featured Combs on a track. Combs plunked down a reported $25,000 to rent out the Parisian Palace in Las Vegas, and his businesses Revolt and Cîroc were affiliated with the event. As Combs mingled with his friends, making sure Huynh wasn't caught by his side by the roaming photographers, Huynh wished Meek Mill a happy birthday and shook his extended hand. Combs caught the blip of interaction, and they left the party twenty minutes later. When they got inside Combs' waiting Escalade, he went ballistic. "He grabbed my hair and cursed me out for doing that," Huynh said. "When we got to the hotel, it got even worse. He took one of my heels and tried to throw it at me. He mushed my face really hard."

The violence escalated from there. Huynh said Combs once hit her in front of her three-year-old daughter at his Miami home. He punched her repeatedly in the head, dragged her by the hair, and stomped on her stomach. "I couldn't breathe," Huynh said of one attack. "He kept hitting me. I was pleading to him, 'Can you just stop? I can't breathe.'" Members of his team were present, but no one stepped in. "Everyone else just allowed it to happen," she explained. "They wouldn't say anything. They would just watch him, [well] not watch it, but just walk away and leave us alone."

George Kaplan, one of Combs' personal assistants, ended up quitting as a result of the abuse he witnessed during his tenure. His breaking point was an extended fight between Combs and Huynh at the mogul's Star Island mansion in the second half of 2015. For some reason, Combs was furious and hurled decorative apples at Huynh, who was trying to shield herself from the sting of the flying objects. "The tension and anger in the room was scary," Kaplan explained. "I've never seen or been a part of anything like this. I was naive enough to think that these were hyperbolized moments that happened in bad movies." Later that night, Kaplan was summoned to Combs' bedroom to bring his boss his medicine bag. Kaplan felt the tension in the atmosphere and saw Huynh standing far away from Combs in a corner. Hours later, Kaplan, who was in bed, was disturbed by the sound of a distressed Huynh shouting at security to open the mansion's front gate and allow her to leave. It was the final straw. Kaplan informed his boss, Khorram, of what had happened and put in his resignation notice. Khorram seemed disappointed but told Kaplan she understood his choice. "In my heart of hearts, I told myself I knew what was happening and I also definitely felt an element of guilt to not be stopping it," he said. (Despite his moral code compelling him to walk away from a once-in-a-lifetime opportunity, Kaplan would stay in touch with Combs, sending him well wishes over the years.)

In October 2015, Combs flew Huynh out to Atlanta to join him for the BET Hip Hop Awards after-party he was hosting with Lil' Kim. Sometime during that trip, Combs attacked Huynh, leading Offord to put his boss on notice that not only was Combs' behavior out of line, it could lead to serious ramifications. "Once they put the cuffs on you, your life and career is over," Offord warned Combs over text. "Puff, really all over her. Puff, really, your family is going to go down the hill. . . . Newspapers and magazines will be paying her top dollar to tell everything." Combs seemed unfazed by his longtime confidant's plea. "Thanks," he responded. "I feel you."

Huynh soon found herself living a life that seemed to parallel Ventura's, and she was kept hidden away from Combs' public life. "I had to play my position," Combs reportedly told Huynh when she became upset at being kept in the shadows. He allegedly beat her into submission, but she continually forgave him, and he pacified her with gifts and some financial support, like help with her living accommodations. "I grew up watching my mom get beat by my dad, so that's all I knew. I just thought it was normal, and I thought it just meant he loved me," she explained.

In truth, Combs was seeing multiple women, spending private time with them at hotels. Even his assistants weren't exactly sure how many women Combs had on the go at once, only knowing to differentiate between his "girlfriends"—Porter, Ventura, and Huynh—and other female "guests." It went back to what he told *Essence* in 2006: He believed he had every right to date as many women as possible—though his girlfriends weren't entitled to the same liberties. He kept a hierarchy. Porter occupied the top spot as Combs' best friend, the mother of his children, and his forever lover, who would also have baby-oiled and video-camera hotel nights throughout Combs' relationship with Ventura, who was essentially girlfriend number two. And Huynh ranked third in Combs' lineup. This priority system was also apparent in how he booked their flights. In travel records documenting hundreds of flights that Combs paid for between 2012 and 2014, Ventura primarily flew business or first class; Huynh was always in coach; and at least one other woman Combs was pursuing alternated between first class, business, and coach.

Between the heavy drug use, sex marathons, and keeping his

love life straight, it was a marvel that Combs still managed to maintain his intense business schedule. But that's what his terrorized team was for: keeping an eye on his professional obligations while also running interference for Combs in a personal capacity. D-Roc was tasked with keeping tabs on both Ventura and Huynh. In one conversation with D-Roc in September 2015, Combs quickly switched between talking about his "shorty, G" and Ventura. When it came to Huynh, Combs gave D-Roc explicit instructions on how to mess with her mind. "You have to act like I said I'm not fucking with her. And you're wondering what's going on," Combs texted. Then he flipped to Ventura, telling D-Roc it was time for the "ice." He followed up with "Does the eye look better? How is she holding up?"

The juggling act imploded in October 2015 when Ventura discovered Combs was openly flaunting Huynh at his Revolt Music Conference in Miami. Ventura was in South Africa, getting ready to film *Honey 3: Dare to Dance*, and she spotted Huynh in a social media video. More than a year earlier, Ventura had become suspicious of Huynh after seeing an email exchange in which Huynh was mentioned, but Combs vehemently denied dating Huynh. While Ventura could begrudgingly accept Porter, whose position in Combs' life was clear, she drew the line at Combs entertaining other women. Ventura admitted she was "insanely jealous" and freaked out over small suspicions, like the possibility of an ongoing romantic relationship between Combs and Sarah Chapman, the mother of his daughter Chance. Realizing that Combs had flat-out lied about Huynh, Ventura decided to focus on her own happiness. She broke up with Combs while overseas, sending the video she had seen to him and to his personal team, whom she also felt betrayed by.

Combs couldn't handle it. He immediately began spamming Ventura's phone. When she stopped taking his calls, an irate, irrational, and slurring Combs began laying into his personal assistant

Mia, whom he had sent to South Africa along with Ventura. "He was threatening my job and threatened to kill me," Mia said. "[He was] telling me that he was on the phone with HR, even though I knew that wasn't true."

Then came the true threat. "If you don't call me now, fuck it all, and I am gonna tell everything and don't ever speak to me again," Combs texted Mia. "You have two min. Fuck her. Call my house now or never speak to me again. Fuck ABC and all lawyers. Let's go to war." The meaning was clear. Mia believed Combs was warning her that if she didn't comply, he'd spin their nonconsensual sexual encounters into something else entirely. "As though I had a part in it," Mia said. She felt trapped, anxious, and deeply ashamed, all the more so because she had grown close with Ventura in the years she had spent working intimately with Combs. He was also threatening to pull out of a deal he and Mia had just announced with ABC to develop a comedy show about their working dynamic. It had been Mia's dream to work in television. Combs was now both weaponizing the show and imploding her friendship with Ventura to force Mia to do his bidding.

Both Combs and Khorram continued to spam Mia's phone, paying no mind to the six-hour time difference, as they worked to get Ventura on the phone. Ventura continued to ignore Combs' attempts to reconcile, especially after he was photographed leaving a sex store, Hustler, with Porter and a handful of shopping bags in December 2015. Ventura responded by starting up a flirtatious relationship with actor Michael B. Jordan. They spent a quiet New Year's Eve together in South Africa, after her friends encouraged the pairing. Combs found out while he was celebrating at his annual bash at his Miami compound. Seething, he allegedly called up director Ryan Coogler—who had just worked with Jordan on *Creed*—to threaten that he wouldn't "have the star of his movie" if Jordan didn't back off. The actor also received a menacing phone call, prompting the then-still-rising star to call it quits and shamefacedly tell Ventura to give Combs a call. By early 2016, Combs and Ventura were back together, with Huynh kept in the wings.

---

To the general public, Combs and Ventura were boyfriend and girlfriend, when in reality their relationship dynamic didn't function in the traditional sense. They dated for more than a decade but never lived together. Combs just paid for her rent. A sore spot was the holidays: Ventura never spent Christmas with Combs. That was his designated family time, spent with his children, his mother, and Porter. And although he threw a massive New Year's Eve party every year, Ventura watched the highlights alone, from her phone.

"As much as you think that you're Bruce Willis, you aren't," Ventura messaged Combs on July 2013, shortly before he left to spend the July Fourth holiday with Porter and his children. "He's married and before he was married, the family as a whole went on trips together. Or just with him and his woman. Eddie Murphy & Paige took his kids away on their own. He didn't go with his ex because that's not who he's in love with. I've been at the edge of tears this whole week. I don't think you sympathize with my feelings. I understand you feeling like you need to protect your children but after a while, it's like for what? They've never known you and Kim to be together. Unless there's something that I just don't know about. They were babies when we started dating. The more time that goes by, the harder it is to understand. I'm here ready to be THAT woman and I'm in a constant fight bc you won't ever allow it. This isn't what I want. I can't become THAT woman this way. I'm bracing myself for pictures that are going to break my heart. That's where my head is at."

"Man I'm gonna spend time with my kids. I'm sorry you feel that way. I won't let no picts be taken," Combs responded.

"I don't trust that after the type of sexual relationship you've had with me. You had that with her and have in the recent past," Ventura added.

Kept at a distance from his family life, Ventura came to feel like she existed for one reason in Combs' eyes: the freak-offs. The arc of their relationship could be separated into three distinct stages. Early on it could have been considered fun and exciting. Sex was a central aspect of their relationship, and they sent countless messages expressing a deep, mutual love, as well a longing to be with each other, along with a heavy volume of sexting and planning for sex marathons. "I'm so horny!!!" Combs messaged Ventura in the middle of the day in August 2009. "How you feelin'? Talk to me!!! You supposed to be seducing me all day." Ventura took a moment to reply to Combs' leading message. He expected her to pique his fantasies in the lead-up to the freak-offs. "Lol I'm sorry!!! I'm nervous!!!!" she eventually replied. "I feel like I wanna fuck." It was a relatively tame start to a string of explicit sexual messages Ventura sent to Combs that day, as she edged her boyfriend in the middle of his jam-packed workday. Of course, even then it was rocky and darkened by domestic violence, but overall, this early period was a time in which Ventura described herself as wanting to make Combs happy by engaging in freak-offs with him.

She initially bought into Combs' pitch that the freak-offs were intimate, bond-building experiences. To outsiders, Combs was the Teflon-tough titan who had the world at his disposal. But in those hotel rooms, in those early years, Ventura felt she was being entrusted with a secret. Combs had shown her his most vulnerable side, something very few others were allowed to see. Somewhere in the 2010s, things became less fun. Ventura became reluctant to continue, but she was worried about what would happen if she denied Combs. It wasn't simply a physical response that she feared; she was apprehensive about emotionally rejecting him. "I didn't want to make him upset," she said. "I didn't want to make him angry and regret having told me about this experience that was so personal. His trust meant a lot to me at that point."

Ventura's quality time with Combs was often spent in dark hotel rooms, taking Ecstasy, ketamine, and other drugs while lining up men, sometimes as many as three, to stop by. The drug use in the rooms was constant. To numb herself from the reality of the sexual encounters, Ventura developed a crippling dependency on painkillers, both in and out of the rooms. It caused friction between the couple, despite Combs also being addicted to opiates. The couple struggled with their opiate addiction together, at different points, trying to wean themselves off the painkillers without assistance. Ventura once had a bad reaction while on GHB during the middle of a freak-off in 2013. "I blacked out," she said. "I woke up nude in the shower, and [the male escort] and Sean were just freaking out outside of the bathroom. . . . I didn't see myself, but it wasn't pretty." The trio proceeded to have sex once Ventura was alert.

In the hours leading up to the freak-offs, Ventura acted more like a travel agent or a personal assistant to Combs, coordinating the men's availability and arrival times. And because Ventura was handling the administrative work—reaching out directly to male dancers and Garren James, the owner of escort website Cowboys4Angels—she had to deal with the men in her downtime. They often reached out to her in the hours and weeks after sexual encounters. A dancer saved in Ventura's phone under the name "Islander" routinely hit her up, sending selfies, Happy New Year texts, pictures of his breakfast, and check-in messages in apparent hopes of keeping her attention. Others sent compliments, reminiscences of their encounters, fantasies, and vulgar messages. Ventura saw her interactions with the men as purely transactional. She never reciprocated the tenor of the conversation. If she did end up responding, it was always polite and brief. Although Ventura mainly used Cowboys4Angels, she had no real way of knowing the men who walked into the room. One time, Islander apologized for getting "so drunk" that he was "embarrassed" by his behavior, telling her he wouldn't drink again. Two escorts later went to jail. Ash Armand, born Akshaya Kubiak, pleaded guilty to voluntary manslaughter for beating his friend Herleen Dulai in July 2020 during a bad psychedelic mushroom trip. Miami-based Jonathan Oddi was arrested after firing a round of shots inside Trump National Doral golf club in 2018, ranting against President Trump.

Combs always remained the boss in control of the freak-offs, which he almost always set into motion. Ventura learned the "cues" Combs would throw out to indicate he wanted a freak-off. On the surface, questions like "What's your plan?" and "What you trying to do?" seemed harmless, but to Ventura, the subtext was clear. Are we having a freak-off or not? If Ventura denied him, she worried he'd seek his thrills elsewhere.

Before she hit her breaking point, there were moments where Ventura tried to gently push back against having sex with other men. In April 2010, after the couple was apart for a few days, Ventura messaged Combs, "I really need 2 fuck." He responded, "So who u gonna fuck. Wanna call someone?" Ventura was disappointed and exasperated. "I wanna fuck you! R u crazy," she asked. Later, she broached the topic. "Wanna talk to you about something," she messaged. "Tomorrow. Going to sleep. Love you."

Combs was immediately annoyed. "Is it gonna stress me out? What is it about," he demanded.

"Freak off, it can wait," she responded. "It's not a big deal."

"Now you don't wanna do [it] anymore," Combs complained. "I already know. You so predictable."

It was typical for Combs, Ventura said, to downplay and dismiss her wishes when it came to the freak-offs. Sometimes, he seemed to agree to take things slow and just be by themselves, but he almost always got his way. Ventura was conflicted. "I didn't want to upset him or make him angry with me," she said. "I just treaded lightly when I would bring it up. When you really care about somebody and you're in love with them, you don't want to disappoint them. I just never wanted him to feel like I judged him for it, but I wanted him to know that this made me feel horrible. It made me feel worthless, like, I didn't have anything else to offer him."

In Combs' mind, this was part of the cost of being with someone like him. "If I'm in a relationship with you, 25 percent of your time, you're gonna just feel like, 'Aw, man, I hate being here, this guy cheated on me, he lied on me,'" Combs explained, his young son Christian beside him, on *The Breakfast Club*. "But then there's 75 percent of 'I'ma make you the happiest woman in the whole wide world. I'ma be there to support your dreams. I'ma be there to hold you, listen to you. I'ma be there to be your best friend. And I promise you'll smile the most. You know who I am, this is what it is.' Which deal would you choose?"

---

By 2016, a full decade had passed since Ventura had released an album. It wasn't for lack of trying. Combs was effectively keeping her music career hostage.

In the early years, Combs gave Ventura the "lion's share" of Bad Boy's resources and support. He connected her with industry giants, like rapper Lil Wayne for her 2008 single "Official

Girl," Akon in 2009 for "Let's Get Crazy," and Nicki Minaj for "The Boys" in 2012. Ventura booked an appearance as Kanye West's "Black Kate Moss" in his 2007 music video for "Stronger," and she popped up in music videos for Jay-Z, Chris Brown, and Mario.

An apparent fight between the couple in April 2012 spilled over to involve the heads of Bad Boy. Ventura sent an email with "thank you team" as the subject line and said she was calling off an upcoming performance on BET's *106 & Park*. "For everything," she began. "With regret, I have been informed that I cannot perform on Monday due to overages in costs. I have worked very hard, but I cannot support myself on the things that I need in order to move forward and make this show happen and run smoothly. I appreciate everyone and I hope that you can understand. Again, I am very sorry and doubly sorry for any drama I have caused at Bad Boy or at Interscope. I have tried my very best. I wish everyone the best. Anyone not attached on this email I will contact directly so not to disrupt anyone's travel and/or schedule."

Combs' 4:00 a.m. response was warbled and incoherent: "Mk sure you stleven hill and let him know your not ready and you do wanna embarrass yourself again."

"If that were the issue, I would so since you no longer want to support your artist I have to pull out," Ventura fired back. "No label support, no show, no?"

Over the years, Combs continued to dangle a carrot to keep Ventura pacified, allowing her to release random singles and film music videos. He'd send her to the studio to work with various producers and songwriters to do what she considered busywork. Despite Ventura recording "hundreds of songs" over the course of her relationship with Combs, it would be generous to estimate that 10 percent wound up being released.

Combs weaponized his position as label boss to block Ventura's releases. "When he would be upset and they would fight, it would be, like, 'Show is over, all bets are [off],'" explained Capricorn Clark, who returned to the Bad Boy fold for a third time in 2016 as Ventura's creative director. "Their fighting led to fluctua[ting], 'No, you're not doing that video. OK, you're doing that video. No, you're not doing that photo shoot. OK, you're doing the photo shoot.'"

In April 2013, Combs broke a promise he'd made to distribute Ventura's mixtape *RockaByeBaby*. The deal was that if the project did well, Combs would put it up on streaming platforms and make it available for purchase. The thirty-five-minute project put Ventura's full creative and artistic aptitude on display. With a partially shaved head, Ventura embraced a more risqué and mature image, rapping and singing on the tracks, which also featured rap juggernauts Pusha T, French Montana, Wiz Khalifa, Rick Ross, Fabolous, and Jeremih. The free mixtape garnered rave reviews from critics. *Pitchfork* rated it a 7.8 out of 10, writing, "What's clear now is that Cassie's no longer just competing in the R&B game anymore. While *RockaByeBaby* has aspects that invite comparisons to risk-taking singers like Jeremih and The Weeknd, it really deserves to be held up against the output of melody-intensive rappers like Drake and Future, and it stands up against either. There's not only not a bad song on the record, but not even any that start becoming skippable after repeat back-to-back listens." It was high praise, which should've resulted in Combs making the mixtape available for purchase. He never did. Instead, it sat online for free.

It seemed like Combs had no real intentions of helping Ventura's career. And her own aspirations seemed to dissipate, especially after the free release of *RockaByeBaby*, Clark noted. Instead, Ventura seemed to care more about being Combs' girlfriend than her career. Ventura acknowledged the slip in her work ethic when it came to her music, but by that time, she was occupied elsewhere. "When I wasn't working on my music, I was recovering from partying," Ventura said. "That took a big chunk out of my life. Plainly, the freak-offs became a job where there was no space to do anything else but to recover and just try to feel normal again." Her drug addiction also significantly impacted her creative output. "I could see that her drug use was preventing her from the opportunities that were before us," Clark said, observing that Ventura seemed "much worse off" than she had in 2012 in the four years Clark wasn't with Bad Boy.

Songwriter Tiffany Red began working with Ventura in 2015 on yet another album that would never see the light of day. She was helping Ventura craft lyrics for personal songs, some that alluded to how she was feeling in her relationship with Combs. "I don't know what is real, I just know how I feel, and you keep acting like you don't know what you did wrong, trying to get me to chill," Ventura sang on an unreleased track called "Loyal." Although Ventura was pouring her heart into what another songwriting partner described as "therapy sessions," she kept a tight lid on what was happening between her and Combs. "When Cassie's album didn't come out," they explained, "we just chalked it up to: They're in a relationship, that she's not thinking about music right now." But, they noted, they had "only seen struggle" when it came to Ventura's music being released compared to other Bad Boy artists.

In 2017, Ventura released a short film titled *Cassie*, an outlet for her confusion and pain, composed of an emotional and raw body of music that Ventura was working on with Red. It reflects an unfolding era in which Ventura was "pushing back" creatively. In a voice-over, Ventura analyzes a fictional relationship's volatility and questions whether she is with the right person. While her on-screen partner helps her float away from her reality, she battles significant doubts. "How do you just walk away from it and escape it? . . . I want to be free," she says in the video.

---

It might have been dawn, but the after-party at Star Island was just getting started in spring 2018. After a night out at the packed club LIV, a group of partiers had come back to Combs' Miami mansion to welcome the sunrise with mimosas. Women skinny-dipped and tipsy guests memorialized the wild night by clamoring into Combs' "Team Love" photo booth. As Combs openly flirted with women, a high-looking Ventura roamed around the party. "I always looked at Cassie like this boss, pretty, happy girl," recalled one party guest. But in person, "she looked very sad. She had her head down the whole fucking time." She looked lost, the guest concluded.

After more than a decade with Combs, Ventura found herself in the same place professionally she had been as a naive twenty-one-year-old. Only now, she was in her thirties, struggling with addiction, and feeling jaded. Ventura still hadn't been fully integrated into Combs' family, and she began to wonder if she'd ever have children of her own. The beatings hadn't stopped and the freak-offs were just as consistent. And her dream of a fulfilling career was collecting dust on a shelf.

A series of messages between Combs and Ventura in the last year of the relationship shows how much things had deteriorated. "Nothing good comes out of fos anymore. You treat me like you're Ike Turner," Ventura messaged Combs in January 2017. "I told you I feel like this is all I'm used for and that's that. . . . I didn't leave you. I saved you from beating me up. And losing another week of my life to recover. That's why nothing gets done. Always healing. You don't even understand because you don't have to look at it once you get with Gina or Kim but you beat me up. You said you would stop and that's not who you are and you haven't."

In mid-March, Combs and Ventura posed courtside at a New York Knicks versus Brooklyn Nets basketball game honoring The Notorious B.I.G. They coordinated their outfits, wearing heavy furs and giggling into each other throughout the game. Hours later, during a freak-off, Combs beat her head in twice, causing her to flee the room in the middle of a session. "You treat and make me feel like I don't matter," she told him. Combs immediately shifted the blame onto Ventura. "You started all of this," he shot back over text. "You really think you can have me jerk my dick for 10 hrs and not come. Your nuts. One minute you down asking about shit. Then the next you acting like you doing something you don't want to. Make up your mind. I'm trying to figure out how I get this nut out my dick . . . Imma make sure I bust after 10 hrs. Your crazy. You can play but I can't? Something ain't fair about that. You just got a dick out your mouth so it shouldn't be a big deal. And I'm keeping it real. You really ended us. Did you ever get any female escorts numbers? It ain't that dramatic when you enjoying yourself. So it shouldn't be dramatic now. Send me those numbers."

Days later, Ventura responded. "You're at a point in your life where you want to party and have a good time and I'm at a point where I have to focus or I'll never become anything," she wrote. "I'm not saying I can't ever party. I had so much fun in Miami but then I realized doing that opened the door to that being my sole purpose in seeing you. I knew if I said no to it in NY it would have been a problem. Those were my last nights with you. You only see me one way. You treat me like a hooker to be honest. You always want to call one so bad and you have one. This hooker has been here for 10 years. . . . Please don't play victim. If you can, go to our last messages. That's all you wanted and that's why I was upset. I love our fos. When we both want it."

And at what would be one of their last major events together, Combs basked in Ventura's beauty at the Met Gala in May 2017. As she jutted out a hip in an On Aura Tout Vu gown, a voluminous black number with an exaggerated spiky train tediously crafted out of black plastic straws, Combs stretched out on the carpeted steps to watch flashbulbs snap around Ventura. He seemed the proud partner, watching his lover enjoy her moment. The night, like so many before, ended in violence. "I want to be with you but I can't get pregnant dragged down a hall," Ventura wrote. "You hurt me so bad. I'm so fucked up. And so heart broken. I never intended to show you disrespect if that's what you felt but some of your wires are loose. All I wanted was to have a good time and you took all of your anger out on me per usual. I know I don't treat you badly. I might say some bullshit here and there but I'm not a bad person. I just appreciate and love you. I can't sleep. I've been crying since I got here. I don't understand what you expect of me sometimes. I smile. I'm happy. I love you. I give you love and as soon as I turn my head for a second and you get fucked up, you drag me down the hall by my hair. I'm 30 years old. This isn't play anymore. I felt like I was dead last night and it wasn't happening to me bc my night was so beautiful."

She continued, "The love you have for me shouldn't equate to what you 'do' for me. I'm so in love with you, you can't even see it. My heart is shattered that you acted the way you did. [Someone] had to tackle you, Puff. That's not love, that's possession. I have bleeding cuts."

Combs was immune to her pleas. "That makes 2 of us," he coldly responded. "But I'm not gonna let someone shit on me when all I've done was be nice. You broke my heart this time. You were negative all night. . . . You don't treat me like the king. Any other woman in the world would have been so happy. But not you. Your wack for not keeping it real. I'm not gonna go back and forth when I and everyone knows you were acting like a bitch. I can't take it anymore. I want after a night like that for my woman to be so happy. You are a different type of unappreciative chick. You did me fucked up."

---

A large kitchen knife was wedged inside the door handle of Ventura's Hollywood home. "I was getting a lot of unannounced visits from Sean where he was angry," Ventura explained. "[I was] trying to kill two birds with one stone, to lock it and have a weapon."

Things were growing increasingly irreparable between the pair by 2018. Huynh had cropped up again, seen in the background of one of Combs' Instagram videos while Ventura was in Chicago. Unable to continue convincing herself that being a human sex doll for Combs was enjoyable, Ventura gave him an ultimatum. "I said, if I catch you with her again, then I'm done," she said. It was also an excuse, a way to anchor herself to her own vows. So, when Combs was photographed at dinner with Huynh in July, Ventura called things off for good. "They were seen out, and I was in Connecticut, so I was out."

As Combs kept himself occupied with Huynh, Ventura began quietly seeing Alex Fine, a handsome professional bull rider, aspiring actor, and a personal trainer. Combs had hired Fine to help whip him into shape, and he also paid for sessions for Ventura and her best friend Kerry Morgan. Combs didn't discover the romance until October. Until then, he and Ventura tried to navigate their uncoupling, swapping mournful texts about how they missed the other and how they hoped to remain friends. Their conversations could turn combative in a flash, a decade of hurt and resentment spilling over. They agreed to have dinner in Malibu in hopes of gaining closure amicably one night in late summer 2018. Ventura alleged that Combs ended the night by raping her on the floor of her living room while she cried. "I don't even know if he noticed, honestly," Ventura said. The lighthearted man who had been laughing with Ventura over dinner just a few hours before had disappeared, replaced with someone whose eyes had gone dark. "It was just, like, somebody taking something from you," Ventura said. "I know I look bad to you," Combs messaged later. "I could tell I didn't turn you on yesterday. I fell off. But I'm about to get my shit together."

They saw each other once more in person, at a birthday dinner for Andre Harrell in September. "It was a really nice night that we've never really had before," Ventura said. "Everything went smooth and happy." The evening was only dampened when Ventura received a call from Fine while she and Combs were being intimate.

When Combs learned about Fine, he was incensed. Nash overheard a voice note that Combs sent Ventura, screaming and cursing her out. Spitefully, Combs planted stories at TMZ in which anonymous sources painted Ventura as a cheater and Combs as the "betrayed" partner, despite being already linked to at least two other women. He alternated between sending Ventura threats and guilt trips. "I was paying 50k for this nigga then 18 for you and Kerry," he raged. "And you fuckin me both ways. Fuckin fuckin foul." Combs demanded that Fine repay him, and Ventura shot back that she could "make sure your lawyer receives pics of my face and body every time you beat me up." Combs was even-keeled. "Release the videos also," he responded.

Ventura packed up her belongings and moved out of the apartment that Combs had fronted payments for. She returned the Jaguar that Combs had gifted her. Nash said they personally arranged for a tow company to scoop up the luxury vehicle and dump it off at Combs' nearby compound. "We sent that shit back," he said.

Unlike previous attempts. Ventura was resolute in her decision to break up. She had fallen in love with Fine. That did little to deter Combs, who continued his bombardment. He laid off the threats and began laying it on thick, trying to win Ventura back through public displays of affection. He posted longing photos of Ventura giggling in a bubble bath and begged her to listen to Michael Jackson's "The Lady in My Life." A large swath of the public discourse was sympathetic to Combs, who was begging Ventura not to abandon him. (Others felt Ventura had stuck around long enough, having invested a decade in the relationship with no children of her own and no ring on her finger.) "Diddy Isn't Giving Up on Cassie Just Yet! Sends her a SWEET Post-Break up Message," read a headline from Hot 97. "Diddy Is on a Mission to Get Cassie Back and He's Asking for Help," BET wrote.

This was part of his age-old pattern, Tiffany Red explained. Combs refused to let the women in his life freely walk away from him. "Everybody is a part of his story," she said. "'You can't leave me. You will always be with me. You'll always be my girl': That's always going to be the narrative." In an act of defiance after Combs posted the bathtub photo of Ventura, she went public with her relationship with Fine in late December 2018, kissing him squarely on the mouth in a photo booth snapshot.

# CHAPTER 8 BROTHER LOVE

**KIM PORTER'S THROAT** began to throb on November 7, 2018. The forty-seven-year-old had been busy. That June, she had marveled at lazy lions and graceful elephants on a safari in southern Africa, played captain while sailing off the coast of Ibiza with old friends in August, and arranged for her ecstatic eleven-year-old twin daughters and their half-sister Chance to meet Beyoncé backstage in September. And she was every bit the proud mom as she stood beside her oldest child, Quincy, at the premiere for his Netflix movie, *The Holiday Calendar*, in late October. Surrounded by Combs and their blended family, Porter seemed content and healthy. "I laughed, I cried, I got in the holiday spirit, but most of all I got to see Quincy live out his dream," she wrote on Instagram.

It had been a nonstop four-and-a-half months of cross-country and international travel. Plus, Porter had spent the weekend partying with Combs for his forty-ninth birthday extravaganza. Newly single from Ventura, Combs danced with Porter under the glow of red lights at West Hollywood hotspot Ysabel, surrounded by longtime celebrity friends Usher, LeBron James, Snoop Dogg, and

Janelle Monáe. More than two hundred people followed Combs back to his $39 million Holmby Hills estate for an after-party that included a food truck serving fried chicken to tipsy guests. Cops eventually shut down the event after the rowdiness spilled into the early hours of the next morning.

Back at her Toluca Lake home, which Combs had purchased in 2009, Porter chalked up her sickness to exhaustion. She called a doctor to prescribe her a routine antibiotic to stave off what she believed could be strep throat. Five days later, her condition worsened: sweats and body aches, on top of a sore throat and a 102-degree fever. Tests for both flu and strep throat came back negative, so Porter's doctor gave her a shot of the anti-inflammatory drug Toradol, and a nurse administered a vitamin-packed IV drip in hopes the combination would help fight off whatever cold Porter was battling. Her fever lifted, but it took her appetite.

By November 14, Porter was coughing up phlegm streaked with blood. A second IV drip did nothing; neither did a deep-tissue massage. Trying to relax, Porter spent the night curled up on the couch watching movies. Around 11:30 p.m., she crawled into bed. A close family friend went to check on her the next morning around 8:00 a.m., but they decided not to disturb her when they thought she was asleep. But by 11:30 a.m., the friend had called 911. Porter had died in her sleep. An autopsy would find she died of lobar pneumonia, a bacterial infection in her fluid-filled lungs. Her shell-shocked friends, including a red-eyed, makeup-free Kimora Lee Simmons, stood helplessly in her garage and watched the city coroner's van slowly pull away, slipping past her fleet of luxury vehicles and turning onto the typically quiet residential street, which was now abuzz with a circling helicopter, news vans, and morbid onlookers.

A distraught Combs arrived at Porter's house in a state of raw shock. The moment he heard the news, he began screaming and crying in disbelief. All the turbulence from their romantic relationship—

the petty fights, betrayals, and constant reconciliations—had long ago softened into something stable and concrete. They had an understanding. Yes, Combs had public girlfriends like Ventura and flings like Gina Huynh and many others, but through every chapter, Porter was his constant gravitational center. They didn't put a label on things; they didn't even know how to quantify it themselves. They could be platonic coparents, but just as easily slip back into something more. They were lovers, confidants, ride-or-dies, and partners until the end. Her sudden death rocked him, and it devastated their children. Combs forced himself to compartmentalize his own grief and "jumped into mommy mode," dispersing his team to intercept his children to make sure they learned of Porter's death from a familiar voice, even if that meant cutting off a traveling Christian's cell phone service so he wouldn't get the news midflight. Some of Porter's last words to Combs gave him his marching orders: "Puffy, take care of my babies." It was a chilling foreshadowing. "She actually said that to me before she died," Combs told *Essence*.

Combs pulled together a private memorial service for Porter at his Holmby Hills mansion. In the entryway, flickering candlelight cast a soft glow over the several enlarged portraits of Porter and their shared family memories that Combs had displayed around the house. Roughly a hundred people gathered to pay their respects. Combs broke his silence that night. "For the last three days I've been trying to wake up out of this nightmare," he wrote on social media. "I don't know what I'm going to do without you, baby. I miss you so much. Today I'm going to pay tribute to you, I'm going to try and find the words to explain our unexplainable relationship. . . . We were more than best friends, we were more than soulmates. We were some other shit!!"

The following week, Combs brought his family to Porter's hometown of Columbus, Georgia, for an elaborate funeral service.

More than 2,500 people came to bid farewell, including old friends Mary J. Blige, Lil' Kim, Usher, Kimora Lee Simmons, and Kandi Burruss. It was a solemn affair. Celebrity pastor T. D. Jakes officiated the service, and Faith Evans performed a heartrending version of "His Eye Is on the Sparrow." Porter's best friends—her "village"—dressed themselves in all white to huddle together onstage, as they spoke of Porter's class, grace, and beauty.

Wearing dark sunglasses, Combs approached the podium with Porter's oldest son, Quincy Brown, at his side. For a moment, they both stood silently, looking down at Porter's golden casket beneath them, which was covered in white and blush-pink roses, their soft scent wafting through the air. The room fell silent as Quincy began to speak; Combs kept his hand firmly on Quincy's back, hugging him when he couldn't make it through his remarks. When it came time for Combs to deliver his eulogy, he removed his tinted sunglasses and steadied himself at the pulpit. When he finally spoke, his voice was low and thick with emotion, as he reminisced about the day he first laid eyes on Porter. "I can't put our relationship into a certain box," Combs said. "She always told me she felt like God sent her here to help me out. I didn't really understand how to love. . . . She just really started breaking down the exterior of any shell that I put up. . . . As time went on, our relationship took so many different changes. From being boyfriend and girlfriend to being lovers to being best friends to being just straight up homies, like somebody that you know you can count on. Somebody who has your back."

During the fifteen-minute tribute to the woman he described as his life partner of nearly twenty-five years, Combs spoke directly to their children. By no means was he absent, but Combs would later acknowledge that he often felt like a part-time parent, choosing work over family and allowing the bulk of the parenting to fall to his children's mothers. That day, he vowed to change, pledging that he would "always be there for you" and "always take care of you." He had grown up without a father and carried the weight of how the loss had shaped him. Specifically addressing his twin daughters, Combs said they would be entering "some different type of times" and offered himself up as their safe place. "I want you to be able to talk to me about everything, and I mean everything," he said.

Ventura sat in the pews, listening. She felt an obligation to show Combs her support despite their recent and ongoing breakup. She also wanted to pay her respects to Porter, a woman Combs had unfairly pitted her against. After more than a decade with Combs, Ventura got the clarity she needed in the words of Combs' eulogy and his social media posts grieving Porter. "I need to be real with you," Ventura texted him after the service. "I know how crazy and painful this all is and you want my support but you compared me to Gina the other day and then the baby sitter was there last night and then you posted that Kim was your soulmate. What was the 11 years all about? 11 consistent years. I know you're going through a lot, but that hurt my feelings. . . . I totally understand. I'm not upset. I know that you have to honor your friendship. Just makes me wonder was I Gina?"

The mask of strength Combs was wearing slipped at Porter's graveside. Sitting alone, without the crowd and his children around him, his shoulders finally sagged. The shades had come off, and his eyes were blank, as he clutched a funeral service program. Porter's death was seismic, and with Ventura gone, for the first time in many years, Combs found himself alone, without a solid partner to seek solace in. He steeled himself for this next chapter, now as a primary caretaker. He'd lean into his image of a widowed, single father, publicly grieving Porter and being strong for his young family. Privately, he'd soothe himself with the same vices he'd always sought escape in. On November 21—three days before

Porter's funeral—Combs had his staff book him a suite at a Los Angeles hotel.

---

Porter's death coincided with and deepened a dark period for Combs. It had begun years earlier, and he couldn't quite articulate what was weighing him down. He told *GQ* in 2016 that he felt depressed, spiritually adrift, and addicted to his phone, so he decompressed among the red rocks and the spiritual vortexes of Sedona, Arizona. The timing coincided with the aftermath of attacking Ventura at the InterContinental Hotel. Was it the drugs? The toll of fame? The suppression of something else? Whatever it was, a midlife crisis was brewing, and Porter's sudden absence only magnified it. Rapidly approaching fifty, he began to wonder what was left for him to conquer.

Professionally, Combs had reached a staggering peak. In 2017, *Forbes* crowned him the wealthiest man in hip-hop with a net worth of $820 million and declared that he was well on his way to becoming a billionaire. Bad Boy Records accounted for only a fraction of that. His accounts had been padded with an estimated $70 million in late 2016 when he sold a third of his Sean John clothing line. By then, he had become a bona fide business mogul. He was the face of Cîroc and DeLeón as part of a partnership with Diageo. Actor Mark Wahlberg brought him into a deal to own a majority stake in Aquahydrate, a brand of electrolyte-infused bottled water. Beyond beverages, Combs had Revolt, his television network that had grown into a multi-platform media company hosting programs like *Drink Champs* and televising *The Breakfast Club*.

He even got in on the singing competition craze and served as a judge on Fox's *The Four: Battle for Stardom*. When his own albums stopped dominating charts, Combs went back to what he knew best: remixes. Banking on his own nostalgia, Combs reunited Bad Boy's original roster, including Mase and Faith Evans, for a multicity tour in 2016, then released the documentary *Can't Stop, Won't Stop,* a victory lap on film, in 2017.

Moments of violence escaped from the containment of Combs' inner circle, but even when the public glimpsed this side of him, he didn't teeter from his professional pedestal. In December 2014, he reportedly decked Drake at Miami nightclub LIV after the Canadian rapper scooped him on a beat for his song "0 to 100/The Catch Up," which wound up earning two Grammy nominations. An incensed Combs allegedly told him, "You'll never disrespect me again," before swinging his fist.

And in June 2015 Combs was arrested for exploding at Sal Alosi, a strength and conditioning football coach at the University of California, Los Angeles, where his son Justin played defensive back. According to two sources familiar with the incident, the controversial former New York Jets coach—who resigned from the team after he was caught tripping a Miami Dolphins player—had "definitely" said something "out of pocket" to Justin during a practice. Later that afternoon, a fired-up Combs barged into the Bruins' fifteen-thousand-square-foot weight room with Justin and security in tow to discuss what he believed was Alosi's bullying of his son. The meeting went sideways when Combs lunged at Alosi, scratching him and tearing at his shirt. As staffers tried to separate the two men, Combs briefly choked an intern, put another member of the coaching staff into a headlock, and then picked up a kettlebell and tried to hit the nearest person with it, according to the Los Angeles County district attorney's office. Combs was led away in handcuffs and charged with assault with a deadly weapon, making terrorist threats, and battery. Officials decided to drop the matter the following month. Although the incident was the talk of the locker room afterward, purported videotape of the incident never saw the light of day. The affected parties went mum. "It was one of those things, it disappeared," said a source.

In an effort to assuage his anxiety, Combs decided to expand his philanthropy. In 2016, he opened the Capital Preparatory Harlem Charter School and donated $1 million to Howard University, which had awarded him an honorary degree two years earlier. Tax filings for his nonprofit, the Sean Combs Foundation, show that between 2018 and 2024, he donated more than $2.4 million to various educational, health awareness, and entrepreneurial charity programs. Still, he couldn't shake the heavy fog that seemed to hover over him.

Although Combs readily described himself as a man of faith, he often referred to this extended dark period as one in which he felt "far from God." He didn't let his wavering show publicly; he took every opportunity to acknowledge a higher power. Having grown up Catholic, he knew his Bible stories. Combs called God his "best friend," attended Sunday services, gravitated toward nondenominational Christian evangelical preachers such as T. D. Jakes, and was always the first to lead a group in prayer. On his neck, he has "God's child" inked across the left side of his jugular, and on his forearm, a portion of Psalm 23: "Though I walk through the valley of the shadow of death, I will fear no evil: for you are with me." And in 2017, acclaimed portrait tattoo artist Nikko Hurtado covered his back with a depiction of a Black Madonna and her crowned child.

Combs was firm in his conviction that God had radically blessed him and had specially chosen him. But those who knew him well saw that first and foremost Combs worshipped at the altar of himself. In his mind, he had been anointed, and the praise for his success belonged to him and him alone. "Y'all witnessing Jesus walking on water or Jesus having a breakthrough," a serious Combs once told his music team. "Because I can only compare myself to the Son of God."

Seven Güzel, an aspiring R&B singer who met Combs in fall 2017, noticed that he frequently invoked God and the Bible. The pair seemed to share similar desires to dive deeper into their spirituality. Combs would heap praise on the musician for bringing him positive energy and coaxing him "from his shell" amid his depression. But Güzel alleged that Combs was slowly grooming her, manipulating her trust by lavishing attention on her, reassuring her about her talent, and dangling the carrot of his backing. By the time her relationship with Combs ended in 2021, Güzel still had no real music career. Instead, Combs allegedly humiliated her in public, plied her with alcohol and drugs, and sexually assaulted her multiple times in various cities, including New York, Los Angeles, Miami, and Washington, DC, once in a room adjoining that of his staff. (A friend of Güzel's from the time confirmed the two had been in a relationship but couldn't speak to the veracity of her claims.)

Amid this spiritual emptiness, Combs decided he needed yet another reinvention. It was time for a new name; it was time for Love. The inspiration struck him on his forty-eighth birthday in 2017 while strolling the beach in Punta Mita, Mexico. In a self-filmed video, he announced, "I have some very serious news. I've been praying on this, and I knew it was risky, 'cause it could come off as corny to some people. I decided to change my name again. . . . I'm just not who I am before. I'm something different."

At first, it seemed like another stunt. Another iteration of "Puffy" becoming "Puff Daddy," or introducing himself as "Diddy" or whatever suited him at that exact, strategic moment. But Combs was serious, telling *GQ* about the name change in 2018, and in 2021 he continued to tout his "Love" agenda in the form of a September *Vanity Fair* cover story. They pushed the assignment through in early July; a few days later, the interviewer,

Tressie McMillan Cottom, was in a car on her way to a $25 million Malibu shorefront mansion for the interview.

Of course, Combs was running late when she arrived. He had a habit of intentionally keeping people waiting, a calculated power move. McMillan Cottom didn't seem to mind. A curated playlist kept her company, as did an impressive spread of hors d'oeuvres prepared by Combs' private chef. A team of nameless staffers buzzed around the secluded house, as Combs' tardiness was half-heartedly excused as an inescapable factor that came with being a mogul. Then, just as McMillan Cottom's glass of red wine was about to be replaced with chilled champagne, Combs appeared in all his glory, descending a floating staircase to wrap McMillan Cottom in one of her first hugs with a stranger since the start of the COVID-19 pandemic. He still needed to step away to take a few unavoidable important calls, but an apologetic Combs made up for his otherwise rude absence by personally swaddling McMillan Cottom in an ebony pashmina.

Combs' charm was sickly sweet, borderline rehearsed. He spoke of the peaceful Malibu retreat as if he owned it, even though it was a rental. His team kept asking McMillan Cottom about the angle of the story but refused to provide anyone meaningful from his circle for an amusing anecdote about Combs, an anomaly for a celebrity profile. The rushed timing made little sense to anyone, except maybe Combs. His team looked shocked when he mentioned that he was in the studio, working on music that would become *The Love Album: Off the Grid*. He wasn't ready for an official rollout just yet, but Combs was eager to start priming the world for his next era.

In hindsight, McMillan Cottom reflected that the experience felt calculated. The conversation veered into MeToo territory, something Combs brought up unprompted. "When they said in the #MeToo, when it was over, it was over," Combs offered. "The movement inspired me. It showed me that you can get maximum change." It was a vague, half-baked thought. To McMillan Cottom, who tried to press him further, there seemed to be no actual conviction behind the statement. "He did get very uncomfortable when I asked follow-up questions," she told British newspaper *The Independent*.

What McMillan Cottom didn't know was that just weeks earlier, in that same Malibu mansion, an actress he'd been casually seeing named Kat Pasion claimed she woke up terrified when Combs emerged from a bathroom high on a pink powder substance and allegedly forced himself on her.

Against the backdrop of the alleged assault, Combs' team was hammering out the deal for the *Vanity Fair* cover so he could continue in rolling out his new persona, Love. For no apparent reason, he insisted that his three teen daughters pose alongside him for the cover shoot. In the pictures, they stand and sit regally, like props, behind their father, who didn't seem to directly mention them at all during his hours-long interview with McMillan Cottom. And as *Vanity Fair* printed stacks of issues with Combs looking triumphant on the cover, his fist raised high and the word *LOVE* tattooed in large block letters down his side, Combs was allegedly threatening Pasion. He was furious that she had ceased contact with him, and in retaliation, Combs said he had half a mind to contact the United States embassy and have her deported back to Canada.

Weeks later, when the cover story was rolled out, *Vanity Fair* released a behind-the-scenes video. A faceless assistant handed Combs an elegant champagne glass, although he already gripped a lemon-garnished beverage in his other hand. Blind to his own hypocrisy, Combs crowed about his newfound calling to spread love while his personal barber perfected his high-top fade. Combs had his guard down, and it was barely noticeable, but the whites in his eyes were nearly bloodshot, and he was slightly slurring his words. "This is a very serious mission, [a] very high-risk mission that God sent me on," Combs deadpanned. "And if you see the devil, tell him I'm looking for him."

---

As Love, Combs was outwardly transforming himself into a softer, wiser, more spiritually evolved persona. He posted about his children often, and on Janice's eightieth birthday in December 2020, Combs gifted her a $1 million check and a Bentley "in her favorite color." To outsiders, he was a serene, spiritual patriarch. He preached empowerment and pursued harmony. But behind the curated Instagram posts, business launches, and motivational speeches, his private life slid deeper into unchecked hedonism.

Combs' recreational drug use showed no sign of slowing down. He had been addicted to opiates for two decades and had been taking Ecstasy continually for somewhere between ten and fifteen years. One former assistant recalled being in the room when Combs was speaking with a doctor, who stressed to Combs that his rampant drug use was leading him to have trouble experiencing natural highs because his dopamine levels were constantly shot. Though there was no way to prove it, those around him believed this was why he thrived in chaos and seemed to seek it out, and why he continued to be drawn toward drugs and long, intense sexual sessions with women, which he juvenilely began calling "Wild King Nights." They made him feel alive.

Now that Combs' relationship with Ventura was decidedly over, he embraced his newfound bachelorhood. He found a sense of freedom in no longer having to hide his romantic exploits from cameras or a public-facing significant other. His sexcapades weren't as intensely followed by media outlets as they had been in his heyday in the early 2000s, but if eagle-eyed observers knew what to look for, it wasn't hard to identify whom Combs was seeing. He had a specific type: notable models and social media influencers in their mid-twenties to early thirties. They were almost always women of color, whether African American, Latina, Asian, or mixed-race, and they had an effortless, almost innocent beauty. Combs had a habit of meeting these video vixens and Instagram baddies as guests at his events and sliding into their Instagram DMs. Others were introduced through his son Justin, whose circle of models, influencers, and aspiring artists made for a convenient pickup pool. As in the past, women who worked for Combs weren't off-limits. Dana Tran met the mogul through her job as a lymphatic drainage masseuse after Combs had a cosmetic surgery procedure in 2021. (She gave birth to a daughter, the youngest of his children, naming her Love in 2022.) The women could be seen accompanying Combs on his over-the-top vacations and on his son's social media feeds. They often wore colorful $5,000 Van Cleef bracelets on tanned wrists and carried lambskin Chanel bags. His favorites were gifted gold or diamond-encrusted "Love" necklaces after Combs insisted upon the new name. They posted social media videos of the Cîroc and DeLeón swag bags dropped off at their front doors, and at least one woman made a brief cameo in his liquor commercial.

At any given moment, Combs seemed to be in conflict with at least one girlfriend, sparked by jealousy between the women or by his belief that someone had disrespected him in some fashion. To keep control, he relied on a tactic he had learned from Janice as a child and which he believed was a fail-safe tool: money. It wasn't the seriousness of the given fight that dictated his response, but the boundaries he believed he could push. Women who seemed ready to walk away were given the red-carpet treatment and bombarded with messages urging reconciliation. They received oversize bouquets of flowers, were taken to upscale restaurants, and gifted designer handbags or fine jewelry. If he genuinely wanted to smooth things over, the word *sorry* rarely came, but a luxury getaway to a Caribbean island or an invitation to the Amalfi coast would. But when he wasn't in the mood to make amends, he would instead double down—belittling the woman and threatening to cut her off for good.

Gina Huynh briefly broke ranks in June 2019. She had spent five long and painful years feeling like Combs' third choice, and he was still treating her like an option, even with Ventura and Porter gone. He insisted on keeping their relationship under wraps, and he discouraged her from posting photos of them together. Meanwhile, he seemed to be pursuing model Lori Harvey, whose intimate photos Huynh claimed to have seen on Combs' phone. That, combined with two abortions and the physical abuse, was more than Huynh could take. "I just had enough," she told gossip vlogger Tasha K, her voice quavering. "You need to be held accountable for your actions. . . . I'm not the first and maybe not the last person you are gonna do this to. He can say he loves you, but if he's putting his hands on you, that's not love." Huynh eventually returned to the relationship.

He began dating Yung Miami, a.k.a. Caresha Brownlee, half of the popular Miami-based rap group City Girls. Brownlee was a departure from the women Combs was normally linked to. She had an established, successful career, a visible name, a monetizable platform, and a firecracker personality. And, more importantly, Combs was openly claiming her. It caused friction with Huynh, who antagonized Brownlee on social media after he brought both women to the Billboard Music Awards in May 2022. Brownlee went low to fire back, mocking Huynh for engaging in sexual acts with both men and women when Combs "feel[s] like it." Brownlee taunted Huynh, "I have a career, hoe. You are [a] certified freak." Combs and Brownlee's relationship had a transactional element. Brownlee was constantly promoting Combs' liquor brands on her social media, and Combs seemed to reward her with a podcast series titled *Caresha Please* at his media company, Revolt. Combs was Brownlee's very first guest in 2022. Within the first minute of the show, the camera cut away to Combs' DeLeón tequila for a brief advertisement before Combs began promoting his new R&B label, Love Records. They addressed their own relationship status: Combs said he was single, but they were dating. "We go to exotic locations," Combs said. "We have great times." They'd later giggle about their sex life. "Let me tell you all something," Brownlee said. "This nigga don't go to sleep, I be like 'goddamn.' I really thought that I was gonna make him tap out. You gotta be energized, you gotta be charged up like a Tesla."

While Combs didn't have Ventura for freak-offs anymore, he still had Wild King Nights. It was unclear whether Combs always brought male escorts into these occasions, but almost everything else about the encounters was virtually the same. Assistants stocked his hotel suites with baby oil, sex toys like a power banger sex machine, red lights, candles, booze, and drugs, before Combs and a female guest would go dark inside the suite for twelve to forty-eight hours. Combs believed he was treating women to a luxe experience. A spread of expensive toiletries was on display to enhance the ambiance as Combs tried to seduce his paramour further. Although Combs intended the rooms to be inviting and seductive, some women emerged from them rattled.

Afterward, as usual, his personal team was sent inside to mitigate the damage. Phil Pines, who worked as Combs' personal assistant between 2019 and 2021, became visibly upset when trying to describe the aftermath of Combs' Wild King Nights. The smell of baby oil still makes him physically sick, he said, after seeing hotel room floors so slick with the substance that someone could easily slip and fall. He was responsible for cleaning up the shattered glass, discarding used condoms, and collecting blood-stained towels. It was demoralizing that what Pines had believed could be a life-changing job turned out to be maid service. Pines had a front-row seat to this purported newfound "Love" era. He had been part of Combs' wider world since 2017, working with one of the mogul's ancillary businesses before becoming his personal assistant. Pines, who wanted to be a music supervisor, jumped at the opportunity to learn from Combs, whom he considered a hero. He quickly realized that a third of his responsibilities would revolve around Wild King Nights. Combs relied heavily on his personal team to juggle the many women he was seeing and to keep them in the dark about the others. His travel manager sorted the women's travel schedules and booked Combs' hotel suites, while his newly named chief of staff, Kristina Khorram, helped ferry the girlfriends in and out, careful to make sure they didn't overlap. Pines estimated that throughout his nightmarish two-year tenure, there were maybe "seven to eight times" that Combs did not have a woman stay the night with him. "He was never alone," he said. To Pines, Combs seemed to rely on sex and women to constantly reassure others—and himself—that he was a "macho alpha male." It was a perpetual insecurity, Pines observed.

The job quickly took a toll on Pines, who dropped tens of pounds and became an anxious wreck. His phone was constantly pinging with audio messages from Combs, who expected an instant response. "He has that ability to make you feel like his world comes first," Pines said. "Even if it's at your expense, that's his need, and his life is before yours." Combs expected subservience from his assistants. Pines braced himself for Combs to toss food in his direction if it wasn't "Godly" enough for him, withstood constant threats to his livelihood, and was on the lookout for random outbursts of anger. "As you enter his life, you start to realize that there is a personality there that is on the spectrum of a dangerous, violent individual," he said.

There was at least one moment during Pines' employment that spilled over into violence. Outside Combs' Miami home in January 2021, Combs became furious with a woman he was casually seeing. Kicking her to the ground, Combs roared that he had warned her that he was "crazy," as he aimed hard blows at her stomach. Out of breath, Combs then demanded his sweatshirt back, leaving the terrified woman topless. Pines ended up giving her the jacket off his back, so she'd have something to wear for her Uber ride home. Pines said he was shocked when the woman turned up at the house soon after, pacified by Combs' taking her on a shopping trip.

Pines tried to bury his unease when Combs was fully undressed around him, but it seems Combs was priming Pines for a devastating moment in fall 2020, when a high "out of his mind" Combs summoned Pines to his bedroom in the middle of sexual activity with one of his female guests. Combs wanted him to take a shot with them, then a second. Then Combs delivered his instruction to Pines: "Prove your loyalty to me, King." He wanted him to have sex with the woman in front of him. Stunned, Pines went on autopilot and ultimately acquiesced out of fear. He received consent from the woman, who put a condom on him, and engaged in sexual activity briefly, then left the room. Pines was deeply shaken by what he categorized as a coerced encounter, but at the time, Pines felt he had no other option, fearing Combs' unpredictability.

---

On a fifty-plus-meter yacht off the coast of southern Italy, Combs was untethered. In the background, amid soothing waves, was the distinct sound of flirtatious, high-pitched giggling from a gaggle of beautiful young women who were accompanying Combs and his entourage on what was becoming an annual holiday trip. After spending years schmoozing with the world's socialites in Saint-Tropez, Combs decided that Italy was more his speed. The vessel roamed the turquoise waters of the Tyrrhenian Sea, dropping anchor so Combs and his guests could race each other on Jet Skis and lazily tan on sunbeds as stewardesses waited on them hand and foot. And when they wanted a change from the yacht's private chef, Combs and his crew would visit eateries along the Amalfi Coast. This was la dolce vita. This was his "Love" era.

His yacht trips were on another level of hedonism. Word among experienced yachties was that several boat companies had blacklisted Combs after his extended stays involving around-the-clock partying, heavy drug use, and extensive damage in the form of baby oil stains. But money was money, especially a $500,000 check for a week's stay, and there always seemed to be at least one new boat owner willing to take on the risk. When Combs stepped on board, he was determined to make the most of the seven-star service. Seasoned crew members were used to dealing with the world's top 1 percent. The rich and powerful are always some degree of high maintenance, but according to crew members who worked on Combs' charters over the years, he was in a league of his own. He once decided a boat's bed wasn't up to his standards and sent crew members on an hour-long tender ride to Naples to pick up a brand-new California king mattress requiring half a dozen people to figure out how to get it aboard the yacht. A yacht crew member recalls an intoxicated Combs declaring "fuck technology" before throwing his custom 24-karat-gold iPhone into the marina at 5:30 a.m. Minutes later, a frazzled personal assistant informed the crew that someone needed to squeeze into diving gear and retrieve the device. "He always liked to go a little bit beyond what was available," said the crew member, who worked for him in 2017. "Like, I can do better."

Beyond being demanding, Combs seemed to be either high or drunk throughout his trips. And depending on what he was on, the atmosphere around him changed. The crew member from 2017 recalled being summoned to Combs' primary suite to adjust the room's temperature. After noticing that the room was a mess, with baby oil everywhere and dirty towels littering the floor, they spotted a cowering Ventura. "Cassie was in the cabin hiding her face, and she was crying," they said. Combs "either didn't care or was too intoxicated to notice." A later girlfriend felt the need to stay up all night with Combs during a charter in 2021, effectively babysitting him, after noticing he was making some stewardesses uncomfortable with his lewd, intoxicated behavior.

Christmas aboard the *Victorious*, a 280-foot superyacht, in the Caribbean in 2022 was a perfect example of his duality. A crew member from the yacht described feeling unsettled by Combs' "Dr. Jekyll and Mr. Hyde" routine, which allowed him to pull himself together depending on who was around. On what was supposed to be a holiday vacation, Combs was filming lighthearted scenes with his children for a family reality show for Hulu tentatively titled "Diddy +7." For the cameras, Combs perfectly played the role of the doting father, wearing matching onesie pajamas with his children. Yet, he was intoxicated for the majority of the charter. "He would do certain things for the video cameras and then switch into a different person," said the crew member. "He was high on some drug. We don't know what it was, but his switching of personality was so unnatural."

The two-week charter was described as a period of unparalleled chaos. "We litty like we got five titties in our mouths," Combs slurred and yelled in an Instagram story while drinking with his sons. He allegedly exposed his penis to his mother, Janice, during a card game, and instructed assistant Brendan Paul, a recent college grad, to stay inside his master suite during an orgy "just in case" he might need something. Things turned dark when women started panicking and passing out from suspected laced DeLeón shots that Combs' entourage was handing out. And the captain had to get involved when an inconsolable woman locked herself in the boat's private massage room, insisting that she felt unsafe and needed to be escorted off the boat. "She had been trying to get away from Christian," the crew member said.

Stewardess Grace O'Marcaigh also tried to escape Christian, the youngest of Combs' sons who was a Combs look-alike. He was staying in a villa onshore, but he and his own guests would party on the boat until the early hours of the morning. O'Marcaigh was on the late shift, 6:00 p.m. to 6:00 a.m., responsible for ferrying drinks to the rowdy group. On this particular night, Christian arrived at the boat late, already intoxicated. He settled in the boat's makeshift recording studio and began demanding that O'Marcaigh pour out shots from a DeLeón tequila bottle he brought and insisting that she take one herself. Feeling pressured but slightly eased by the presence of others in the room, she obliged. Christian continued to egg her on and insisted that she hang out with him. Eventually, she became woozy and suspected the drink had been spiked, and Christian began touching her. "Excuse me, you don't touch my legs like that," O'Marcaigh said, the studio's system picking up the audio. "You can take your hand off my ass for the first thing." Still working and growing increasingly intoxicated, O'Marcaigh claimed Christian asked for a bed to be set up for him. She proceeded to show Christian to the yacht's movie theater room so he could crash there for the night. Once they were alone, O'Marcaigh claimed Christian cornered her, stripped off his clothes, and tried to force her to perform oral sex. The alleged assault was interrupted by a fellow crew member who came looking for O'Marcaigh. (Christian has denied O'Marcaigh's claims. Another crew member corroborated details surrounding O'Marcaigh's account of her encounter with Christian, including that O'Marcaigh was uncharacteristically inebriated.)

The next morning, O'Marcaigh informed the captain of what had happened, but she was admonished and accused of partying with the guests. When Combs learned of her accusation, he left a hefty tip, making the matter all but disappear until O'Marcaigh filed suit against Combs and Christian in 2024.

---

The atmosphere for the filming of Combs' "Gotta Move On" music video in 2022 seemed more akin to a packed Los Angeles bar than a production set. The floor was sticky from sloshing alcoholic drinks, the dance floor was alive, and Combs was on the prowl. "I want you, I want you," he called out, referring to certain women who were hired as background dancers for Combs' new song with Bryson Tiller for his upcoming album *The Love Album: Off the Grid*, the R&B project he had been tinkering with for the past two years. Armed with his own DeLeón liquor, Combs wanted the women to loosen up. "It was a few young ladies, [and] he was trying to force them to drink," said one background dancer hired for the video. "He's basically being flirtatious with them. He had his own drinking cup and [was] forcing them to drink from his cup."

It seemed odd to the dancer and another production member that not only was alcohol brought to the set, but Combs' entourage was handing out drinks to people working on a professional music video shoot. But they brushed it off as a mega-famous rapper still behaving as if it were the nineties. At least Combs seemed to be in a better mood than he'd been in on the first day of filming, when he'd walked in and immediately insulted the casting directors' choices. "He said, 'Have any of you guys ever partied with Diddy?'" recalled a second crew member. "Of course, no one had. Then he goes, 'Do you think any of these bitches look like they party with Diddy?'" The three-day shoot—directed by Teyana Taylor—was grueling, with long hours and overnight setups. When the production finally wrapped, a crew member tasked with clearing out Combs' trailer found the clothes of a woman Combs had been flirting with in a heap on the floor.

A close reading of Combs' interviews over the decades shows that he's a master at deflection and denial. He'd be incredulous at the suggestion he'd carry a gun, while having just been in court over the same accusation. He'd preach peace, while delighting in havoc. But he has always been strangely transparent when it came to his sex life. To the point of oversharing, Combs spoke openly of his fondness for pornography and hours-long sessions. But his commentary around *The Love Album: Off the Grid* is perhaps the most revealing look at how he viewed sex. In short, it was sexy, baby-making music. Combs' goal for the hour-and-a-half album seemed to mirror his clandestine personal habits when it came to his sexual relationships. Combs explained he hoped people could go off the grid for forty-eight hours, listen to the album in full, and "turn off your phone and lock in with a significant other. Laugh, dance, cry, make love, eat, chill and do it all over again. That's important."

As with all Combs' solo projects, he leaned heavily on his vast Rolodex of connections to assemble the album, calling in favors from Mary J. Blige, John Legend, Kehlani, H.E.R., Busta Rhymes, French Montana, 21 Savage, Summer Walker, Swae Lee, and many others. Of the twenty-four tracks, only the instrumental "Intermission" lists Combs as the sole performer. In every other song, another artist does the heavy lifting. Some tracks are overt, like the longing tribute "Kim Porter," while others—such as "Gotta Move On"—are more ambiguous in their inspiration. But nestled in the ad-libs of "Homecoming," the intended recipient is unmistakable. Whispering Ventura's nickname, "CC," Combs urges her to "bring the kids" and "come on home."

Since their split in fall 2018, Ventura had largely managed to escape Combs' all-consuming orbit. She had settled into her new relationship with Alex Fine, and by June 2019, the couple announced they were expecting their first child.

Ventura began making music again, teaming up with songwriter Tiffany Red, singer-songwriter Ronnie James Tucker, and producers Chris-n-Teeb. Throughout that summer, on what she declared were Free Fridays, Ventura dropped new music, including "Excuses," "Hungover," "Don't Let Go," "Speaking Of," and "Rollercoaster," some which hinted at Ventura's inner struggle in tearing away from Combs. "We released a record every week for like ten weeks," Red said. There was no money to make in the endeavor, as the singles were freebies posted on SoundCloud, but it was an outlet for Ventura, who was still tied to her Bad Boy contract. "She just wanted to move on with her life," Red said. Ventura began talks with Bad Boy to get out of her contractual obligations. It was a delicate dance, said Red, who was part of her management team at the time, because "it's not like we were negotiating with her record label"; rather, "we were negotiating with her abuser." Still, things were moving as smoothly as they could—until Combs demanded that a non-disparagement clause be added to Ventura's separation agreement. "We were just like, 'What the fuck does that have to do with her record deal?'" Red said. "It just didn't feel right, it didn't feel fair." The respective teams went back and forth until somehow Combs relinquished the final sticking point a few days before Ventura's birthday in late August. She was free.

Days later, her father linked his arm with hers as he led a radiant Ventura down a stone-paved aisle atop a Malibu cliffside.

Seven months pregnant with her daughter Frankie, Ventura wore a structured yet soft and billowy dress designed by her stylist team of close friends, who had been by her side from the very beginning. "As soon as I saw Alex, any nerves that I did have went away, and I just couldn't stop smiling," she told *Vogue*. In front of an intimate crowd of family—fourteen guests in total—the couple emotionally exchanged personal vows. A few days later, Fine completed a fifty-mile ultramarathon to raise money for a domestic violence charity. After crossing the finish line, he collapsed into Ventura, who silently hugged him and kissed his cheek. "It was emotional but for all of us it felt like a moment of closure," Fine wrote in a blog post, revealing that his mother was a survivor of domestic violence. "I felt like I made peace with my anger and feelings of helplessness."

Combs publicly congratulated Ventura on her growing family, and from the outside, it seemed that the two were amicable exes. Yet, Combs had demanded his $50,000 back from Fine and threatened Ventura with freak-off tapes. "You have too many iPads full of skeletons. If I was you, I would get me my money," he warned in March 2019.

After Ventura's pregnancy announcement, Combs gradually softened toward Ventura, his messages growing friendlier. "Sending you love and light. Hope all is well. Had a dream about you last night," he texted her in June 2019. "Smh. What a difference a year makes. Really happy for you. Have a blessed day. Just sending love." He'd sporadically check in, making a heartfelt confession to Ventura in March 2020, shortly before the worldwide COVID-19 pandemic set in. "Shit has definitely been rough without your friendship," he wrote. "I pray for a day that I can sit down with you and let you know all the things I've reflected on. You were there for me throughout everything. You were my ride or die and I've got nothing but love for you always. My heart is filled with joy to know that you don't hate me. . . . I thank God for the time that we had together, and you're one of the greatest woman [sic] in the world and don't you ever forget that. Love."

The response knocked Ventura back, and she took a full day to respond. "Sorry, I needed a second to gather my thoughts," she wrote. "The things you said blew my mind a bit. First, I don't hate you. I never have. I wouldn't be at this beautiful point of my life without having been with you. I definitely think of the same day to sit down and just talk because I know that we need closure and understanding."

"Tears of joy," Combs responded. "I don't even know what to say but I'll always love you. And one day I hope you can forgive me. I pray for the day we can have closure but most importantly talk. We're honestly lucky to be alive. We went hard. God was really watching over us. You deserve the world. And I'm happy you found someone that loves you the way you deserve to be loved and respected."

Ventura grew her family, giving birth to a second daughter, Sunny, in March 2021, and began to eye a serious return to music. She performed at the Lovers & Friends festival in May 2022. It was the first time she'd been onstage in six years. The last time was during Combs' Bad Boy Family reunion tour, where she was relegated to a brief appearance to sing her hit "Me & U" during the Brooklyn tour stop. "This was the first time in my career that it was on MY TERMS," she wrote about the Lovers & Friends festival.

Yet—almost as if he could feel Ventura standing on her own—Combs attempted to suck her back into his world. In March 2022, he begged to see her. "There's some important things I need to tell you," he texted. "And to be honest I need closure. So asking for a favor just to speak to you for 10 min. It's all respectful. Tomorrow is not promised. I've been carrying so much in me that I need to say to you. Please." Ventura didn't respond. In June 2022,

Combs called Ventura out by name as he stood onstage at the BET Awards to accept a Lifetime Achievement Award. Speaking of battling through a low period, Combs thanked several friends and confidants who were "really there for me," before he stared directly into the camera and said, "Cassie, for holding me down in the dark times. Love," he added, holding up a L sign toward the crowd.

The entire gesture unnerved Ventura. She had made painstaking efforts to quietly and peacefully untangle herself from Combs. But he refused to let her. That night, he performed a snippet of his single "Gotta Move On" with Bryson Tiller, a song whose lyrics seemed to apply to Ventura and her new life. It had been years since their split, and Combs was still "infiltrating her news feed and still disrupting her life because you feel like you have a point to prove—and that is abuse in itself," said close friend and stylist Deonte Nash.

Ventura had tried to bury her uneasy feelings, but on the set of a music video in February 2023, "horrible flashbacks" resurfaced. When she got home late that night, Ventura broke: "I just remember telling [my husband,] you can do this without me. You don't need me anymore. I couldn't take the pain that I was in anymore so I just tried to walk out the front door into traffic, and my husband would not let me." Ventura checked herself into an inpatient rehab and trauma therapy facility for forty-five days. In both her music and public platforms, she alluded to finding her voice again and making up for the decade that was taken from her. And so, in rehab, she began writing, hoping Combs would understand the pain he put her through.

In spring 2023, a lawyer for Ventura reached out to Combs' team to inform them that Ventura was interested in writing a "tell-all" memoir, tentatively titled "Dark Times." In a recorded eight-minute call, the attorney vaguely laid out the book's framework. A proposal hung in the air: For a certain sum—the representative reportedly floated the figure $30 million—Combs could own the exclusive rights to Ventura's book. If the content wasn't to his liking, he could do with the work as he saw fit. In short, Combs was being offered the equivalent of a catch-and-kill fee before the book would be shopped around to publishers.

Combs weighed his options. At fifty-three years old, he was thoroughly enjoying the successes of his firmly established and celebrated career. He was considered a respected elder of the music industry, championing new artists and hosting black-tie affairs that celebrated Black excellence. While Combs could coast on his undisputed legacy, including creating Bad Boy and molding The Notorious B.I.G., he could as easily jump back into music production and put together a Grammy-nominated record. He possessed the grit to weather a legal war until he could declare victory and force his adversary to crawl away from the battle.

For decade after decade and scandal after scandal, Combs had not only handily beat the odds when the cards were stacked against him but flourished when he was backed into a corner. After all these years, why would he think Ventura's tell-all book would have a different outcome? He knew the game better than anyone else. With that in mind, Combs dismissed Ventura's supposed memoir offer. The feedback made its way back to Ventura, who had reached out to Kristina Khorram to gauge Combs' response. "She said it wasn't taken seriously," Ventura said. "They didn't think that I would do something like that."

---

Around the same time, Combs was also weighing whether he wanted to wage his own war against Diageo, the British liquor behemoth whose annual revenue topped $20 billion in 2025. After a lucrative decade-long partnership that began in 2007 when the company had tapped Combs to be an ambassador for its then-struggling vodka brand Cîroc, the business relationship had drastically soured. Diageo believed Combs was entitled, while he believed he was being shortchanged.

The discontent began in 2013, when Combs encouraged Diageo to acquire the award-winning tequila DeLeón. He immediately applied the playbook that he had perfected with Cîroc. Along with his three sons, Combs constantly promoted the label, hosting branded events and sending gift packages of the decanter-style bottles to close friends. A cross-promotional savant, Combs not only rapped about his liquor in his music, but Usher, Lil Wayne, Yung Miami, Busta Rhymes, Fabolous, and French Montana also had tracks that name-dropped his booze. Combs was intent on making DeLeón as much of a cultural force as Cîroc had been. If anything, he let the established vodka brand fall by the wayside in his championing of DeLeón, although that revenue was the backbone of his liquor income stream.

Yet, DeLeón's sales were abysmal. The brand accounted for a weak 0.4 percent of tequila sales in the country and struggled to sell more than 120,000 cases a year. Meanwhile, Diageo had scooped up George Clooney's Casamigos tequila brand for $1 billion in 2017. The celebrity-backed label quickly became a go-to, top-shelf brand despite its higher price point. Combs seethed as he watched sales for Casamigos soar, nearly doubling in percentage every year. While DeLeón limped along, Casamigos pulled in 3.2 million cases in 2022—putting its sales volume in league with established powerhouses like Patrón and Don Julio.

Combs always reveled in his status as the original celebrity influencer. Now, he was watching from the sidelines as his celebrity peers cashed in on something he'd been doing for nearly two decades—but making off with hundreds of millions of dollars more than he was. Combs was especially furious that he didn't receive a payout as high as Clooney's or the $610 million actor Ryan Reynolds earned when Diageo acquired his Aviation gin in 2020.

In Combs' mind, Diageo was purposefully shortchanging and mistreating him because he was Black, while his white peers were enthusiastically being given blank checks. Combs complained of DeLeón's faulty bottle redesigns, inventory issues, and manufacturing delays. He claimed Diageo had "sabotaged" and "neglect[ed]" DeLeón, which was being typecast as an "urban" and "Black brand." On the liquor company's side, managers and executives were reportedly growing tired of Combs' working style: He arrived at meetings hours late, summoned the Diageo team to whatever city he happened to be in, and burned through the tequila's three-year $15 million marketing budget within eighteen months, according to *Bloomberg*. Combs had only invested a shocking initial $1,000 of capital contribution, while Diageo had sunk more than $100 million into a partnership that was supposed to be 50–50. Now Combs was making what Diageo believed to be unreasonable demands, without a hint of the sales that would have justified funneling him more cash.

Combs didn't really care what Diageo thought of him. He was not a man to be slighted or viewed as less than. So, Combs did what he had always done: He made it clear that he wanted his just deserts. In a steady stream of complaints to Diageo executives, Combs began leveling accusations of discriminatory treatment against the company. He claimed Stephen Rust, Diageo's president of Reserve and New Business, told him that the Diageo executives were resentful of all the money Combs was making. Further fueled by the social justice movement of summer 2020 following the police murder of George Floyd, Combs threatened to "burn the house down" and go public if Diageo didn't pay him the same $100 million it was donating to pandemic-impacted liquor establishments.

In May 2020, Combs fired off an email to Diageo boss Ivan Menezes. "I will not continue to be treated this way," he wrote. "If Diageo is truly committed to diversity, you can never treat another person of color this way again." In November 2021, the once-simpatico partners tried to start fresh with a new agreement with language stating, "The DeLeón brand will be treated at least as favorably as Diageo's other tequila brands." But by 2023, Combs was complaining of unfair treatment again.

It was a character trait that traced back to Combs' childhood: a deep desire not only to fit in, but to feel welcomed and accepted. As he got older and climbed his way to the top of the social stratosphere, that feeling only intensified; now Combs wanted to be exalted. At any hint of rejection or a lack of deference, Combs would tap back into his mother's edict from his youth. He needed to hit back ten times harder when he was wronged.

But this wasn't the music business, where he could speed-dial fellow A-list artists to call in a favor or rant at a record label head until an issue was fixed. Nor was this a space where simply being "Puffy" meant things magically went his way. Combs was dealing with a giant corporate entity, headquartered in well-mannered London. He couldn't as easily strong-arm his way into his desired outcome. Combs needed to abide by the gentleman's game: legal action.

On the brink of filing a lawsuit against Diageo, Combs traveled to Los Angeles, where he met with Khorram, whom he had recently called his "soul sister" and credited for keeping his world spinning. Khorram had proved herself time and time again, like when she sweet-talked the InterContinental Hotel guard into handing over the damning footage of Combs beating Ventura in 2016. Now in her late thirties, Khorram earned $600,000 a year for managing every aspect of Combs' life. She was more than an employee; she was an indispensable part of his family. Using Khorram as a sounding board, Combs was deliberating a scorched-earth approach against Diageo, publicly calling the company out for alleged discriminatory treatment.

Half-heartedly listening to the boardroom war talks was Chelsea Marie Lovelace, a model and entrepreneur, one of the many women Combs was casually dating. The two had met in the Turks and Caicos Islands during Combs' wild, booze-soaked fifty-first birthday celebration in November 2020, and Combs' team members flew Lovelace at least once a month to the various locations the busy executive would flit between. On this particular visit, Lovelace found herself summoned to his family's California residence, a gleaming white mansion in the neighborhood of Holmby Hills. Lovelace was patiently waiting for her boyfriend to finish up his meetings when a single question made her ears perk up.

Combs had been discussing his assets, specifically *Past Times*, the visually arresting Kerry James Marshall painting that was gloriously displayed in the central hallway of his seventeen-thousand-square-foot home. Purchased at a Sotheby's auction for $21.1 million in 2018, the nine-by-thirteen-foot piece by the Chicago-based contemporary artist depicts Black men, women, and children basking in an afternoon of leisure. It's an idyllic scene that recalls the likes of French artist Georges Seurat's *A Sunday Afternoon on La Grande Jatte*, challenging assumptions about who might be pleasantly wasting a clear-skied day away. A representation of Black excellence, the piece had served as a poetic backdrop at Combs' fiftieth birthday party in November 2019 when Combs, Jay-Z, Kanye West, and Pharrell Williams solemnly posed in front of it. The conversation Lovelace could hear was largely about Diageo; when it shifted to a discussion of what Combs could financially withstand, he referred to the painting as an insurance policy of sorts, something that could be easily liquidated for hard cash. He wanted a direct answer from Khorram. "Do you think we can ride this thing out until the end?" Combs pointedly asked Khorram. His lieutenant's answer was swift. "Yeah, we could do it."

At the time, Lovelace couldn't quite make sense of Combs' urgency in that moment or his underlying tone. A few months later, as she began to mentally retrace her four-year relationship with Combs, it dawned on her that Combs might not have been talking solely about Diageo.

Combs filed an impassioned thirty-two-page lawsuit against Diageo in New York on May 31, 2023. He accused Diageo and its executives of putting "their feet on the neck" of Combs and his brands and treating DeLeón worse than other labels "because he is Black." He claimed Diageo had breached the terms of their contract and sought immediate injunctive relief from the judge, adding that he planned to seek billions in damages in another jurisdiction.

A few weeks after Combs decided to take on Diageo, Lovelace was once again on her way to visit him. Flying into Miami, she tried to call Combs when she landed, but he wasn't picking up. A driver booked by Combs' team took her to his Star Island compound, the heavy, copper-plated gates swinging open as the SUV approached the main house. Padding inside the familiar space, Lovelace was greeted with a beautiful floral arrangement. But the flowers weren't for her. The executives at Diageo had sent Combs three bouquets of black roses. That day, he learned the company was severing their business relationship and would be seeing Combs in court. Distraught and in a state of shock, Combs called emergency meetings with his team. It was the first visible crack in the platinum armor that he'd carefully forged in his childhood and believed was impenetrable enough to last a lifetime. But after a half century, Combs was learning he wasn't as invincible as he thought. Worried that he had overplayed his hand and devastated by Diageo's response, Combs began to sob.

---

His confidence shaken, Combs did what always served him best in the past—he began to heavily market himself.

But unlike in the nineties and aughts, Combs wasn't trying to sell himself as a flashy party host, a slick music executive, or an all-knowing, brash businessman. Instead, he decided to lean into his newfound image as a devoted father who wanted to pass down his legacy, and, above all else, as a steward and champion of Black excellence.

Most of Combs' publicity stunts were lip service, later revealed to be hollowed-out shells created simply to promote Combs. For example, in July 2023 he unveiled Empower Global, an online marketplace that exclusively sold products from Black-owned businesses. More than seventy brands across a number of industries, including clothing, beauty, skin care, and jewelry, were announced as being signed up to the platform. "This is about building our own infrastructure and ecosystem," Combs said of the launch. "I'm not doing this for profit. This is about us." Combs sank $20 million into the venture after acquiring the Nile List, Harvard alum Khadijah Robinson's e-commerce directory of Black businesses, in 2021, and seemingly transforming it into Empower. Business owners later admitted the entire process seemed rushed and disorganized, despite Combs having had nearly a two-year head start to prepare the platform for a full-scale debut. Roughly eight brands said they never saw any meaningful revenue from Empower. "It felt like a vanity project for Diddy," said the founders of New York–based clothing line The Label. "They did not invest in brand visibility or marketing."

Combs' biggest vehicle for publicity was the rollout of *The Love Album: Off the Grid*, his first solo album since 2006. It was the long-awaited peak of his self-declared "Love" era. In the lead-up to the album's September 15 release date, Combs came to New York City, where he was being honored at the MTV Video Music Awards with the Global Icon Award. One of Combs' strengths throughout his discography of hits was bringing an air of nostalgia to the tracks he produced. Using his time onstage as a walk down memory lane, Combs ran through a medley of his biggest records during the eight-minute set, including "It's All About the Benjamins," "Bad Boy for Life," and "I Need a Girl Part 2." His performance invoked his legacy, not just as the founder of Bad Boy Records, but for his family. Combs' twin daughters with Porter were spotlighted as backup dancers, and Combs hyped up the crowd for his son Christian to perform a portion of Biggie's "Mo Money Mo Problems," a glaring slight to former Bad Boy artist Mase, who had performed on the track. Later, a sweaty Combs proudly accepted his golden Moonman with some of his children and Mary J. Blige by his side. "I thank God for this choice that he made for me to be able to touch you with my music, give you a good time, make you dance, make you feel good," he said. "That's the only intention."

Days later—after picking up the keys to the city of New York from Mayor Eric Adams—he stopped by the *Today* show. Sitting outside the show's Manhattan studio with hosts Savannah Guthrie, Hoda Kotb, and Carson Daly, Combs promoted the album, speaking of his inspiration to "be love and give love." Positioned in the background behind Combs were students from the preparatory schools he had helped establish in Harlem, the Bronx, and Connecticut.

The segment also touched on Combs' recent splashy announcement that he was giving a slate of Bad Boy artists and songwriters their publishing rights back. Combs claimed that he had been approached by investors looking to take the Bad Boy music portfolio off his hands, but he had passed on the offer, deciding instead to give the rights back because it was "the right thing to do."

"Right now, I'm a person that's asking for change from the world, I'm asking for change from certain institutions," Combs said, perhaps in a thinly disguised shot at his ongoing litigation with Diageo. "I have to be part of that evolution to look within. When I look within as a businessman on the other side of artists, I was like this is the right thing to do. Contracts that were done twenty, thirty years ago, things have to evolve."

It was a major gesture of goodwill. The Notorious B.I.G.'s estate, Faith Evans, 112, the LOX, and even Mase—who previously had railed against Combs in a fight for his publishing rights—were among the artists whose publishing rights were assigned back to them. In the fine print that was not disclosed in the press release, the offer came with strings attached: a non-disparagement agreement. "They're like, we don't want you to say anything disparaging about [Combs] and his mother, his kids. I don't even know who the fuck are his kids," said Craig Mack's ex-wife Roxanne Alexis Hill-Johnson. She said she refused to sign. There were wrinkles of protests from some artists, including Danity Kane's Aubrey O'Day and rapper Mark Curry, who both said that being offered the rights some fifteen years after their hit songs came out meant a payday that amounted to a few hundred dollars. "He knew this was happening," Curry said, looking at the offer in hindsight.

"That's why he said, 'Let me give you guys back some publishing, make myself look good.' You say, 'Wow that is a really good gesture, a really good deed to do.' But your son is on TV with a million dollars on his necklace. It's like come on man."

Combs' last stop on the publicity train was his old stomping grounds at Howard University, where he made a surprise visit to the institution's homecoming celebration, Yardfest, in October 2023. He performed his hits "It's All About the Benjamins" and "I Need a Girl Part 2" on a large makeshift stage to a crowd of cheering students. Combs' impromptu visit was to make good on his vow from the BET Awards stage the year before: He dropped off a $1 million check to the university. His black Bottega Veneta sunglasses stayed glued to his face as he spoke about the donation with local news crews. "The concept is revival this year," he told a reporter. "This pledge is a way to revive the alumni to understand we got to keep sowing the seed. They've given us so much—we got to consistently, not just every now and again, sow the seed to this university because it is the most important Black institution ever."

His good deeds accomplished, Combs headed back to Los Angeles. After six months of nonstop publicity, Combs felt like he could finally relax. He had masterfully laid the groundwork to establish himself as a goodwill ambassador, particularly within the Black community. Now, it was time to celebrate. His birthday was on the horizon, and he was about to earn his fourteenth Grammy nomination for Best Progressive R&B Album for *The Love Album: Off the Grid*. He posted a clip of himself singing a rendition of Elton John's "I'm Still Standing" in his Los Angeles mansion, with *Past Times* proudly displayed in the background. "I'm still standin' better than I ever did," a jovial Combs bellows, a chilled glass of white wine resting in his hand as he struts about his home. "Lookin' like a true survivor, feelin' like a little kid."

Three weeks later, on a relatively quiet Thursday night on

November 16, 2023, a wrecking ball crashed into the fortified wall that Combs had spent months assembling. *The New York Times* published a story headlined, "Sean Combs Is Accused by Cassie of Rape and Years of Abuse in Lawsuit."

Across thirty-five pages that came with a trigger warning in bolded, all-caps, red letters, Ventura laid bare in her lawsuit the reality of her relationship. It was intensely personal, vulnerable, and explicit, going into extreme detail about the sexual encounters that the world now knows as freak-offs. She gave dates and locations of the beatings she endured and detailed why she felt like she had no choice but to stay. She named Combs' enablers who encouraged her to return to the arms of her abuser, listed Bad Boy staffers who cried when they saw the extent of her injuries, and noted her own friends who were victimized simply because of their proximity to her. Ventura wrote of her recurring nightmares and how she returned to abusing substances to cope with processing the aftermath of a deeply traumatic and abusive relationship. She admitted she contemplated suicide at times. In a statement about the lawsuit, Ventura said, "After years in silence and darkness, I am finally ready to tell my story, and to speak up on behalf of myself and for the benefit of other women who face violence and abuse in their relationships."

It was a jaw-dropping account that stunned the world into an almost immediate, collective reaction: We believe her. That support was bolstered by Mescudi, who confirmed that his car partially exploded in his driveway after Combs discovered his fling with Ventura. "This is all true," he said through a representative. Former Danity Kane members Aubrey O'Day, Dawn Richard, and D. Woods, whose paths crossed with Ventura's during the girl group's time on *Making the Band* and their short-lived Bad Boy Records deal, were among the first to applaud Ventura for coming forward. "It isn't easy to take on one of the most powerful people in this industry," O'Day said. "May her voice bring all the others to the table, so we can start having more transparent conversations about what is actually happening behind the scenes."

While the public and social media recoiled from the accusations, even more talk was occurring in private. The link to the *New York Times* article pinged across multiple group chats. Former Bad Boy staffers began questioning who among them had known about this—had they ever witnessed any signs of trouble between the couple? Long-whispered rumors about Combs' behavior began recirculating. And for dozens across the country, the news hit like an unexpected punch to the stomach. They all now had confirmation that they weren't alone in their experiences with Combs. And thanks to Ventura's bravery, there was a path forward in sharing the truth with the world.

Combs' team was quick to categorically deny Ventura's accusations, describing her complaint as "riddled with baseless and outrageous lies." They accused Ventura of "seeking a payday," claiming she made a "persistent demand of $30 million, under the threat of writing a damaging book about their relationship." Yet there were numerous people in Combs' inner circle who knew elements of Ventura's account were truthful. They had all seen her bruises and overheard their ferocious fights, and members of his personal team were privy to aspects of Combs' sex life and out-of-control drug use. As Combs scrambled to reach out to old friends and employees, his lawyers headed to the negotiating table.

Both sides admitted there was a period of negotiation. Combs had known for months that Ventura was on the verge of going public. She had sent Combs a copy of the memoir she had written while in rehab. According to Ventura's attorney Douglas Wigdor, who was declared "America's most prominent #Metoo lawyer" by the *Financial Times,* Combs had offered Ventura an eight-figure settlement to silence her and squash the lawsuit. "She rejected his efforts," Wigdor said. Though each side disputed elements of the initial negotiation period, what became clear was that Combs had been given the chance to keep Ventura's accusations hidden, and for whatever reason, he failed. From the outside, it looked like Combs had made a baffling error in judgment. Maybe Combs believed that Ventura wouldn't be willing to expose herself so nakedly. And if she dared, maybe he thought he could weather the storm, telling himself that his star power, famous connections, stacks of cash, fandom, and the decades of music he'd created would overpower any fallout from Ventura's claims. Or perhaps, Combs truly didn't think that what Ventura was accusing him of was really that horrific, or he remembered the points of contention vastly differently. Whatever his logic, once the accusations were made public, it was clear that Combs had made a massive miscalculation. Less than twenty-four hours later, the parties reached a private settlement. Combs would pay Ventura $20 million. "I have decided to resolve this matter amicably on terms that I have some level of control," Ventura said in a statement released by her attorney. In acknowledging the settlement, Combs' team was adamant that it should not amount to a concession of any wrongdoing on Combs' part. "We have decided to resolve this matter amicably," he said. "I wish Cassie and her family all the best. Love."

Apart from the eight-figure settlement, there was another stipulation that Ventura would not waver on: Combs could never say her name publicly again.

# PART III

# CHAPTER 9 | AN IMAGE SHATTERED

**AS NEWS OF VENTURA'S** lawsuit dominated headlines, many in Combs' orbit and those who managed to escape it collectively held their breath to see if the notoriously slippery Combs would finally have to face real consequences. Of course, there were the anticipated, immediate reactions from social media as spectators began weighing in, unearthing old rumors from Lipstick Alley, and weaving together a decades-long timeline of Combs' documented bad behavior, like the 1999 nightclub shooting and the UCLA incident in 2015. The public discord meant Combs had to skip the Grammy Awards despite *The Love Album: Off the Grid* being up for Best Progressive R&B Album, Combs' first nomination in eight years. The Recording Academy effectively warned the fourteen-time nominee to stay away, hinting that the organization was weighing the decision to rescind his invite. "We are taking this matter very seriously, and we are in the process of evaluating it with the time and care that it deserves," a representative said weeks before the ceremony.

While Combs could withstand the short-term effects of his cancellation, the institutional and corporate fallouts stung much more. Howard's board of trustees unanimously voted to revoke his honorary degree from 2014. He resigned as chairman of Revolt, the media company he had proudly founded in 2013. Diageo used Ventura's filing to end their business relationship for good, agreeing to pay Combs a flat $200 million for his remaining shares of DeLeón. "Sean Combs and Diageo have now agreed to resolve all disputes between them. Mr. Combs has withdrawn all of his allegations about Diageo and will voluntarily dismiss his lawsuits against Diageo with prejudice," a joint statement from January 2024 read. "Diageo and Mr. Combs have no ongoing business relationship, either with respect to Cîroc vodka or DeLeón tequila, which Diageo now solely owns."

A day after he settled Ventura's lawsuit, a stressed-looking Combs sank into a cushioned couch on the edge of his Star Island dock. Overlooking Miami's main channel, he anxiously raked his hands over his head and clutched his stomach. There to console her distraught boss was Khorram, robed and makeup-free and looking equally as unnerved as Combs. She had hitched her career to Combs. Now, her phone in hand and laptop cracked open, Khorram looked blankly ahead as Combs hung his head in despair. Eventually, Combs peeled himself off the couch and began making phone calls while pacing along the waterfront. He was ready to fight.

Despite the severity of Ventura's accusations, Combs believed he could salvage his reputation and protect his beloved and hard-earned legacy. Safeguarding his wealth was also a priority. After decades in which money was a second thought, Combs needed to drastically rein in his spending now that Diageo had pulled the plug on one of his primary liquid revenue streams. "No more Uber Eats," a terse Combs dictated to his household members and guests. "If you get one water, you better drink the whole thing." After crisis talks with his team of lawyers and financial advisers,

Combs was buckling down. "We are now in the times of war," was his frequent reminder to anyone within earshot. "He was like, very spooked," Lovelace said. "Very, very spooked."

The partnership with Diageo had brought in estimated annual earnings of $66 million; with it out of the picture, *Forbes* slashed Combs' overall net worth, estimating that he now hovered around the still impressive $400 million mark, with $200 million in cash, as well as pricey artwork, and a fleet of twenty cars. With future business stalled, Combs needed to batten down the hatches until he could sort out a long-term plan for his finances. But if he held firm, Combs was sure he could emerge from this nightmare with minimal lasting damage. Staving off any other calamitous accusations from going public was paramount.

His first priority was keeping a particular girlfriend quiet. "I feel like I'm reading my own sexual trauma," the woman who came to be known as Jane emphasized to Combs just three days after Ventura's lawsuit was made public. "It makes me sick how three solid pages, word for word, is exactly my experiences and my anguish."

The text message sent Combs into a panic.

Jane knew almost as much as Ventura did. Although she had been participating in freak-offs with Combs for the past few years—or what she called "hotel nights," which also involved sex with male escorts—there were several entries in the notes app of her phone that expressed how she no longer wanted to continue them. Desperate to stop any more women from coming forward and seemingly aware of the danger of criminal repercussions, Combs reacted to Jane's message frantically, calling her from a different cell phone and begging her not to put anything else in writing. Khorram recorded the conversation in which Combs tried his best to pacify Jane. "I'm not even supposed to be talking on the phone," Combs stammered. "Like, please don't send no texts or d-do nothing. People misread and shit." Combs proceeded to try to feed Jane a false narrative of events, saying any trauma she might be experiencing stemmed from acts she had willingly engaged in.

When Jane wouldn't budge, saying it was "not how she saw things," he switched up his tactic. Combs pleaded for her support and friendship. But she was undeterred. "He just threatened me about my sex tapes that he has of me on two phones," she later texted Khorram. "He said he would expose me. Mind you, these sex tapes where I am heavily drugged and doing things he asked of me for the past three years."

---

Combs met Jane in November 2020, during a fun girls' getaway to sunny Miami while the rest of the country braced for winter amid the COVID-19 pandemic. Jane, who was in her mid-thirties, had been invited by a friend who was casually seeing Combs at the time. Jane and Combs subtly flirted throughout the trip, and eventually Combs asked for Jane's number. "That's when we decided we should have a nickname," Jane said. "And he said Bert and I said Ernie." By January 2021, Jane was back in Miami for a whirlwind first date with Combs that would last five days. They discussed how Jane shared a child with a famous rapper who Combs wasn't particularly fond of, but mostly they basked in each other's company and made love for hours and hours. "I remember it was just amazing," Jane said. "I was pretty head over heels for Sean."

When Combs learned that Jane's birthday was in February, he jetted her to Turks and Caicos on his private plane and took over an entire oceanfront villa for the week, reserved exclusively for the two of them and his staff. Jane felt she was being swept up into a fairy tale created especially for her. Early in the trip, while sipping cocktails poolside, Jane took Ecstasy for the third time in her life.

Combs handed her the pill, assuring her it would make the day more fun. Moments later, while strolling on the beach, a sudden rush of euphoria knocked her to the ground, her body convulsing in the sand. Scrambling, Combs' personal team—Khorram and his butler—hauled Jane into a shower, hoping a stream of tepid water would calm her nervous system. Slowly, Jane's body settled. The incident didn't end the drug use. Over her remaining time in the Caribbean, Combs continued to feed Jane Ecstasy, only in smaller doses. Nearly two weeks later, when they finally went their separate ways, Combs had his business manager wire Jane $10,000. At the time, she understood it as a thoughtful gesture, meant to repay her for any missed work opportunities while she was away. Only later would that generosity feel less like a gift and more like a tool of manipulation.

For the next three months, Combs and Jane were in a love-induced haze. He'd fly her out every other week to spend time with him in Miami. There, they'd take drugs—mainly Ecstasy, sometimes cocaine and ketamine—whenever they had sex, and Combs introduced Jane to his highly specific preferences when it came to sex. It was thrilling for Jane to seduce Combs. She'd wear flimsy lingerie and seven-inch stripper heels, continually applying baby oil to herself as the two would make love for anywhere between twelve and twenty-four hours. "I felt like Sean was really passionate, and he brought out a lot of passion out of me too," Jane said. "The way he would compliment me and be so into me and just really like enjoying one another, it made me feel really good inside."

During one of these extended sex sessions in May 2021, while watching pornography, Combs pushed Jane to openly fantasize about bringing another man into the bedroom while he watched. They had been wired for the past fifteen hours, having sex and taking Ecstasy, and a high Combs said he could turn the fantasy into a reality in that moment. "I said okay," Jane said. Within a few hours, Jane found herself inside a Miami hotel suite that pulsed with red mood lighting with Combs and a man from Cowboys4Angels. As he had with Ventura, Combs allegedly puppeteered the encounter between a nervous Jane and the male escort, guiding them through escalating sexual acts while he masturbated. Afterward, when the man left, a pleased Combs and giddy Jane made love for hours. "I felt exhilarated from that experience," she explained. "I felt that I had did something that I had never done before. I felt excited. I was happy. It was taboo. It was fun. I had a good time with my partner." They slept off the drugs and spent the next day partying on a yacht before Jane returned home, happy and content with the state of her relationship.

Jane thought the encounter with the male escort would be a one-time thing, something that was "crazy, taboo, and fun, and sexy." But that trip, Jane said, opened Pandora's box. "It just completely set the tone for our relationship moving forward," she said. Having sex with other men in front of Combs became a dominant aspect of the couple's relationship. Jane found herself increasingly "scared" by how often these encounters began occurring and unsettled by Combs' presumption that she'd continue having sex with men she didn't know. At no point, Jane insisted, was she interested in having sex with other men. She was only agreeable to the arrangement initially because she wanted to "satisfy" Combs. In texts, Combs would always push for Jane to initiate his fantasy, telling her to "lead" him and to "be explicit." Jane felt obligated to play along. "I just wanted to make him happy, and I feared losing him," she said.

Though Jane was desperate to experience the smallest semblance of normalcy, like going out for dinner together, the trips always ended too soon, and a strung-out Jane was back on a plane before she felt she had been able to spend quality time with Combs.

And Jane was uncomfortable with the idea of Combs having other girlfriends. Early on, Combs had been clear with Jane that he was dating other women, describing his wishes to keep all his relationships open. Jane accepted his terms; she was in love with him. But as she spent most of her visits with Combs inside dark hotel rooms, she became envious of his other girlfriends, like the rapper Yung Miami of the duo City Girls, who seemed able to enjoy Combs' company outside of sexual encounters. Other girlfriends were being gifted designer handbags and taken on extravagant trips, while Jane felt she was being used to fulfill his sexual desires.

This was a recurring fight between the pair. If Combs wanted to continue their hotel nights, Jane expected things from Combs in return. In the bluntest of terms, she was a beautiful woman accustomed to dating high-profile, high-net-worth men who treated her to luxury experiences. She was now dating a self-professed billionaire, yet she was receiving no tangible benefits from being with Combs, apart from his professions of love. Jane felt that if she was going to continue to share her body with other men for his fantasies, Combs needed to make her feel valued through quality time, vacations, and tokens of his appreciation—things she believed Combs' other girlfriends were receiving without having to endure hotel nights.

To ratchet down the growing tension, Combs offered what he described as a "love contract" in March 2023: a $10,000 monthly allowance. Jane readily accepted, believing "there was some sort of balance in our relationship," a generous gesture that mirrored the love she had shown him in their sex life. (Unbeknownst to Jane, Combs was easily spending between $5,000 and $8,000 on each hotel night. The suites he rented were pricey and he often incurred thousands of dollars in damage charges for the baby oil–soaked mattresses they left behind. That was before he paid the male escorts between $1,500 and $5,000 for their company.) Jane used the entirety of the allowance to rent a beautiful house on the West Coast, complete with extra bedrooms and a large backyard for her child to play in. The new space was supposed to be Jane's safe haven, but it would also serve as the new go-to destination for Combs and nights of "debauchery."

Combs would soon weaponize the house against Jane, along with the other gifts he gave her. After he paid for her veneers, he'd remind her about her "pretty" smile if they got into a fight. He arranged for Jane to get her nipples pierced, then complained when she took the jewelry out because it snagged on her lingerie and the piercings were frequently infected. "Where are my piercings? This is the last time I see you when you don't have any piercings on," Jane said Combs would bark. The hefty rent on the house came to feel like an anchor, an obligation to continue having hotel nights with Combs.

Still, Jane never stopped trying to tell Combs how she felt. In numerous text messages, as far back as fall 2021, she begged Combs for quality time and to scale things back sexually. She wondered if they had "taken things too far and now you look down on me," and in a burst of anger she told Combs to play out fantasies with his other girlfriends. "I'm not an animal. I'm not a porn star," she texted him in October 2023. She continued, "Our experiences are desensitizing sex for me. It's been 3 years of me having to fuck strangers," "Sex is sacred to me, and I can't be used like this anymore," "I just wanted to make u happy but it's creating a war inside me," "It's loveless for me. And nothing satisfies u and u always push me to do more n more," "U make it crystal clear exactly what u want me for."

Combs groveled. "Let's spend the day. Just me and you. No strangers. Please," he pleaded. Later, he took a backhanded swipe. "You the one with the house and me holding you down. So, you know I want you."

It had been less than a month after the pair's latest fight when Ventura's lawsuit both validated Jane's feelings and ripped through the couple's thinly held together peace treaty. In a phone call confronting Combs, Jane laid out for the nth time how hotel nights made her feel sick with herself but she felt she had little choice in the matter, since if she stopped them, Combs would pull his financial support or break up with her altogether. Combs tried a variety of tactics to calm her down until he found one that hit home. Careful not to say anything directly, Combs hedged that if he could count on Jane for her continued support, she wouldn't have to "worry about nothing else." Jane immediately read between the lines; Combs was referring to her home. His generous offer to alleviate her worries was a blatant wink and nod to what he truly meant: Keep quiet and his monetary support will continue. Once they hung up, Combs instructed Khorram to ensure his financial manager, Tri Star's Robin Greenhill, was "not doing anything dumb . . . like not having that rent paid on time."

---

After Combs managed to keep Jane subdued for the time being, he shifted his attention to Chelsea Lovelace, who had gone into a tailspin in the aftermath of Ventura's accusations. When the news of the lawsuit broke, she found herself wondering, could it be possible that she was in love with a rampant abuser?

Lovelace had never directly seen the version of Combs that Ventura described, although she had seen flickers when he would turn "demonic on benders." There were times that she acquiesced to his specific sexual demands—like holding certain uncomfortable sexual poses for lengths of time—because she feared what might come next if she refused. There was an alleged early nonconsensual encounter in April 2022 when Lovelace said Combs ignored her request not to have sex that night. "He would always take it to a point that I was fearful for my life," she said. He'd push her boundaries in other areas, nudging her to take Ecstasy with him and forcing pills that she believed to be laced with ketamine inside her mouth. He couldn't stand to hear the word *no*, especially when Lovelace refused to drop everything to come see him. Once, after screening both Combs' and Khorram's incessant calls, Lovelace was surprised when a hired driver turned up unannounced at her house on Combs' orders to take her to the airport. She caved and packed her bags to take the next flight out.

The incidents gave Lovelace every reason to keep her guard up. Yet there were so many other happy moments she could easily recall. Although Combs was a bona fide celebrity, Lovelace saw their relationship as normal. They doubled over in fits of giggles, went on romantic candlelit dinner dates, and binge-watched *Dateline* episodes. She was friendly with his mother, and she'd baby a needy Combs when he felt sick. These moments didn't necessarily erase or excuse Combs' darker episodes, but they tended to take the sting out of any perturbing memories.

Combs did his best to quell Lovelace's alarm regarding Ventura's accusations. There was absolutely no sex trafficking, Combs insisted. It was Ventura, he claimed, who first confided in him that it was her fantasy to be with two men. A giving and accepting partner, Combs had simply obliged. Now Ventura was bitter and financially struggling, so she was turning her desires back on him for a quick buck, Combs told Lovelace. When it came to physical abuse, Combs was adamant it was in the past. He blamed his actions on substance abuse, which he had overcome through rehab stints and professional help. He veered into conspiracy territory, suggesting that vengeful executives at Diageo had encouraged Ventura to sue him and were paying for her high-powered attorney. The company had dug into his past in search of any minor transgression to push him out and sever his contract on an immorality clause. For the moment, Lovelace tentatively accepted Combs' version of events.

Although Combs managed to calm both Jane and Lovelace, it was too late for him to stop the lawsuits. Ventura had filed her complaint under a special look-back window in New York State called the Adult Survivors Act, which was set to close on November 24, 2023. The legislation gave a one-year period to alleged adult victims of sexual abuse to file lawsuits that would normally fall outside the statute of limitations. (Prior to 2019, a claimant typically had three years to file a civil lawsuit on the grounds of sexual assault. The statute of limitations has since increased to twenty years, but it is not retroactive.) Days before the look-back window closed forever, two women who had met Combs while he was still a budding music executive in the early nineties filed complaints. "It's about making sure the world sees that this man who rose to the level of an 'icon' is actually sick and has left so many victims in [the wake of his] unpunished disgusting behavior for years," Joi Dickerson-Neal said in a statement of her decision to come forward. She was the first person, after Ventura, to sue Combs, confessing that she harbored an "ocean's depth of shame" from her traumatic encounter with him in 1991.

Liza Gardner's complaint followed the same day. The North Carolina resident said she was forever haunted by the 1990 night at Uptown singer-songwriter Aaron Hall's New Jersey apartment, where Combs and Hall allegedly took turns assaulting her as Jodeci member DeVante Swing leaned against a wall and watched.

Anna Kane, now a mother in her thirties, was triggered upon reading Ventura's lawsuit and immediately retained the singer's attorneys, Douglas Wigdor and Meredith Firetog. For the past two decades, Kane had believed that what she had experienced as a high school junior was an isolated event. But now, she knew that being lured onto a private jet by Bad Boy president Harve Pierre and flown across state lines to be plopped into Combs' lap wasn't just an inebriated, naive teen being taken advantage of, it could also be considered an act of sex trafficking. Supported by a handful of digital photos that she had saved from 2003, Kane filed her sexual assault lawsuit against Combs and Pierre in December 2023 under another specialized look-back window in New York City that pertained to gender-motivated violence, which was open until March 1, 2025. (In court papers, Pierre has denied Kane's allegations.)

Going into damage-control mode, Combs' attorneys attempted to discredit the three women by painting them as opportunists who were shamelessly looking for an easy check and questioning the merits of their "decades-old" claims. But Kane's lawsuit, which included four photos of herself posing inside Daddy's House studio and perched in the lap of a posturing Combs, set him over the edge. He launched a ferocious attack on his accusers in his first personal statement since settling Ventura's lawsuit. "Enough is enough," he wrote in all caps. "For the last couple of weeks, I have sat silently and watched people try to assassinate my character, destroy my reputation and my legacy. Sickening allegations have been made against me by individuals looking for a quick payday. Let me be absolutely clear: I did not do any of the awful things being alleged. I will fight for my name, my family, and for the truth."

---

In early February 2024, music producer Rodney "Lil Rod" Jones finally hit his own limit. For the past few months, the Chicago musical prodigy had been trying to amicably resolve a dispute with Combs over being stiffed out of royalty points, publishing rights, and an estimated $180,000 for nine songs he had produced for *The Love Album: Off the Grid*. For thirteen months of work, Combs was offering Jones a measly $29,000. Frustrated and behind on bills, Jones felt his only option was to take his fight public.

Combs was unaware that Jones was sitting on a pile of footage of him. Over the years, the image-obsessed Combs had hired personal photographers and videographers to trail him day and night, capturing countless hours of his personal and business life. The videos were often archived and saved for undetermined projects, and the making of *The Love Album* was no different. While working on the record, Jones wound up with access to the hard drive. Now, months later and fed up, Jones wanted the world to see firsthand how cruel Combs could be.

Tabbing through the video drive, Jones dug up a clip in which Combs gleefully taunted him by having A&R executive DeForrest Taylor read aloud from a text conversation in which Combs discussed withholding Jones' publishing rights. "Lil Rod ain't worth giving this kingdom to if we don't control his publishing," read one text from Combs. "He's a piece of shit human, but we do not need his talent unless we can work with him." Watching Jones' reaction while Taylor read the text aloud to the entire studio, Combs cackled. "I run shit," Combs gloated. Jones sat in silence, refusing to show any sign of embarrassment. "He was hoping for some commotion between [Taylor and me]," Jones explained. "He's that type of messy person. He'll put two people against each other and laugh just watching them going at each other."

The veil had finally lifted for Jones, and he clearly saw how he was exploited and humiliated by someone he had considered a hero. The revelations in the growing number of lawsuits against Combs helped jumpstart his awakening. Although he had never crossed paths with Ventura, Jones began to understand how his hazy memories and unsettling experiences might fit into a long-established modus operandi: There was Combs' alleged unwanted touching and groping of Jones and his insistence on holding meetings in his bathroom naked; the nights Jones said he was expected to recruit women from the popular strip club Booby Trap on the River, wearing Bad Boy merch and leading a group back to Combs' home for a raucous after-party; and the mornings Jones claimed he woke up sore and in bed with women, and sometimes Combs, with no memory of the night before, leading him to believe he had been drugged.

Watching Combs adamantly deny these women's experiences while Jones processed his own, Jones could already see how the master marketer was preparing to lay out his chessboard to emerge from this crisis unscathed. Combs was already shamelessly sharing photos of his children, particularly his young daughters, as a tactless buffer against the sexual assault accusations being leveled against him. "That's a manipulative way of him trying to start slowly coming back outside," Jones said. "He is trying to be very, very strategic about coming out in public and winning." Aware Combs always had cameras rolling, Jones was convinced that he was still filming this exact juncture of his life to save for his eventual comeback tour. "I'm sure he's still recording the process because he's doing a documentary of his life," Jones said. "[He's] hoping that he comes out victorious."

Jones sued Combs in late February 2024, becoming the first man to accuse Combs of sexual harassment and assault. In the months afterward, more than two dozen men would follow with similar claims. In his lawsuit, Jones laid out Combs' dependence on illicit substances, his penchant for women, and his late-night parties. He alleged that Combs proudly brandished a stockpile of guns, bragged about getting away with shootings, and once threatened to eat his face. At the time, Jones said he was receiving threats from men in Combs' inner circle and he was growing afraid for his family's safety. He hoped that the lawsuit would afford a measure of protection. "He needs to know it's unsafe to touch me," Jones explained. "For anyone who would think that they would act on his behalf to think about it. He made people loyal to him, but he's loyal to nobody."

Combs' lawyers dismissed Jones' claims as fantastical and sensationalized. Yet a team of all-women prosecutors from the Southern District of New York found that some of his claims had merit. Federal investigators had begun looking into Ventura's sex trafficking claims after the explosive filing landed in their jurisdiction. Even though she had reached a civil settlement with Combs, that paperwork did not restrict her from talking to prosecutors who were weighing whether her experience amounted to criminal charges. Before the end of 2023, Ventura sat down for an interview with prosecutors and retold the harrowing details of her decade-long relationship with Combs. She handed over cell phones and iPads, the broken and old electronics containing several videos of freak-off encounters. She shared the names of close friends; people on her team of managers, stylists, and makeup artists; Bad Boy employees and executives; male sex workers; and other witnesses who might be able to help corroborate her claims. Ventura gave prosecutors a road map to build what would be an extensive federal criminal case against Combs, and by January 4, 2024, prosecutors had access to a trove of emails and text messages that tied back to two of Combs' iCloud accounts. One was linked to his Bad Boy Worldwide email address and a second to an Apple account—pdteam69—that he and his staffers frequently used. They began planning for secret grand jury sessions, and when investigators heard Jones' allegations, they also brought him in for an interview, gleaning alarming information about possible firearms and allegations of drug dealing that enabled them to expedite the next stage of their investigation.

---

The only warning of what was to come on March 25, 2024, was the whirl of a helicopter drawing closer to a residential Los Angeles neighborhood. In a matter of moments, heavily armed Homeland Security agents in tactical gear leaped from armored vehicles and swarmed Combs' Holmby Hills mansion, automatic weapons drawn. The palatial grounds that had served as the backdrop to Combs' countless self-celebratory parties, where he had toasted himself and his many successes with chilled DeLeón shots and Cîroc cocktails, was now teeming with law enforcement. They stormed the house and flew a drone down a gallery hallway dotted with Combs' family photos.

Officials detained two of Combs' sons, pinning twenty-five-year-old Christian against a wall and leading him out of the house. Seconds later, thirty-year-old Justin emerged from a room with his hands held above his head as agents trained a bright red laser on his chest. Both looked shell-shocked as they sat handcuffed outside their father's home. Neighbor Ridley Scott, the famed director of *Gladiator*, *American Gangster*, and *Alien*, similarly stood dumbfounded as he watched a spectacle that wouldn't be out of place in one of his movies unfold behind yellow police tape.

Agents scoured the compound, picking through Combs' personal items. His bedside table drawers hung open while a nearby Bible and the self-help spiritual enlightenment book *The Power of Now* sat untouched. In a primary closet, random papers and boxes were strewn around the room in disarray. A handmade Father's Day poster was left leaning against a mirror, and a teddy bear with a frozen smile was splayed out on a dressing room ottoman. Combs' offices were ransacked. Multiple dual-bolted safes were cracked open, and jumbled wires hung uselessly after hard drives and electronics were ripped from the walls. Even his teenage daughters' rooms were turned over, their oversize stuffed animals tossed aside and their personal items dumped on the floor. Perhaps the starkest image of all, Combs' three cherished Grammy awards—for *No Way Out*, "I'll Be Missing You," and "Shake

Ya Tailfeather"—stood atop a gutted console. Once markers of Combs' success, they now seemed more like relics amid a rapidly disintegrating empire.

Over in Miami, a similar scene was unfolding simultaneously. Longtime Hitmen producer Steven "Stevie J" Jordan was detained outside Combs' Star Island home, later saying he was "traumatized" by agents training red lasers at his chest. "It felt like they had come to kill somebody, like they just wanted to come and kill somebody," he told a local Miami news outlet. "My man would never break the law. We're law-abiding citizens. That's what we do. You know this is another crucifixion of a Black man." Agents meticulously went through every inch of Combs' main Star Island property, leaving the neighboring villa Combs had purchased from singers Gloria and Emilio Estefan in 2021 untouched. Christian later teased the decision in a diss track titled "Pick a Side," which mocked investigators and took shots at Combs' fair-weather friends. "Knocked them walls down like when the Feddy boys ran in both of our cribs," he rapped. "Too bad they ain't know we bought the one next door 'cause that's the one they missed."

Officials would find enough in the one home. Hidden inside Combs' primary bedroom closet were two broken-down AR-15 rifles with their serial numbers scratched out and loaded with 10-round and 30-round magazines of .223 ammunition. In Los Angeles, a similar bored-through automatic rifle was discovered among six other legal, registered firearms and several boxes of bullets. Officials found ample evidence of Combs' raucous Wild King Nights: Boxes of tall stripper heels were stored in his closets and more than a thousand bottles of baby oil and personal lubricant were stockpiled around the properties. As evening arrived, officials departed with boxes of paper records, electronics, and any shred of potential evidence that might prove helpful in the case, leaving the overturned mansions quiet.

Misa Hylton, Justin's mother, was beside herself. Posting surveillance footage of SWAT members training their weapons on the young men inside the Holmby Hills home, she railed against the "overzealous and overtly militarized force." "If these were the sons of a non-Black celebrity, they would not have been handled with the same aggression," she wrote. "The attempt to humiliate and terrorize these innocent young BLACK MEN is despicable!" Echoing Combs' earlier words, she added, "Enough is Enough! Did Justin need several laser beams from firearms pointed at his chest?? Did Christian need a gun pointed at the back of his head while he was handcuffed?? How many times have we seen young UNARMED BLACK MEN not make it out of these types of situations alive??" Lawyers for Combs used similar language, labeling the raids a "gross overuse of military-level force."

Combs was not at either residence. Instead, the mogul was a few miles away from his Miami mansion with his twin daughters and members of his personal team, about to board a private jet bound for the Bahamas. Officials surrounded a casually dressed Combs on the tarmac as they informed him of the dual raids. They never took Combs into custody, but they led his twenty-five-year-old personal assistant Brendan Paul away in handcuffs. Jones had described Paul in his lawsuit as Combs' drug mule: The recent college grad's main job was to keep Combs' supply of pills and powders on his person at all times. During the search, Miami-Dade police officers said they found cocaine traces and marijuana-laced candy in Paul's baggage. (Although he was charged with drug offenses, Florida prosecutors dropped the case after Paul completed a drug diversion course.) Combs seemed to be caught off guard by the ambush. He was later seen on the edges of the Miami–Opa Locka Executive Airport looking distressed, aimlessly pacing like he had done on the dock of his home just four months earlier. He was caught in a storm of his own making, and his legacy and empire hung in the balance.

---

If the March raids were the alarm that signaled the feds were closing in, stomach-churning surveillance of Combs beating Ventura would be the firestorm that engulfed Combs.

Released by CNN on May 17, 2024, the footage came from March 2016 when Combs attacked Ventura at InterContinental in Century City, Los Angeles. Unfolding across two camera angles, the scene of domestic violence is profoundly upsetting. The encounter had been briefly highlighted in four short paragraphs in Ventura's lawsuit. Ventura knew a tape of the attack had existed at one point, noting that alarmed hotel security staff seemed to have watched it and urged her to get far away from her domineering boyfriend, but she didn't think that it would ever surface. She believed that whatever footage existed had been destroyed after Combs paid the security guards to hand over what he believed was the only copy of the footage. Yet the video hadn't been wiped away. The tape had been secretly stored for eight years until it found its way to reporters at CNN.

Ventura wasn't warned that the video would leak, sources close to her said. When she received word through her attorneys that the network planned to air the distressing footage in full, she booked a flight out of the country, unable to stomach rewatching her abuse. When she felt ready, Ventura decided to say her piece. While her lawsuit had earned her a wave of initial support, the public is notoriously fickle. Doubters and armchair experts increasingly picked apart Ventura's experience, questioning her motives and floating the idea that a larger conspiracy against Combs was at play. The footage shocked onlookers back to reality: Ventura was telling the truth about what happened that day. It lent credibility to the rest of the nightmare she claimed to have endured. "My only ask is that EVERYONE open your heart to believing victims the first time," Ventura wrote in an Instagram statement, thanking people for the outpouring of support. "It takes a lot of heart to tell the truth out of a situation that you were powerless in." She added, "Domestic Violence is THE issue. It broke me down to someone I never thought I would become. With a lot of hard work, I am better today, but I will always be recovering from my past. Thank you to everyone that has taken the time to take this matter seriously."

What little support that Combs retained, even privately, dissipated when the video aired. He had confidently and definitively dismissed Ventura's entire lawsuit as a flat-out lie. Now, there was indisputable video evidence of Combs beating her, almost precisely as she had detailed in her lawsuit. The public's outrage finally forced Combs' presumed allies to abandon him. His longtime spiritual adviser, megachurch pastor T. D. Jakes, broke all ties. What unfolded on that security camera was "atrocious, degrading, demeaning debauchery," he told his thirty-thousand-person-strong congregation. "I know who it was, but as a man, I saw my daughters. And it made me angry. Let me tell you a couple of things before we pray, both for the victims and the perpetrator. There's something you need to understand. If you've got a rage you can't control, if you have an emotional problem, a mental health issue where you're bipolar, and your kids get scared when they hear your car coming home, you gotta get some help, dude."

John Legend, who was featured on *The Love Album: Off the Grid*'s soulful tribute "Kim Porter," made known his absolute support of Ventura and condemned Combs' behavior on CNN. "My default stance is to believe women when they make these accusations and to make sure that we do whatever we can to support women," he said. Even some of Combs' closest and oldest friends expressed shock at witnessing the very same abuse that Ventura described in her lawsuit play out before their eyes. "I didn't know he had that in him to do that," producer Stevie J told TMZ. "I just know that he was in a dark place in his life, as he described to me. He was just doing a lot of drugs, and it was just dark for him."

Even Hylton felt compelled to speak out. She was outraged over officials' show of force during the raids, but even before Ventura's lawsuit, Hylton had been stewing. For years, she had watched from afar as Combs' above-the-law, fast-and-loose attitude trickled down into her son's actions. She took to Instagram to blow off steam after Justin was arrested on a DUI charge for speeding through a red light in the early hours of the morning in June 2023. The then twenty-nine-year-old was able to eventually take a plea deal and avoid serious repercussions, but Hylton blamed Combs. "I'm not protecting no one anymore, just my son," she wrote at the time. "Everyone has to sit around for years and act like there isn't anything wrong with you. This [is] where the buck stops for me. I should have kept my child with me. . . . Everybody. Can get it." She added, "The statement 'a fish rots from the head down' means that, in addition to being a major contributing factor in a family or organization's success, leadership is also the root cause of its failure and demise."

Seeing the CNN tape brought back a flood of painful memories. Hylton was one of the first women to experience Combs' violence firsthand—in Bad Boy's offices and even in an incident in front of her parents back in the nineties that had led to the cops being called. She had to fight financially with him, when he was paying only $2,795 a month in child support for Justin until she dragged him back into family court. His recklessness resulted in the death of her close friend during the City College of New York tragedy. The footage was a jolting reminder of Hylton's own relationship with Combs. "I am heartbroken that Cassie must relive the horror of her abuse, and my heart goes out to her," Hylton wrote on Instagram.

"I know exactly how she feels, and through my empathy, it has triggered my own trauma." Though Hylton could relate to Ventura's experience, the situation was complicated. She had remarried, had more children, and continued a successful styling career, but she was forever tied to Combs through their son. In the wake of Porter's death, Hylton was also a mother figure to Porter's three children. This was her family. Sharing photos of Combs' children in the Instagram post, Hylton wanted to remind the world that children shouldn't bear responsibility for the sins of their father. "These young people were raised by women that want the best for them—we put God and education first and have always been united in our mutual effort to support their dreams. Two of the youngest do not have their mother here, and it has been our duty to support them."

After forty-eight hours, Combs finally emerged. He also had no warning the video was about to implode his narrative. One of Combs' sons woke him up to break the news, pulling him away from a sleeping Jane to have crisis talks with his team and family members. Since she had confronted Combs about "hotel nights" and their subsequent fight in November 2023, the relationship had been strained. As Combs huddled with his team, Jane lingered in the background, left to figure out what they were discussing by picking up her phone. She skipped breakfast after watching the video. The rest of the day, Jane was mostly left alone as Combs and his team crafted what they hoped would come off as a sincere apology. Jane read a draft of the statement, which mentioned Ventura by name and struck her as genuine.

Combs ushered away his flocking crisis team to record a brief video on his patio. He looked numb and spoke slowly and deliberately. "It's so difficult to reflect in the darkest times of your life, but sometimes you gotta do that," he said in the minute-long video amid a hum of whirring generators and muffled shouts of excitement in the background. "I was fucked up. I mean, I hit rock bottom. But I make no excuses. My behavior on that video is inexcusable. I take full responsibility for my actions in that video. I'm disgusted. I was disgusted then when I did it, I'm disgusted now. I went out and sought out professional help. Had to go into therapy, go into rehab. Had to ask God for his mercy and grace. I'm so sorry. But I'm committed to being a better man each and every day. I'm not asking for forgiveness. I'm truly sorry."

The public quickly clocked that Combs didn't directly mention Ventura, the victim of his aggression and violence, although her name had been part of his draft apology just a few hours earlier. Industry rival, rapper 50 Cent, gleefully twisted the knife, posting Combs' apology and asking, "Who is advising him right now?" He added, "This is not going to work. SMH, bad move."

Combs' heart was already evidently beginning to harden against any further shows of remorse. The following month, he wiped his Instagram account, erasing the apologetic admission of his abuse of Ventura. Then, he committed another violent assault, this time of Jane.

---

Combs' apology video disappointed Jane, who felt the final version was tonally different from an earlier version that was run by her. The initial draft sounded sincere, she said, but what was shared to Instagram seemed like "there was no heart in it." It took some time for Combs to discuss with Jane the physical violence that was on display in the video, with Combs insisting that was the lone time things had escalated to that level. When it came to Ventura, Combs "said that she was a hitter and that she would hit," but Jane couldn't exactly recall what Combs said his role was in the dynamic.

Leaving Miami on a somber note, Jane didn't see Combs in

person again until he was in Los Angeles in mid-June, about a month later. The couple planned to spend a chill date night alone at Jane's home, until the romantic evening took a turn when Jane accused Combs of secretly seeing another woman during his annual family summer trip. She shoved Combs' face into her marble kitchen countertop and hurled glass candles around the room, the hot wax splattering all over Combs. He snapped. Over the course of a prolonged physical fight, Combs chased Jane throughout the house, kicked down four sets of locked doors, put Jane in a chokehold, punched her, and repeatedly kicked her while she was on the ground. There were several moments in which Combs could have cooled off, including when Jane was able to flee her home in the dead of the night, yet when she returned, he resumed his attack. "He started saying all kinds of things, [like] I was trying to take him away from his kids and his family," Jane recalled, before he dragged her inside the house by her arm and hair.

Eventually the violence subsided. Taking a bleary look at herself in the mirror, Jane saw knots and welts the size of golf balls forming on her head, as well as a black eye. "I remember being so exhausted and sitting there, just in the towel. Then Sean said, 'Put some ice on it and put an outfit on.'" A numb Jane understood what was about to happen: Combs was inviting over a male escort, and she needed to get ready. "I remember him opening his hand with a pill in it, and he said, 'Take this fucking pill. Take this fucking pill. You're not going to ruin my fucking night. You better go out there. You're not going to ruin my fucking night. Get out there. Suck his dick. Fuck him. I don't care, just you're not going to ruin my fucking night,'" Jane recalled Combs telling her. When Jane refused, Combs leaned in, inches away from her throbbing face. Combs didn't care that he was under investigation for the very same behavior that he was currently subjecting a bruised Jane to.

In fact, he used a word that demonstrated he understood exactly what he was doing. "Is this coercion?" he allegedly snarled.

Jane swallowed the Ecstasy pill, and when the male escort arrived, she performed oral sex on him for what "felt like forever" until he ejaculated. "I just felt sick," Jane said. "I felt like I wasn't even in my own body. I felt disgusted. I felt terrible." Combs watched the entire encounter with a blank stare and later departed with his security, leaving Jane alone to clean up the mess at her home, tend to her injuries, and arrange payment for the male escort.

---

Behind the scenes, Combs' team was bracing for an indictment. Combs' at-the-ready attorneys sent emails to prosecutors asking for an introductory meeting as they prepared to mount a defense. "I know we have never met, but I would like to speak with you and provide you with information that has come to my attention over the last couple of weeks," read one of the first emails lead defense attorney Marc Agnifilo sent to Southern District of New York prosecutors. He followed up on his unanswered request five days later. In the coming weeks, an ever-expanding list of seasoned and expensive attorneys was added to Combs' representation roster as they received a flood of subpoenas for records of Combs' various businesses going back decades. Combs' team's greatest priority—and what would prove to be a Herculean task on the heels of the damning hotel surveillance video—was to lay the groundwork for Combs to receive bail if he was arrested and charged. While he awaited his fate, Combs diligently worked to build "trust" with the court, Agnifilo would later tell a series of judges.

It began with Combs' attorneys preemptively taking his passport in April 2024 and keeping prosecutors abreast of his movements, alerting officials anytime Combs left his home base in

Miami. (By that June, his elderly mother, Janice, and four daughters, including his toddler, Love, also handed over their travel documents.) It was determined that the mogul's sleek black Gulfstream G550, owned by the LLC Love Air, had to go, and his team began trying to offload the aircraft. Selling a plane is no easy business, Agnifilo would later acknowledge. The plane was leased out for chartered rentals until they could find a deep-pocketed buyer ready to pony up roughly $20 million. His attorneys also convinced the notoriously stingy Combs to pull $18 million from his coffers and pay off the remaining mortgage on his $48 million Star Island compound so he could use the estate as collateral when it came time to present a bail package.

By then, Southern District of New York prosecutors were sending subpoenas to people in Combs' orbit—friends and foes alike—and holding secret grand jury proceedings as they worked toward an indictment. Combs launched an outreach effort of his own, believing it was imperative to keep a handle on those closest to him. Ventura might be cooperating with prosecutors, but they wouldn't be able to build a complete and compelling case if they had no corroborating witnesses. A worst-case scenario would be if the government was able to expand its investigation with more alleged victims to demonstrate a decades-long pattern of behavior with multiple women. Combs covertly tried to manage—or at least be aware of—the flow of information to investigators. When Lovelace received a letter from prosecutors asking her to sit for an interview, Combs immediately set her up with an attorney and offered to foot her legal fees. Combs also reconnected with an old acquaintance, a male sex worker who had been frequently hired for freak-offs. The man received a grand jury summons in June to testify about his sexual involvement with Combs. How was he? Combs wanted to know hours after what was supposed to be a secret testimony. He was later accused of deleting the messages from his phone.

Under investigation, cash-conscious and without his passport, a stressed Combs needed to blow off some steam. Typically, he spent his summers island-hopping in the Caribbean or lounging on superyachts that bobbed against the picturesque backdrop of the Italian coast with his children, family members, and romantic interests. Unable to leave the country, Combs was determined to make the most of his summer by exploring the natural beauty of the United States. He flew to Los Angeles to attend his oldest daughter Chance's high school graduation before piling his family into oversize RVs for an epic road trip through Arizona and Utah in June. Intent on spending quality time with his children while he could, he offered $1,000 cash to whoever could go the longest without their cell phone. Together, they marveled at the rock formations in Antelope Canyon, danced in the kitchen to "Warning" by The Notorious B.I.G., and spent hours on a lake. "I'm enjoying watching y'all have the greatest time," Combs called out to his brood from the shade of a rented boat. For an early July Fourth vacation, he jetted off to Jackson Hole, Wyoming, with his latest flame, model and clothing designer Jesse Mae, and his personal photographer, Mike Oberlies. They stayed at the ultra-luxe Amangani hotel, lounging by the pool sipping espresso martinis and going on a whitewater rafting excursion. A hiccup occurred on the second day when the couple reportedly got into a verbal spat after a meal of steak and fries, and a "pissy" Mae stormed off to their room.

Combs got on his phone and called Lovelace, begging her to jump on the next flight out. "He said some girls were there, but he was trying to make it like [Mae] was just a friend," Lovelace said. There was no chance she would go: She was uninterested in sitting through what she knew would be a rowdy, party-heavy vacation. "I knew what time they're always on," she said. "They're always doing, like, white people drugs." Instead, Lovelace agreed to see Combs when he landed back in Florida.

As soon as she arrived, Combs started pursuing an old topic, one that Lovelace had hoped they had long put to bed. Early on in their relationship, Combs had asked her, "Would you ever be interested in a threesome?" They had been dating for only a few months when Combs sprang the question on her. The conversation began as one of those innocent, playful moments that new couples tend to have when getting to know each other: talking vaguely about past flings and sheepishly disclosing their fantasies. Combs wanted to know if Lovelace would entertain having sex with two men. She quickly assured her new boyfriend no, explaining that she considered herself monogamous by nature. It was a genuine answer, but Lovelace was also trying to gauge whether Combs was testing her. Self-conscious about the weight he had gained during the pandemic and his maturing age—he had taken to dyeing the gray flecks in his short-cropped hair—Combs surely must have been feeling out if Lovelace was attracted to him for reasons other than his fame or sizable bank account.

Combs' response surprised her. "I'm okay with you seeing other people, other guys," she recalled Combs reassuring her. The comment irked her. In her mind, Combs was hinting that he was giving her a hall pass so that he could do the same, guilt-free, when she wasn't with him. "Okay, well, if I see you with somebody else, you're cut off" was Lovelace's stern warning. Combs later floated the idea of having a threesome with a woman, but Lovelace shot that down, too. As their relationship progressed, Lovelace began to understand that Combs was slowly trying to warm her to the idea of bringing another man into the bedroom. She delicately tried to play it off, saying it wasn't something she was that interested in. But her dismissals did little to stop Combs from bringing it up again throughout their four-year relationship, and Lovelace somehow managed to wriggle her way out each time.

When she arrived in Miami in July, a frenetic energy clung to

Combs during what would be Lovelace's last visit. As soon as she entered the mansion, Lovelace said Combs shoved two unknown pills into her mouth. The rest of the night was a blur, but Lovelace did remember Combs "pounding it in my head" that they needed to find a man to bring over. "I was in and out that night," she recalled. "He was pressuring me into it. He was like, 'You need to find the person and set it up.' I was like, 'Fine, next time' because I knew there wouldn't be a next time. I'm gonna say yes, so he leaves me alone, and I'm never coming back. I am never coming back after this."

In hindsight, Lovelace believed Combs was once again trying to control and manipulate her, now against the backdrop of a looming sex trafficking criminal investigation. "I don't know if it was really like the desperation of him wanting this fantasy with me," she said. "I think it was more so, 'Okay, she does this with me, now I got something on her'—just like he does with everybody else. He'll record a video of somebody, not to show people, but to be like, 'well, I got this on you if something were to happen.' I feel like he was trying to get me to facilitate it because then, now, I'm not a victim," she added. "I'm the doer."

---

By late August, the initial grand jury hearings were coming to a close. Combs' attorneys knew he was on the brink of being arrested, and his team was intent on Combs self-surrendering when the inevitable came. They wanted to avoid a dramatic, SWAT-style arrest in which lurking paparazzi could snap pictures of Combs being led away in handcuffs, images that would be splashed across newspapers' front pages. An amenable Combs agreed and he boarded a plane to return to New York City.

It was unclear how long Combs could be waiting for an indictment. His lawyers held out hope that Combs would be released on bond, meaning a temporary residence was necessary. Combs was picky, and until his team scoped out a suitable long-term rental, he made himself comfortable at the luxurious Park Hyatt Hotel, one block south of Central Park.

The five-star hotel was in a familiar area, a brisk five-minute walk from where Combs' Bad Boy office had once occupied a plum piece of real estate off Broadway in Midtown. The offices had become dormant after Combs departed New York City for sunny Los Angeles in the 2010s. The gold lobby doors were now tarnished and boarded up, soiled cardboard pallets were left under the awning, and the Bad Boy Worldwide nameplate was in tatters. After sitting vacant for years, the building was demolished in July 2024, just a few weeks before Combs' arrival. Within minutes, a once-towering beacon of Combs' untouchable empire turned into dust and rubble. The irony was not lost on Combs, who remarked on the coincidence as he sat in the living room of his hotel suite with his dwindling entourage. "This shit is not fucking funny," Combs said, holding a blunt in one hand. "There's a whole lot of crazy shit going on. I went and saw they knocked the Bad Boy building down. That shit was crazy to me that that shit wasn't there. Which is a sign to me, like time to go to the future. 'That was a little building compared to the building I got ready for you, son.' It was a sign to me."

The moment on September 10, 2024, was captured by a freelance videographer, hired by Combs to document what he saw as the early phases of his inevitable comeback. The finish line wasn't even visible, but Combs was focused on his victory lap and he wanted to preserve this period of struggle and turmoil he was sure he'd be able to overcome. Footage of Combs giving himself a pep talk, cutaway shots of police officers positioned by coincidence on a nearby roof, and strategy sessions with his legal team would all make for great content for a documentary down the line. However, the raw footage—which would land in the hands of his rival

50 Cent—also captured a side of Combs unlikely to make the final cut. "We have to find somebody that'll work with us," Combs stressed to his attorney Marc Agnifilo, as he strategized how to reach potential jurors as he was being rocked by negative press. "It has to be somebody that has dealt in the dirtiest of dirtiest of dirty business of [the] media and propaganda."

Combs' mind was working overtime. As always, he was five steps ahead. He had moved past worrying about a looming indictment and arrest, and now he was concerned about what future jurors were currently seeing about him in the interim. As a result, Combs wanted to project an image of confidence and went to lengths to treat his indefinite stay like a homecoming. Flying in his children later that week, Combs took them on a tour of his old stomping grounds in Harlem, the neighborhood Janice had been determined to leave behind after his father's bloody murder. Accompanied by the twins, Chance, and Quincy, plus the son of his late mentor Andre Harrell, he was spotted outside the local soul-food spot Melba's. One passerby gawked and excitedly exclaimed, "I'm not lying!" as locals caught sight of Combs. Many were old enough to recall the height of the music executive's fame in New York City. Others might have been stunned that Combs was showing face and raised their phones to document the moment. Combs didn't seem to mind, chatting with fans around the city. After mingling with some fans at a bar, happily taking shots, Combs climbed into his waiting SUV and dropped the act. He demanded that someone find him "some hand sanitizer," only halfway joking that he needed a steaming hot bath because he'd been "in the streets amongst the people."

The freelance videographer would capture how Combs could easily flit between different moods. Earlier that night, for example, he FaceTimed a woman while in the car. He lit a joint and acted like he didn't have a care in the world, bragging that he was on his way to a bank to deposit a $200 million check. The woman shrieked in excitement, proclaiming that Combs was in his "Puff Daddy bag." Combs laughed along before asking the woman if she'd fly out to New York and visit him.

A few hours later, when Dawn Richard filed a lawsuit alleging breach of contract and sexual battery, Combs was equal parts bewildered and enraged. "Dawn Richard just dropped a lawsuit on me—from Dirty Money!" he told his old friend and stylist Groovey Lew, security guard Faheem Muhammad, and anyone in earshot that night. "I don't know what the fuck level of brokeness disease is going on," he complained. "Look at this shit. It's fucking dozens of liars." As the night bled into the early hours of the next day, Combs puffed on a vape, his black Louis Vuitton medicine bag and orange prescription bottles visible on his nightstand. His speech became slightly garbled as he adamantly insisted that God instructed him to "do nothing" to counteract Richard's claims. Still, Combs reasoned, "He's not saying he doesn't want Justin to use his brain and everybody to use their brains and fucking to figure out whatever." When his attorney Teny Geragos, daughter of famed celebrity defense attorney Mark Geragos, said she found a clip of Richard praising Combs, his mood brightened. "I think you have the atomic bomb," he celebrated. Meanwhile, he phoned Kalenna Harper, the third member of their Diddy-Dirty Money trio, laying it on thick with a brotherly love act and asking Harper to release a statement disputing Richard's versions of events. Earlier that year, Harper had swallowed her pride and asked Combs for $5,000 as she tried to manage a legal custody situation. Combs refused to help. Now, Harper told Combs she'd have to sleep on it. Combs called and texted Harper fifty-eight more times. She eventually acquiesced.

Combs felt the walls closing in and needed to blow off some steam. Since the June assault, Combs had made up with Jane, and they resumed having drug-fueled hotel nights with male escorts.

He decided he needed to see her, asking Jane to send him explicit videos and begging her to come to New York. Jane resisted, suspecting he was already keeping company with another woman. "I'm alone," he texted her on September 9. "Are you trying to start with me this morning because if you are. Don't please. And you responsible for that you got me fucked up you got me paying for jobs and talking this shit to me if you feel like that way about me then you shouldn't accept the gift from me. And it is your responsibility you want new titties new teeth a house. Are you still wanna up in the morning and fuck up my day with dumb shit. You have a nice day and now I'm really really really really really mad."

He also began to fear that Lovelace was about to turn on him. The last time he had seen her was in Miami in July, when he allegedly forced two pills into her mouth. Lovelace recalled little of the evening, her memory hazy apart from the moments Combs pressured her to have a threesome with a man. "I do remember bits and pieces," she said. "The whole night was just craziness. I was trying to run away into another room, but he kept following me everywhere." The morning after was crystal clear. Combs' bedroom was destroyed. There were multiple wine bottles, dirty towels, baby oil bottles, lube, a hookah set, and half-eaten food strewn about the room. "This was the worst I've ever seen the room," she said. Even Combs seemed to realize he took it too far. "I know he was paranoid because if I went anywhere, like to take a shower, he would be right there," she said. "He would get so pissed that I would have two seconds to myself. He obviously knew he drugged me, so I think he was nervous that he threatened me and said all these crazy things. He's nervous that I'm gonna leave him or I'm gonna tell somebody. So, he would not let me have a second to myself." On guard, Lovelace played nice until she could leave the compound without arousing his suspicions. But she had reached her breaking point and was firm in her conviction that she would never see him again. Combs spent the following weeks trying to persuade her to return to Miami, yet she invented various excuses to keep physical distance between them.

Fast forward to mid-September: Combs saw Lovelace posting cryptic quotes about the mistreatment of women and women's rights on her Instagram Story. Attempting to be casual, Combs reached out to her. "How are you," he texted on September 14. "Checking on you." Lovelace took her time in responding. "Truthfully, I don't really know how I'm feeling," she replied the following day. "Just giving it time." The panic was clear in Combs' response. "What are you giving time? What's wrong?" he immediately wrote back. Her phone began vibrating; Combs was calling. "I really just need you to come to New York," he kept repeating, adamant that they could talk through whatever was upsetting her in person. Lovelace made sure to seem open to the idea on the phone, though she fell short of accepting his offer to fly her out. She was wary of his intentions. "I thought it was either to try and keep me silent or to threaten me in some type of way," she said. She was particularly concerned that Combs would be expecting her to deliver on her promise from July, forcing her to find a random man to have sex with. "I just was scared," she explained. "I was not gonna go." Ultimately, Lovelace didn't have to worry about going to New York. "The next day, they came and picked him up," she said flatly.

On September 16, Combs was headed back to the Park Hyatt Hotel with his entourage in tow. Although he seemed fixated on Lovelace visiting him, Combs wasn't alone. Designer Jesse Mae had flown out to celebrate her birthday with Combs. She kept a relatively low profile during the trip. While Combs roamed the city with his children, Mae caught a *Hamilton* performance on Broadway and read the adult high fantasy novel *Fourth Wing* back at the hotel. On her birthday, hotel staffers decorated her suite and Mae pampered herself, having her nails done as she waited for Combs to return so they could head out for dinner. They would end up missing their reservation. As Combs made his way to the hotel's elevator banks, two plainclothes federal agents intercepted him. They led him into a back room, where they informed Combs he was being charged with sex trafficking, racketeering conspiracy, and transportation to engage in prostitution. The three-count indictment accused Combs of using his billion-dollar empire as a "criminal enterprise," conspiring to commit a range of offenses, including "sex trafficking, forced labor, kidnapping, arson, bribery, and obstruction of justice" since at least 2008. Dressed in an overcoat, gray sweatpants, and a black T-shirt, Combs was handcuffed and paraded past his stunned sons to spend the night in a holding facility.

News of Combs' arrest broke hours later, and a swarm of news crews and spectators gathered outside a Manhattan federal courthouse the following morning. The courtroom was silent as a US Marshal led a downcast Combs to his seat. Wearing the same rumpled clothes in which he was hauled off the night before, a solemn Combs pleaded not guilty to the charges. He didn't speak aloud to the court again, anxiously waiting to learn if a sympathetic judge would grant him bail.

From the outset, Combs' defense team was incredulous that Southern District of New York prosecutors had made the extraordinary leap from what they described as an admittedly toxic relationship between Combs and Ventura to arrive at charges of sex trafficking. While that matter would be addressed in court, Combs' attorneys made the case for him to be released as he awaited trial, presenting the judge a sizable $50 million bond package, which included his $48 million Star Island mansion as collateral. Combs' actions—forfeiting his passport, paying off his mortgage, and voluntarily traveling to New York in the first place—were all signs that the court could place its trust in him, Agnifilo said. When it came to Combs' confessed violent behavior, such as kicking and dragging

Ventura on the hotel security tape, Agnifilo said Combs had sought professional help and checked into rehab to address his substance-use issues years prior. "He has done tremendous things to try to change as a person since then," Agnifilo later insisted. "He's not the same person he was then."

Prosecutors disagreed. The core team of six female US assistant attorneys was led by Emily A. Johnson, a stylishly dressed seven-year veteran of the Southern District of New York and a lecturer at Columbia Law School with a background in violent and organized crime; the serious Mary "Christy" Slavik, a University of Pennsylvania Law graduate who had successfully prosecuted drug-trafficking cases; and powerhouse Maurene Comey, daughter of former FBI director James Comey, whose extensive experience in sex trafficking crimes had led to the jailing of Jeffrey Epstein, Ghislaine Maxwell, and Columbia University gynecologist and sexual abuser Robert Hadden. Also joining the bench was Madison Smyser, a Harvard Law graduate coming up on four years at the Southern District; Meredith Foster, who had a background in drug enforcement and narcotics; and Yale-educated Mitzi Steiner.

The government painted Combs as manipulative and dangerous, saying there were no feasible conditions under which he could be released that wouldn't threaten to endanger the integrity of the trial. They leaned heavily on the CNN footage as an example of Combs' capacity for violence, as well as proof of the lengths he'd go to conceal evidence of his explosive brutality, such as paying $100,000 to hotel staff to bury the tape. Prosecutors also had records of his recent communications with Harper—calling and texting her fifty-eight times—before she released a statement in support of Combs. (The government would later say they found evidence that suggested Combs arranged for payment to be sent to Harper.)

Although the indictment was clearly based on Ventura's experience, the case wasn't solely about her; prosecutors made clear there were numerous victims. And if Combs was coming to court as a changed and rehabilitated man as his lawyers claimed, prosecutors questioned why police had confiscated bottles of baby oil, $9,000 in cash, and baggies of pink powder and other drugs inside his hotel room when he was arrested. It seemed Combs had all the makings for another freak-off that very night. Presiding Magistrate Judge Robyn F. Tarnofsky sided with the prosecution. "The fact that the alleged violence seems to occur hand in hand with times when you are not necessarily in control of your actions because of that substance abuse" was warrant for his detention, Tarnofsky said. "Your lawyer asked me to trust you and to trust him, and I don't know that I think you can trust yourself. . . . I can't reasonably assure his return to court or the safety of the community, or a lack of witness tampering."

After an hours-long arraignment, Tarnofsky's decision seemed swift. Combs rose from his seat dazed as she left the bench. His attorneys whispered assurances they'd be filing an appeal within hours. Combs was about to be led out of the courtroom when it finally dawned on him to check who might be in the room. Spinning around, he looked toward the benches behind him, where his sons Quincy, Justin, and Christian were eager to catch his eye. The men, along with other friends, had arrived at the courthouse hours earlier, forfeiting their phones and tucking themselves into a corner of a quiet upper floor, away from lurking reporters. They offered encouraging smiles and waves, which Combs did his best to return, before he was led away.

# CHAPTER 10 | UNITED STATES V. SEAN COMBS

**THE MAN WHO HAD LIVED** in a townhouse on Park Avenue and kept multimillion-dollar addresses across the country was now spending his days at the Metropolitan Detention Center in Brooklyn. Housed in a general population area reserved for high-profile detainees, Combs crossed paths with the convicted "Crypto King" fraudster Sam Bankman-Fried and shared a lawyer with Luigi Mangione, who was accused of murdering the United Healthcare CEO. Time in the notoriously bleak and run-down facility took its toll on Combs, who couldn't dye his hair on the inside. His tight curls had turned a muted gray, as had his goatee. At a pretrial court appearance in early 2025, he looked noticeably frail and thinner, with his beige jumpsuit hanging loosely around his hips.

Being detained ahead of the trial was not part of Combs' game plan. On the night of his arrest, he'd been scheduled to tour a long-term rental, so he could prep and meet with attorneys from the comforts of a three-bedroom apartment on the Upper East Side. Instead, he was scraping for phone minutes inside a barracks-style unit that housed up to twenty inmates. Three judges in succession denied Combs' release, deeming him a flight risk and a danger to the community. Until they exhausted their appeals, his lawyers had submitted increasingly restrictive proposals to satisfy the court's concern. On top of a $50 million guarantee and half of his children's passports, Combs agreed to submit to weekly drug testing, hire around-the-clock security to monitor his every move, and forgo seeing any woman apart from his female family members.

Prosecutors claimed it still wasn't enough; they said that Combs was allegedly tampering with potential government witnesses from behind bars, calling him a "serial obstructor." A month into his stay at the detention center, officials had seized a notebook with "Things to Do" scrawled on the cover page. One of the missives included instructions for a third party to find "dirt" on two potential victims. Combs was also using an unauthorized messaging service on the facility's computer, making forbidden three-way calls, and paying at least eight different inmates to use their personal jail phone accounts to make calls, prosecutors alleged.

Combs was still trying to win back public goodwill through his children and nostalgia. He wanted to "reach for this jury," he told an associate over the phone. "I just need one." A week before his fifty-fifth birthday in November 2024, Combs plotted a social media campaign with his adult sons. At first, they balked at the idea, citing his lawyers' previous warnings about public commentary on the case, but Combs blew past their trepidations. "I don't care," he said. "It's my birthday." And sure enough, Combs' children uploaded a video of all of them calling the Metropolitan Detention Center and singing "Happy Birthday." His youngest daughter, two-year-old Love, blew out the candles on his cake. Combs deputized someone in his circle to share the video to his Instagram account on his behalf, with the caption, "THIS MADE MY DAY." Meanwhile, Christian took over his father's Instagram page on a mission to "spread good energy, and take y'all down memory lane of all the positive things he did." He posted throwback clips of Combs working in the studio with The Notorious B.I.G. and music videos for "It's All About the Benjamins" and "Victory."

From the outset of Combs' arrest and detention, he was adamant that he wanted a speedy trial, and a trial date in May 2025 was quickly set. It was a risky move for Combs to rush the proceedings, but the defense hoped the aggressive eight-month timeline to prepare for trial would put the government at a severe disadvantage as it pulled together its wide-ranging case.

Prosecutors continually reminded the court that their investigation was ongoing, and Combs wanted to make them work overtime. They needed to construct a cohesive case based on complicated and intricate criminal statutes, all while wrangling dozens of hesitant witnesses with varying motives and gripes. Prosecutors were also holding additional grand jury panels, which returned three superseding indictments, handed down in January, March, and April 2025. The racketeering conspiracy was now backdated to 2004, and Combs was newly accused of abusive treatment and the forced labor of his employees, including a personal assistant whom he manipulated into engaging in sex acts with him, according to the indictment. Prosecutors also added a new central victim to the case: Jane, identified as Victim-2. The government would argue that her repeated pleas to stop participating in hotel nights amounted to another count of sex trafficking and transportation to engage in prostitution against Combs.

It wasn't just the government racing to prepare for trial. To build Combs' defense, his lawyers had to construct a plausible counternarrative to the story put forth by prosecutors. There were dozens of potential witnesses, and the lawyers had to dig into each of their lives, looking for ways to poke holes in their stories, cast doubt on their motivations, or catch them off guard.

Outside the volume of pretrial motions, both Combs' defense team and government prosecutors were also keeping tabs on a Houston trial attorney named Tony Buzbee. In October 2024, Buzbee staged a press conference declaring he had more than 120 potential female and male clients looking to file claims against Combs. Standing in front of a 1-800-number backdrop, Buzbee spoke of horrific assaults, with alleged victims as young as nine, and warned he'd be exposing influential people. Buzbee represented dozens of women and men who filed claims under Jane and John Doe pseudonyms. Their claims dated back to 1991 and were as recent as 2022, alleging they had been drugged and sexually assaulted at Combs' legendary White Parties, during industry events, and at his home following the BET Awards in 2022. As Buzbee steadily continued to file cases in the lead-up to the criminal trial, Combs' team began issuing the same statement to each new claim. "As we've said before, Mr. Combs cannot respond to every new publicity stunt, even in response to claims that are facially ridiculous or demonstrably false. Mr. Combs and his legal team have full confidence in the facts and the integrity of the judicial process. In court, the truth will prevail: that Mr. Combs never sexually assaulted or trafficked anyone—man or woman, adult or minor," a legal representative said.

Others began coming forward, including Bad Boy artists and employees like early president Kirk Burrowes, *Making the Band* singers Dawn Richard and Sara Stokes, and personal assistant Phil Pines. Then there were the documentaries, streaming on Peacock and HBO, tracing Combs' history of violence and an unprecedented fall from grace.

Each side was willing the other to blink first. Combs suffered a slight setback in February, when one of his defense attorneys, Anthony Ricco, inexplicably withdrew from the case. Harlem-born

Ricco bore a sterling reputation and was known for having taken on forty-five federal death penalty cases. (Ricco had a connection with Combs, previously representing Bad Boy artist G. Dep, who confessed to a seventeen-year-old shooting, consumed by the guilt of not knowing if the man died.) Without going into detail, Ricco told the court in a written notice that "under no circumstances can I continue to effectively serve as counsel" to Combs.

And in April, after prosecutors unveiled their third and final superseding indictment and submitted paperwork with Jane's expected testimony, Combs' team waved the white flag. Less than three weeks before the trial's start date, the defense requested a two-month delay, which the judge quickly shut down. Both sides were racing toward the trial in May when the government suffered a possibly fatal blow: One of their main witnesses, Gina Huynh, had disappeared on them. It wasn't surprising that the government would want to speak with Huynh, who had come forward about Combs' beatings and manipulation in 2019. In a sit-down interview with blogger Tasha K, Huynh had wiped her eyes as she told women who may be listening that someone who truly loved them would never abuse them. It seemed like a definitive breakup following her toxic on-off five-year relationship with Combs. But at least by 2021, Combs and Huynh had reconciled. Identified in a superseding indictment as Victim-3, Huynh was not labeled a victim of sex trafficking, though prosecutors believed she fell under the racketeering conspiracy charge. Combs was accused of luring her into his orbit "under the pretense of a romantic relationship and using physical violence, threats, financial control, and coercion" to allegedly compel her to have sex with other men for his pleasure.

On the same day Ventura's lawsuit was published, Huynh was open to speaking with reporters about her experience. "Yes, I'm down to talk about it," she responded to a message seeking an interview. But she had second thoughts and decided to hold off. She quietly retained the counsel of Gloria Allred, a trailblazing feminist lawyer who has litigated some of the country's highest-profile cases holding powerful men to account. By December 2024, Huynh and Allred had silently parted ways. As of April 29, Huynh was still part of the government's case, having agreed to forgo a pseudonym and testify under her real name. In heavily redacted court submissions, prosecutors said Huynh was expected to testify about Combs' "financial coercion and abuse," which she allegedly disclosed to members of his staff. "These statements include notes that [Huynh] drafted in the Notes App of her phone, much like diary entries or first drafts of text messages" that were sent to Combs.

Then, on the eve of the trial, she vanished. Prosecutors were forced to admit they didn't know if Huynh intended to appear even if they tried to enforce a subpoena and have her board a flight from where she lived in Las Vegas to come to New York. Combs' lawyers were persistent in asking the government about whether Huynh was cooperating with them and if she was going to be mentioned in their opening statements. "We are trying very hard to find out because we are having trouble communicating with her counsel," an exasperated Comey explained to the court during the jury selection process. It came as Huynh cryptically posted on Threads, "I can feel the universe is elevating me again."

Sitting in audience for jury selection was famed celebrity attorney Mark Geragos, whose daughter Teny was co-counsel on Combs' case. Throughout the high-stakes selection process, Mark whispered with Nicole Westmoreland, a hard-hitting Atlanta attorney who'd soon join the case. They took copious notes as both sides quizzed potential jurors about their general knowledge of the case. "I wish I did, but no," one woman quipped when asked if she personally knew any of the names on the celebrity-filled potential witness list. The woman was selected as a juror. By May 12, a dozen jurors—eight men and four women—plus six alternates were empaneled to serve. The group skewed older, with only three jurors under the age of forty. Two were retirees who had worked in finance and telecommunications; several worked in the health-care system; and the youngest, at thirty, was a deli clerk.

Before the jury was finalized, US District Judge Arun Subramanian, a typically levelheaded and good-natured Biden appointee, pulled the senior Geragos into chambers and harshly reprimanded him for claiming Combs was being selectively prosecuted based on his race by a "six-pack of white women." He made the offending comments on *2 Angry Men*, the podcast he cohosted with TMZ's owner, Harvey Levin. "I think this is outrageous, and this would not be tolerated in any court from any lawyer anywhere across the nation," Subramanian scolded. "And I'm going to be watching, and I'm going to be listening. All right? You have one more listener for your podcast." The chastisement didn't faze the gregarious showman. "As long as you subscribe, I'm all for it," Geragos replied. After jury selection, Geragos returned to Los Angeles, making a pit stop in Nevada, where he called in from a hotel room to film that week's podcast segment. "Look you're supposed to zealously defend your client," Geragos explained.

By the close of the week, prosecutors told the court they wouldn't be mentioning Huynh in their opening statement and she would not be called to testify. Her disappearance was a detrimental loss for the government: As prosecutors sought to weave together a complicated narrative about power dynamics and coercion, they now had to do so with a central piece of their puzzle missing. It was an early massive win for Combs.

---

When the courthouse opened its doors at 7:30 a.m. on Monday, May 12, 2025, there was a seemingly mile-long queue of journalists; content creators; streamers; attorneys, like prominent civil rights and sexual misconduct attorney Lisa Bloom, who was representing Dawn Richard; and curious local spectators jockeying for the few dozen slots reserved for press and the public. Among the hundred-plus waiting to see if they'd make it inside the courtroom was Rodney "Lil Rod" Jones. "I just want him to turn around and see me," Jones said. "For him to see me and face me." The line had begun to form at 3:00 p.m. on Sunday. Popular YouTuber Stephanie Soo of *Rotten Mango* secured the first three slots, sweetly declining to disclose what time her team had arrived. Professional line sitters, who charged upward of thirty-five dollars an hour, camped out overnight, curling up in mini-tents until news reporters or deep-pocketed content creators relieved them of their posts at dawn. Across the street from the gray stone courthouse, a row of news stations marked their territories with pop-up tents and camera crews, their anchors ready to narrate what was already being called the trial of the decade. Credentialed photographers swarmed the front and side entrances, their heads on swivels in anticipation of a celebrity arrival. It was an all-out media frenzy.

The atmosphere inside the typically dull courtroom was abuzz with a palpable anxious energy. US Marshals led a visibly shaky Combs into the room. Forgoing a suit, he adopted a uniform of neutral-toned sweaters worn over white collared shirts. His beige slacks frequently sagged; federal custody rules note a belt could be used as a weapon. Nerves radiated from Combs, who greeted his well-paid team of reassuring lawyers with hugs and smiles. Lead attorney Marc Agnifilo was a charismatic and diplomatic character, whose spectacles and easy smile made him readily likable. His cheery disposition was a stark contrast to the complex and sometimes dark cases he took on, including NXIVM sex cult leader Keith Raniere and "pharma bro" securities fraudster Martin Shkreli. By his side was Teny Geragos, a well-heeled attorney in the middle of her second pregnancy. She came to court immaculately dressed and prepared, in charge of keeping track of the hundreds of exhibits. Almost stepping into the role of a Bad Boy chief of staff, Geragos became the Combs whisperer, seen giggling with him during breaks and nodding along to his many passed notes. Combs also took to Westmoreland and her unrelenting cross-examination style. Then there was Xavier Donaldson, an attorney who frequently argued cases in the Southern District of New York and who replaced Combs' only other Black male attorney, Anthony Ricco. Rounding out the team was white-collar defense attorney Anna Estevao; aggressive appeals wizard Alexandra Shapiro; and Brian Steel, a laid-back character who carried around a hot pink water bottle. Steel was among the last to be added to the defense lineup, joining after securing the release of rapper Young Thug in October 2024 following a yearslong racketeering trial in Atlanta. Combs had the best defense money could buy, but everything was still a gamble. He bent over an open Bible at the defense table, poring over a passage in the book of Psalms.

Combs' quiet younger sister, Keisha, was the first in Combs' family to arrive. She entered the courtroom with her husband, Stephen Dent, a former Bad Boy producer. Gradually, the rest of his family and loved ones slid onto the hard wooden benches. Combs' sons, Quincy, Justin, and Christian, were followed by his three eldest daughters, Chance and twins Jessie and D'Lila, who grasped each other's hands as they entered. The eighteen-year-olds attempted to put on a brave face but looked more like meek fawns. Janice; Sarah Chapman, Chance's mother; Misa Hylton; and the mother of his youngest daughter, Dana Tran; as well as other supportive figures from Combs' life squeezed into the pews. When he turned around to greet his brood, his daughters made a heart sign to Combs, who returned the gesture, waving and smiling at the rest of his family before returning to read scriptures. Subconscious jitters took over, and his leg bounced under the table.

The all-female team of prosecutors shuffled paperwork at the tables in front of him. The optics would be nothing like the David versus Goliath match New York state prosecutor Matthew Bogdanos tried to stage during Combs' nightclub shooting trial when Bogdanos had faced off against Combs' deep-benched team of attorneys alone. Still, it was hard not to spot the difference between Combs' attorneys—in nicely tailored suits, carrying designer bags, and with a small army of hovering legal associates—and the subdued and plainly dressed prosecutorial team, many of whom looked like they'd been up all night preparing for the trial.

When a loud knock on the jury door signaled the start of the proceedings, Combs jumped up. He clasped his hands in front of him and wasn't shy about looking the jurors in the eyes as they took their designated seats for the next eight weeks. Prosecutors made their opening statement first, with Emily Johnson acknowledging that the jury was likely already familiar with the "larger than life" man who had been awarded the keys to New York City. If jurors didn't know already, they'd come to learn how he built his multimillion-dollar empire out of nothing; that his dogged work ethic inspired his employees; and the many tragic losses throughout his life that had scarred him. But "there was another side to him," Johnson said, and laid out the "criminal enterprise" that revolved around fulfilling Combs' sexual desires with Ventura and Jane. "This case is not about a celebrity's private sexual preferences," Johnson said. "The evidence will show that the sexual conduct at issue in this case was coercive and criminal, because the defendant made women have sex when they did not want to, because he threatened them, he drugged them, he lied to them, and he even used violence to make them do it." Combs didn't act alone, Johnson alleged. The mogul relied on a small but loyal circle of trusted bodyguards, vigilant chiefs of staff, and dutiful young personal assistants to "cover up" his alleged criminal behavior and protect his public image at all costs. "Together, they agreed to commit different crimes, including kidnapping and arson, distributing drugs to other people, exploiting employees for labor, and in [one] case, sex, bribery and obstruction, sex trafficking, and transporting people for prostitution," Johnson alleged. "You will see how all of these crimes and the empire the defendant controlled were designed to fulfill his sexual desires, to protect his reputation, and to keep his power."

Teny Geragos presented the defense's opening with a markedly different approach. She was equally firm but conversational, sometimes pausing as she smoothed her hair behind her shoulders. Off the bat, she conceded that Combs had a notoriously "bad temper" and that he'd get so "angry and jealous" that he could spin "out of control." But putting aside any personal feelings about Combs' temperament, Geragos said there were no real crimes committed in this case. "He is not charged with being mean. He is not charged with being a jerk. He's charged with running a racketeering enterprise." She accused the government of drastically overreaching, prying into "this man's private bedroom" and charging him with heinous crimes. Prosecutors spoke of a sprawling criminal enterprise, with guns seized from Combs' homes and drugs passed back and forth, but, she asked, why weren't these alleged co-conspirators similarly charged? Why wouldn't there be a single witness who identified themself as being part of this so-called racketeering conspiracy? And when it came to the women who were the focal point of this case, Ventura and Jane, "they made free choices every single day for years," Geragos reasoned. "Ask yourselves: What are they getting from being with Sean Combs?" And with that, Geragos concluded, and the government would begin calling its witnesses.

On the second day of testimony, muffled gasps floated up from the gallery when the court officers swung open the heavy, creaky wooden doors and in came Ventura. Combs immediately turned toward the sound, twisting his head to see his ex-girlfriend through the rows of people. Under a figure-hugging brown dress, Ventura's nine-month pregnant belly was a powerful visible reminder that she was sacrificing what should have been a time of rest and peace to testify against the man who had traumatized her. (Agnifilo had lost his bid to shield the jury from seeing Ventura walk in and out of the courtroom, saying her pregnancy could be "a source of potential sympathy" and possibly "prejudicial.") It was the first time either had laid eyes on the other since Porter's funeral in November 2018.

Settling themselves into the first pews were Ventura's attorneys, Meredith Firetog and Douglas Wigdor, and beside them were Ventura's older brother and her husband, Alex Fine. The actor's jaw tensed as he stared daggers at Combs, who snuck a few glances back to his former personal trainer. But when Ventura took a deep breath and vowed to tell the truth, Fine fixed his gaze back on his wife, never flitting away. (The defense also tried to have Fine barred from the courtroom for the entirety of Ventura's testimony, saying they were toying with the idea of having him testify. The request was denied.)

Over four days, through direct testimony and cross-examination, Ventura would go into intimate detail about her relationship with Combs, describing frequent beatings, falling deeper into addiction, and developing a general sense of worthlessness. "He would mash me in my head, knock me over, drag me, kick me, um, stomp me in the head if I was down," she said quietly. In a soft monotone, she confirmed the identities of dozens of men who had been hired for the couple's freak-offs and described some of the degrading sexual acts he compelled her into. "I just didn't feel like I had much of a choice. I didn't really know what 'no' would be or what 'no' could turn into," she explained. "[Make] the wrong face and the next thing I knew, I was getting hit in the face." She was nervous, and her emotions were always close to the surface, but Ventura remained unwavering in her testimony. She reached for tissues when trying to articulate the burden he placed on her, explaining that she felt like she was required to carry the weight of his "own personal shame" when it came to his sexual desires. Ventura was careful in trying to toe the line of expressing herself without making it seem like she was trying to put a label on Combs' sexuality, which had been the subject of much speculation and crude jokes on social media in the aftermath of her lawsuit. It felt like a sacred and heavy responsibility, Ventura said, to carry "the things that were shameful to him . . . the sexual part, the freak-offs. I took on a lot of responsibility with that, that I never should have."

"He brought the concept to me when I was twenty-two, and I would do absolutely anything for him, and I did," Ventura further choked out. "And it never stopped our whole relationship. It was expected of me, and it made me feel horrible about myself, and I couldn't get it out. I couldn't face him with it. I can't carry this anymore. I can't carry the shame, the guilt. I was guided to treat people like they were disposable. What's right is right and what's wrong is wrong. And I'm here to do the right thing."

Combs seemed unmoved by Ventura's tears.

---

Stylist Deonte Nash did his best to calm himself down before he walked into a packed courtroom on the twenty-sixth floor of the Daniel Patrick Moynihan United States Courthouse in Lower Manhattan to face Combs directly for what would be the first time in seven years.

He had remained a steadfast confidant to Ventura in the wake of her breakup with Combs, helping her design her wedding dress and shooting the shit over the phone as she raised her two young daughters in the serenity of suburban life. Ventura's lawsuit brought a surge of repressed emotions to the surface, and Nash had to finally confront the realities of what Ventura and her close-knit circle, including himself, had lived through. The past eighteen months had been brutal, with reporters hounding Nash for memories of Combs mercilessly attacking his friend. He felt overwhelmed by the breathless news reports about Combs' upcoming trial, and by the surge of sexual assault lawsuits. He began spending much of his free time holed up at home, avoiding questions about Ventura and the time he had spent working under the Bad Boy umbrella. He had walked away from the Combs circus nearly a decade before and he longed for quiet and privacy. Then he was subpoenaed.

Nash was initially reluctant to participate in the case against Combs. At first, he was hardly a cooperative witness, cursing out lead prosecutor Maurene Comey at least once during his meetings with the government. But Nash wanted to support Ventura. His outbursts came from knowing what was at risk. He, too, was a victim of Combs: He had been physically assaulted, choked against the hood of a car, threatened with losing his livelihood, and, he'd allege in a later lawsuit, groped and sexually harassed. And so Nash agreed. In late May 2025, he flew from Los Angeles to New York City, nervously playing music from his go-to playlist in a small private waiting room as he waited for a US Marshal to collect him. Then a sharp knock came: The government had called Nash as its twentieth witness.

When he entered the wood-paneled courtroom, all those in the room craned their necks to see him, while he kept his eyes focused on the witness box. Only when he was sitting beside Judge Subramanian, spelling out his name for the court reporter, was Nash able to take in the full sight of Combs, who was sitting on the last row of benches, surrounded by his all-star team of defense attorneys. "He looked like an old man," Nash said of his first reaction to seeing an entirely gray Combs. "He looked a mess."

During Nash's testimony, which often elicited laughs from the audience and jury, Combs came alive. During a break following Nash's verbal spar with a heavy-handed Donaldson, Combs excitedly huddled with his team like he was back on his high school football squad, strategizing on a game plan. Although Nash's time on the stand was expected to last only one day, after that conversation with Combs, Donaldson stretched his cross-examination into the following day, forcing Nash to reschedule his flight home.

Throughout the trial, Combs was an avid listener and silent participant, furiously scrawling notes to pass to Geragos, who'd sometimes pop up and place the sticky note on the cross-examining attorneys' podium. When the measured, almost gentle Anna Estevao began questioning Ventura, Combs' eyes were glued on his attorney, almost as if he were watching a live sports match. He also constantly looked at the jury, trying to gauge their reactions. He adamantly nodded his head in agreement when Estevao made Ventura read aloud her texts to Combs in which she had gushed that she was "always" ready to freak off. He looked triumphant when Nicole Westmoreland successfully tripped up Bryana "Bana" Bongolan regarding the date she alleged Combs dangled her from Ventura's seventeenth-floor balcony in Los Angeles in 2016. Her story was impossible, Westmoreland said, because, on the date Bongolan gave, Combs was on the other side of the country in New York. When prosecutors used choice language about Combs' abusive behavior, he scowled and adamantly shook his head in disagreement. Every morning, he either greeted or eerily stared down the journalists and content creators in the gallery. As jurors watched explicit videos of the freak-offs, Combs bobbed his head to the music, as if he were thoroughly enjoying himself.

So animated were Combs' reactions that Judge Subramanian warned him twice about "nodding vigorously" before losing his temper. "I was very clear this morning that there were not to be any facial expressions, other attempts to have any interaction with the jury whatsoever, any influence on the jury whatsoever, and I could not have been clearer in terms of what I said. You heard me, right?" Subramanian asked rhetorically. "It cannot happen again. If it happens again, if it happens even once, I will hear an application from the government to give a curative instruction to the jury, which you do not want. Or I will consider taking further measures, which could result in the exclusion of your client from the courtroom." Combs couldn't help himself. As he saw it, he was in a fight for his life, and remaining passive went against his DNA.

---

Both men and women shed tears as they struggled to express the toll Combs had taken on their lives. "It's proven to be one of the most complicated pieces of my life," former assistant George Kaplan said, unable to give a decisive answer to whether he considered his time working for Combs something he was proud of. Capricorn Clark choked up as she testified about being taken at gunpoint to Scott Mescudi's house in 2011, crying as she described feeling like a cruel casualty of Combs' and Ventura's never-ending toxic relationship, discarded and unhirable. Although Clark sought employment elsewhere, she claimed Combs blocked her at every turn. At Interscope Records, chairman Jimmy Iovine and executive vice president Larry Jackson invited Clark for a meeting ostensibly about potential opportunities. But when she arrived, "they were there to tell me to leave Puff alone and that this wasn't going to end well for me," Clark said. When she tried to seek employment through the Creative Artists Agency, Combs and Andre Harrell "followed" her around "to talk me out of pursuing my legal efforts." She was "blacklisted" until she felt like she had no choice but to crawl back to Combs for a job after four years without being able to find work in the entertainment industry. And when Ventura broke up with Combs in 2018, Clark was a victim of their fallout once again. "This is my whole life and their shenanigans," Clark said between tears. "I have no parents. My son has autism. He's nonverbal. My stakes are higher."

Combs' former personal assistant, who testified under the pseudonym Mia, physically cowered throughout her three days on the witness stand, unable to look up even at the questioning prosecutor. There was a stark difference between the timid Mia on the stand and the confident and spunky twenty-six-year-old woman pictured in the photos Combs' defense team showed the jury. Mia said she was diagnosed with severe post-traumatic stress disorder after leaving Bad Boy. Harmless questions about her whereabouts, misinterpretations of work emails, or hearing her name shouted across the room would send her into a spiral. "I would be triggered by really normal situations with an overwhelming sense of fear, or [the idea of] being in trouble, just overwhelmed me," Mia explained, her head tilted down. "All those feelings of getting in trouble would come flooding back." When it came to Combs' alleged random and sporadic sexual assaults, Mia said she never told anyone about them because she tried her best to block them out. "I didn't know that you had to tell the bad things that happened to you if nobody else saw," Mia said. "I thought I could just die with it and never tell anyone because it's [the most] shameful, shameful thing of my life." With a faux air of Southern cordiality, Steel peppered his aggressive questions with "God forbid"s and pressed an already shrinking Mia to the point of palpable discomfort in the courtroom. "[If] you were so deeply ashamed and, God forbid, wanted to die, why did you, with all of these messages that the jurors have seen, still communicate with Mr. Combs?" he asked. "Didn't you have time away from Mr. Combs where you could write a note to yourself—'Today, he sexually assaulted me'?"

Jane was one of the last witnesses to testify; her entrance caused muffled gasps as she entered the room with her head high on June 5. Her identity had been kept under tight wraps in court submissions, and there had been rampant speculation as to who she was.

Over six days, the longest of any witness, Jane frequently sobbed as she parsed out her conflicting feelings: her deep love for Combs and her hatred of the never-ending hotel nights with male escorts. "I felt really loved by him because we experienced these things together and because they were something really special for him," Jane said. "As time went on, it was very conflicting for me internally because I'm breaking all of my own boundaries just to make him feel extremely loved in these times." She still loved him, she confessed, and confirmed that Combs was continuing to pay for her $10,000-a-month house and footing the bill for the attorney who accompanied her to court. Throughout hours of cross-examination, Geragos quizzed Jane about her motivations for dating Combs, suggesting she was shallow and dating him only for material gifts, and asking about the cost of a designer handbag. Pushed to her brink, an upset Jane snapped, "How much does my body cost?" and quickly asked for a break, leaving the room. Combs subtly nodded his head, pleased Geragos had provoked Jane.

---

Each day brought a potential media whirlwind, spectators unsure exactly who might enter through the courtroom's double doors. A nonchalant Mescudi turned up on a rainy Thursday, smoking a cigarette as an aide hoisted an umbrella over his head. He elicited laughter from the court when he described Combs as looking like a "Marvel super villain" when he confronted the mogul about his firebombed Porsche at Soho House in Los Angeles shortly after the early 2012 incident. Combs glared at him from his seat. Rumors that controversial rap superstar Ye, a.k.a. Kanye West, was about to show up at the courthouse while Jane was testifying sent Geragos into a panic. She seemed on the brink of tears as she anxiously instructed a court officer not to let anyone inside the room who wasn't on the list of Combs' approved family members. (West's presence in the courtroom could have been a distraction for the jury and for Jane, who was testifying how a meetup in Las Vegas with West and his wife Bianca Censori caused a fight between her and Combs.) When West did dramatically turn up with Combs' son Christian, he was escorted to a near-empty overflow courtroom, sparking a mad dash among reporters to find out where he was watching a live stream of the proceedings. West didn't hang around for long. He was in and out of the courthouse in less than an hour, the jurors none the wiser to his presence.

Outside the courtroom, Combs' personal team and his longtime friends were running offense. An old friend by the name of Charlucci Finney acted as the family's intermediary, turning up every day for Combs' trial, including jury selection. Finney gave interviews decrying the accusations against Combs and handed out "Free Puff" T-shirts to supporters. In a scene similar to the nightclub shooting trial of 2001, Combs' new crisis publicist, Holly Baird, was friendly with credentialed reporters and newcomer content creators alike, happy to be pulled aside for an off-the-record conversation or to chat breezily about the frigid temperatures inside the courtroom. Combs' publicity team offered content creators free copies of the day's expedited transcripts, which cost anywhere from $350 to $450 per day, and, in email blasts, highlighted specific portions of testimony that Combs' team considered relevant. Members of his inner circle began calling key figures around Combs' old party buddy, Donald Trump, now the president of the United States, hoping to lay the groundwork for a pardon if the verdict didn't go their way.

Sitting in the pews every single day was Janice. The glamorous eighty-four-year-old, always well dressed and with a fresh face of makeup, would patiently wait to catch Combs' eye, then give him a reassuring smile and exchange a few brief words before he turned back to his team. Tired of the uncomfortable, solid wood benches, midway through the proceedings, Janice began bringing a thick foam cushion to sit on. During the trial, Janice leaned heavily on her grandchildren, particularly Christian, a dead ringer for Combs. She opted to sit next to him most days, the two taking turns resting their heads on the other. Combs seemed genuinely moved to see his elderly mother show up for him, day after day, especially after her brain surgery in 2024 and continued chest pains due to stress over Combs' predicament. And she was here now, blowing kisses to her prince.

---

After eight long weeks and thirty-four witnesses who flew in from across the country, the trial was coming to a close. Combs would not take the stand, and no one would testify for the defense. In a risky move, Estevao only read into the record a series of messages from Ventura, in which she gushed to Combs about how deeply in love she was, explicitly fantasized about wanting to "fuck for 48 hours," described purchasing baby oil "because I couldn't help myself," and called herself Combs' "lil freak."

During closing arguments, prosecutor Christy Slavik spent five hours giving a methodical presentation showing "crime after crime" Combs had allegedly committed during a two-decade period: kidnappings, arson, distributing a controlled substance, obstructing justice, and sexually assaulting Ventura. "All of this evidence paints a clear picture of how the defendant didn't take no for an answer," Slavik said. "Up until today, the defendant was able to get away with these crimes—because of his money, his power, his influence. That stops now. It's time to hold him accountable. It's time for justice. It's time to find the defendant guilty."

Closing arguments were Agnifilo's time to shine. He'd spent the past sixteen-some months preparing to plead Combs' case, which largely hinged on whether jurors believed the legal standard of sex trafficking could be applied to such a complicated and turbulent relationship as Ventura and Combs'. Agnifilo appeared at ease beforehand, jokingly testing the microphone by performing a rendition of "Copacabana" that earned him several laughs.

But when the jury settled in on Friday, June 27, to hear the summation, he turned thunderous. As his wife, attorney Karen Friedman Agnifilo, watched on, he delivered a forceful speech, pacing in front of the jurors and villainizing anyone not in Combs' corner. There was no sex trafficking between Combs and any of his girlfriends, he maintained. And if Combs liked to record the freak-offs, so what? "I don't think by any stretch of the imagination this is the only man in America making homemade porn," he reasoned, pointedly speaking to the eight male jurors who sat before him. Instead, Agnifilo encouraged the men and the women of the jury to think of the couple's deeply toxic, consistently abusive relationship as "a great modern love story" that prosecutors had twisted into a criminal case. He took cheap shots at Ventura, who alleged Combs raped her in 2018 while she was dating her now-husband. "She has to do the oldest trick in the book," he sneered. "She lies and says that she was raped." Agnifilo used Ventura's words against her, saying she was more affected by the "shame" she carried on Combs' behalf regarding the freak-offs than by any abuse that occurred during their relationship. "I'm asking you to acquit Sean Combs of all the counts in this indictment," Agnifilo implored. "He is not a racketeer. He is not a conspirator to commit racketeering. He is none of these things. He is innocent. He sits there innocent. Return him to his family, who have been waiting for him."

Combs was visibly nervous as the jury finally began deliberations on Monday, June 30. His lawyers managed to put in a word with the court officers, and Combs was granted a moment alone with his family. As the courtroom cleared out, they remained behind until barely anyone was present. It was quiet as Combs led his family in a prayer, begging God for salvation.

Federal cases require juries to reach a unanimous verdict for conviction, and three agonizing days passed as jurors struggled to reach a consensus. Roughly an hour into deliberation, the foreperson notified the judge that one juror, a fifty-one-year-old man with a PhD in molecular biology and neuroscience, "cannot follow Your Honor's instructions." No further details were provided, and Judge Subramanian instructed the jurors to keep going. Another note on the first day caused anxiety in both the defense and the prosecution. The jurors had a technical question. Can someone be held responsible for distributing drugs if the person they gave them to asked for them? They were given the plain legal definition and told to continue working. On day two, they requested portions of Ventura's testimony concerning the InterContinental Hotel assault, Combs kicking her off a yacht during the Cannes Film Festival in France in 2012, and a freak-off in which she ran crying into a male escort's arms after a presumed beating.

With every juror note, both sides fretted, passing around the scrap of paper and trying to glean clues on which way the jurors were leaning and why they had asked for those specific sections of testimony. When another note arrived, indicating that the jurors had reached a partial decision on some of the counts, Combs looked ill. Once more, the judge told the jury to keep deliberating.

Word finally came on Wednesday morning, July 2, that a verdict had been reached. A nervous Combs clutched a printout of Psalm 11, which ends with the promise:

*For the Lord is righteous, He loves righteousness;*
*The upright will see His face.*

As the jury meekly entered the room, twelve faces giving nothing away, Combs gripped his hands together and stared blankly ahead. The room went quiet to hear the foreperson read the verdict aloud. As to racketeering conspiracy, the word "not" had scarcely left their lips before a gasp came from the Combs' family side of the courtroom. When Combs was cleared of count two, sex trafficking Ventura, a full cheer rose from Combs' stunned family members. In disbelief and overcome with relief, Combs put his hand over his face and bowed his head. As he pumped a fist by his side, the crown tattoo on the base of his neck just barely peeked out over his white collar. By the time the complete verdict had been read, Combs was nearly in tears. He was acquitted of the most serious charges—sex trafficking Ventura and Jane and racketeering conspiracy—but found guilty of the two lesser charges of transportation to engage in prostitution. Once again, he had beaten the odds. He had faced up to life in prison, and now he was reassured he would eventually come home to his family, whether that very day or a few short years down the line. Standing to watch the jury exit the room, Combs profusely thanked them, clasping his hands together. He then dropped to his knees, thanking God in fervent prayer.

---

Even before the government began presenting its case, three subpoenaed witnesses had told Southern District of New York prosecutors they had everything wrong. They worried the government was underestimating Combs, a man who kept ten contingency plans ready at all times and was willing to do anything to win. "I feel like nobody really talks about their interactions with the government, because it's so taboo. There's something missing without talking about that experience," said one potential witness who was flown to New York and kept on standby. "I told them bitches exactly what the fuck it was. A group of white women trying to bring a Black man down who don't speak the language focused on the wrong shit."

Prosecutors centered their case around Combs' freak-offs with Ventura and Jane, and they applied two complicated criminal statutes to what Combs' attorneys called an unprecedented case. Under US federal law, sex trafficking involves the "recruitment, harboring, transportation, provision, obtaining, patronizing, or soliciting of a person for the purpose of a commercial sex act in which a commercial sex act is induced by force, fraud, or coercion." Proving intent to coerce is notoriously difficult, and unlike typical sex trafficking cases, Combs wasn't profiting off Ventura or Jane, the alleged victims, for the commercial sex work; nor was he directly paying them. Instead, he was paying consenting male escorts to have sex with the women. And when it came to the racketeering conspiracy charge, the phrase RICO alone inspires imagery of *The Godfather*–like operations, not a record executive and his small team of assistants and middle-aged security guards who could be viewed as helpless staffers being put in the middle of their boss's chaotic love life.

Notably absent from the government's witness list were Combs' alleged co-conspirators, the people accused of enabling his weekly freak-offs, obtaining illicit drugs for him, and covering up any whiff of his misconduct. Security guards D-Roc, Rube, and Uncle Paulie were repeatedly identified by witnesses as the muscle behind

Combs; and his former chiefs of staff were identified as his fixers, but none were called to the stand. (Two months before the trial, Kristina Khorram issued a statement through her attorney, broadly denying the accusations and saying she had left Combs' employment. "The idea that I could be accused of playing a role in—or even being a bystander to—the rape of anyone is beyond upsetting, disturbing, and unthinkable," Khorram said.) One lone Bad Boy executive, CFO Derek Ferguson, testified, essentially to confirm that a vast number of Combs' personal bank accounts were tied to his company accounts, with millions of dollars freely moving between them. The government pinned everything on Combs. Where were the other executives who turned a blind eye to what was happening not just in Combs' "private life" but on the company dime? Combs was the head of his company, yes, but the case also revealed wide-ranging institutional failure.

While forced labor fell under the racketeering conspiracy charge, the prosecution had trouble seamlessly incorporating the idea to jurors that an element of this case was also about how Combs ran his workplace. Almost every main witness had been on Combs' payroll, and a majority detailed the abuse they suffered while also being privy to Ventura's. Mia claimed Combs would randomly sexually assault her when his girlfriends weren't around and explained how she was expected to work for days on end with no sleep. Clark said Combs forced her to go to Mescudi's house at gunpoint and then blackballed her from the entertainment industry over a petty grudge. Nash claimed Combs strangled him on the hood of a car while working on the set of a Bad Boy music video, upset about Ventura hanging out with him. And several personal assistants detailed how part of their job was to obtain and travel around with illicit drugs for their boss.

Ventura also fell under the umbrella of Combs' employ. The jurors were aware that she had signed a ten-year record deal with Bad Boy when she was nineteen years old, but they were given no frame of reference to understand the extent to which Ventura was dependent on Combs. He dictated her career, but she only put out one studio album in 2006. How much money was she earning on her own? Would it have been enough to cover her bills and living expenses without Combs' help? She developed a severe prescription pill addiction after her boss kept handing her powerful mood-enhancing drugs. And then there were the continual beatings that left her on unsure footing and hypersensitive to Combs' moods. Instead of making music, her "job" was serving Combs sexually. Only Jane, Ventura, Mia, and Clark fell under the government's forced labor theory, but it should have been made clear to jurors that rampant abuse occurred within the Bad Boy workplace under Combs' dominion.

Testimony was disjointed; pieces of stories were told without a clear understanding of how they were supposed to fit into the wider picture. Prosecutors laid the groundwork to accuse Combs of obstruction of justice and witness tampering under the racketeering conspiracy charge, but they failed to clearly connect the dots for jurors. One of their examples hinged on Mia's claim that after Ventura filed her lawsuit, Combs' longtime security guard D-Roc acted as an intermediary for Combs, trying to arrange a call between the pair so she could help "jog" Combs' memory. "Let me know how I can send you something," D-Roc texted Mia in February 2024, months after Ventura's lawsuit was settled, as he worked to get her on the phone with Combs. Mia read between the lines. She refused any offer of money, even as a gift. Prosecutors also pointed to Combs' frantic phone call to Jane after she said reading Ventura's lawsuit was like reading her own sexual trauma. Combs had tried "to feed Jane a false narrative of the events. . . . That's witness tampering," Slavik argued. But prosecutors failed to call others who might have been able to better bolster that claim, like Roger Bonds, who had witnessed numerous instances of Combs' physical abuse of Ventura during his decade as one of Combs' most trusted security members. He wrote in his book that Combs called him before he settled with Ventura. "Bonds, if the reporters reach out, let them know that all you saw was regular relationship stuff, nothing crazy," Bonds wrote. "All I could think of was 'Here he goes again, trying to control the narrative.'" Bonds was never called to testify.

When Combs' former personal chef Jourdan Cha'Taun Atkinson received a subpoena, Combs somehow found out and had an attorney inform her of Combs' generous offer to cover her legal fees. Atkinson ignored the outreach. A few days later, her Cadillac was broken into and all her belongings in her car were left neatly organized on the passenger seat. Atkinson couldn't prove it, but in her gut, she felt the perpetrator was someone sending an intimidating warning on Combs' behalf. Atkinson never testified.

Other expected names were missing from the witness list. Combs' personal assistant Phil Pines had testified before a grand jury, later filing a complaint in California, detailing how he was asked to set up hotel rooms and alleging that Combs coerced him into having sex with one of his female guests while he watched. Where was he now? Gina Huynh's participation in freak-offs and the physical abuse she endured overlapped with both Ventura's and Jane's relationships. Was there no way to walk Huynh back over the line? In her lawsuit, Anna Kane said she was a victim of sex trafficking, alleging she was flown by Bad Boy executives on a private jet from Detroit to New York City then gang-raped by Combs and his associates at Daddy's House studio in 2003. Was her experience disregarded because prosecutors couldn't pinpoint a commercialized sex act?

Fifty-plus civil lawsuits against Combs, some that were pending in the Southern District's own court system, painted him as an unchecked serial sexual predator, and if credible, would have helped establish a pattern of behavior to bolster Mia's testimony regarding Combs' "random" sexual assaults. But it was impossible for prosecutors to create a catchall case, in compliance with criminal statutes, that could ever encapsulate the breadth and scope of accusations against Combs.

And as the case grew bigger, prosecutors failed to cohesively tie together a convincing narrative that Combs' activity could be seen as a concerted conspiracy. The jury rejected the notion that Combs' personal team doubled as a criminal enterprise when they secured drugs for Combs or helped facilitate the organization of freak-offs and hotel nights. They gave no credence to the government's example of alleged bribery when Combs paid off the InterContinental security guards for the hotel footage or to his security head kidnapping Clark when she was forced to take a lie detector test over several days. Mescudi could think of only one suspect when it came to the firebombing of his Porsche, but the act of arson is still a cold case. And when it came to the freak-offs, jurors believed prosecutors weren't able to prove that Combs had coerced or defrauded the women into participating in the sexual encounters.

---

Reality kicked back in for Combs after the verdict was handed down. His triumphant attorneys submitted an immediate application for his release pending sentencing. Pulling on "heart strings," Agnifilo reminded the court of Kim Porter's death, saying Combs' children needed him back at home. "He just deserves the chance," he begged. Comey took a different approach. "There is nothing exceptional about his case except for his continued criminality and his willingness to violate the law," she shot back. "He's an extremely violent man with an extraordinarily dangerous temper, who has shown no remorse and no regret for his violence toward multiple victims, not just Cassie and Jane, but multiple other victims, who showed courage coming here and testifying about it." Judge Subramanian sided with the prosecution and sent Combs back to the Metropolitan Detention Center until his sentencing that October.

In hopes that his sentence would amount to time served for the year he'd already spent in detention, Combs pulled together a portfolio of his good deeds. While at the Metropolitan Detention Center, he created a six-week business and entrepreneurship course called "Free Game with Diddy," securing testimonials from fellow inmates. He collected seventy-five support letters from romantic partners, his children and mother, old friends, and business associates. "I've witnessed him doing real inner work," Yung Miami wrote. "He made the choice to check himself into anger management, start therapy, and commit to physical healing through therapy. . . . That's a good man." Combs' circle of loved ones spoke of him as a committed father, describing his inspirational "Horatio Alger-esque rags-to-riches success story" and the blessings he had bestowed upon their lives. "Looking back, my time at Combs Enterprises stands out as one of the most fulfilling periods of my career," wrote Vashta Wilson, a former HR and operations head at Bad Boy. "Under his leadership, a boutique record label evolved into a cultural powerhouse spanning music, fashion, and lifestyle. Mr. Combs was a visionary and a catalyst for change." Many acknowledged that Combs had "wrestled with deep grief and loss" and that his excessive drug and alcohol use had made him lose his way. Several said they were shocked to learn of the accusations that surfaced in the trial but expressed confidence that Combs would emerge as a reformed man if given the chance to return to his children. Still, for all the celebrities who jostled to attend his events, none were among the stockpile of those who supplied letters of recommendation on his behalf to the court.

A surprising submission came from Huynh, who claimed in a full-page letter that she "felt pressured to feel like a victim" in her meetings with the government. "I told them I was not, but they insisted that I was, even when I expressed my truth otherwise," she wrote. "I understand they concluded that I had been sex trafficked and involved in 'forced prostitution.' I did not agree with that conclusion." Huynh was adamant that "during this process," Combs "never once reached out to me or made me feel uncomfortable in any way," asking the judge to allow Combs to be with his family. She made her support known when she turned up at Combs' sentencing in October. Huynh's appearance was bold, given that prosecutors claimed they were unable to reach her ahead of the trial. She attempted to keep a low profile, sitting in the back row of the packed courtroom. Justin Combs came to sit next to her, and Huynh eventually greeted Janice and chatted with Combs' publicist and his accountant, Tri Star's Robin Greenhill, who also managed Britney Spears' account when she was under her controversial conservatorship. Returning to her seat as proceedings began, Huynh appeared anxious as she waited to learn if her letter would hold any sway with the court.

Combs and his arsenal of lawyers worked all the angles to persuade Judge Subramanian to sentence him lightly. The height of his hubris on display, Combs simultaneously argued that he should be released because a federal prison system couldn't adequately treat his complex mental health needs, including post-traumatic stress disorder, while positing that he was well enough to take on a "teaching" speaking engagement in Miami, his first appearance already booked for the following week. His attorney Brian Steel said the combination of "untreated trauma" and a "ferocious drug addiction" stemming from a doctor's prescription for pain meds after a surgery "caused him to hit, on occasion. . . . He would hit the woman he loved. He loved Ms. Ventura." If Combs stayed in prison, he'd have a target on his back. "Every day he lives in fear," Steel added. "The guards stopped a person who was armed with a shank who was right on top of Sean and was about to cut him."

Nicole Westmoreland cried as she spoke of the impact Combs had on her life and the inspiration he provided to "his community, people who are struggling to find their way or constantly hit with barriers, individuals that are trying to achieve their goals and follow their dreams." His attorneys claimed Combs' "money is gone" and that he "doesn't care if he's never spoken about again." All they were asking for was a chance to prove that he had changed.

It's also what his children implored. Clutching each other, his adult sons and teenage daughters stood together, and each took turns begging the judge for mercy. "Good afternoon, Your Honor. My name is Jessie Combs, and I'm eighteen years old," she began, her voice breaking, turning into uncontrolled sobs. "I want to start by saying, throughout the trial, everyone has had their own views on our dad. We know he isn't perfect, and he has made many mistakes, and we aren't here to excuse any of those mistakes. But, Your Honor, he is still our dad, and we still need him present in our lives." The room was thick with the sounds of sniffling and muffled sobs from family members. D'Lila also broke down. "We are scared," she said, choking out her words. "We cannot watch our baby sister grow up fatherless the same way we had to grow up motherless. We are tired of being strong. We have already lost so much. We lost our mother, we lost time with our father, and every day he remains incarcerated, we lose more and more." As they sat back down in their seats, a court security officer looked up to the ceiling, blinking back the tears welling in his eyes.

An unreadable Combs watched his children intensely, ducking his head in shame when they sobbed, yet no tears seemed to flow from his own eyes. But upon seeing the late Kim Porter in a twelve-minute documentary-style home video prepared by his team, Combs was sent over the edge. Letting out a small wail and holding his head in his hands, Combs' body was racked by sobs as he rubbed away his tears. There in the courtroom, he was forced to watch how far he'd fallen. Doubling as a career-highlight reel, the video was a jolting reminder of the man Combs publicly proclaimed to be, while he carried out repeated acts of violence and abuse.

Prosecutors seized upon Combs' duplicitous tour down memory lane, calling him a "master puppeteer of his own image" and claiming he lacked genuine remorse. The government believed a sentence of roughly eleven years was appropriate and urged the judge to heed their recommendation. "He talks about 'my domestic violence will always be a heavy burden that I will forever have to carry,' like he's the victim in this scenario," US Attorney Christy Slavik said, referring to the four-page letter Combs had submitted to the court the night before. "He uses his wealth and power to convey a very specific image to the world, but that image is incomplete, and it's misleading. . . . He was not a changed man then, and, despite what he says now, he's not a changed man now. You can't trust his words. Unfortunately, what this case shows is that despite what the defendant was projecting publicly, behind closed doors, when cameras were off, he wasn't helping others. He was exploiting and violently abusing them."

Then it was Combs' turn to address the judge. He stood up from the same seat he had been parked at on and off for the past few months. Gathering his notes and taking a deep breath, he began: "I want to thank you for giving me the chance to finally speak up for myself. One of the hardest things that I've had to handle is having to be quiet, not being able to express how sorry I am for my actions. I want to personally apologize again to Cassie Ventura for any harm or hurt that I've caused her emotionally or physically. I don't take that lightly. I would like to apologize to her family. I'm so sorry. I would like to apologize to Jane. I didn't mean to hurt you. I'm sorry that I brought you into my mess.

"Domestic violence will always be a heavy burden that I will have to forever carry," he continued. "My actions were disgusting, shameful, and sick. I was sick. Sick from the drugs. I was out of control. I needed help, but I didn't get the help. Because of that, I can make no excuse. I could really make no excuse because I knew better. My mother raised me better. I was taught better. My faith taught me better. I got lost in my journey of life. I'm not this larger-than-life person. I'm just a human being. And I am trying my best. I got lost in the excess. I got lost in my ego. And because of my decisions, I lost my freedom. I lost the opportunity to effectively raise my children and be there for my mother. I lost all my businesses. I lost my career. I totally destroyed my reputation. But most of all, I lost my self-respect.

"I been humbled and broken to my core. I hate myself right now. I've been stripped down to nothing. I really am truly sorry for it all," Combs said. Then with a slight snarl in his voice, Combs emphasized, "No matter what *they* say."

Turning to his children and his "mommy" sitting behind him, Combs' voice cracked, and he began to cry, apologizing for failing them. "Y'all deserve better," he said. "You taught me better. You raised me better.

"I got lost. I'm not this bad person. I'm sorry to my community for letting y'all down. I want Your Honor to know that if given a chance, people can change. . . . I know that I've been changed for the better. I can't change the past, but I can change the future. I ask Your Honor for mercy. I beg Your Honor for mercy. I ask Your Honor for a chance to be a father again. I ask Your Honor for a chance to be a son again. I ask Your Honor for a chance to be a leader in my community again. I ask Your Honor for a chance to get the help that I desperately need to become a better person.

Because I don't want to let God down. I don't want to let my family down. They need me. I let them down. They don't have no other parent. They're scared. I'm scared. And I have nobody to blame but myself. I know I'll never put my hands on another person again. I know that I've learned my lesson. I'm willing to comply with any conditions the court puts upon me. Given a chance, when we talk about the possibility of me sharing my story, it's not for a scheme to try to get less time. It's that this story is real. This story is tragic. And if there's any way, I don't have nothing else. I have my family, and that's all I need. I don't care about the fame or the money or making records or performing. If there's a chance for me to go into and touch some kids and touch some inmates that have lost hope. I feel like if Your Honor gives me a chance by sharing that story, that this will have a positive outcome. This will have a healing effect. So that at least I could help one person for not ending up like this. . . . I would never, ever, ever jeopardize being in this situation again, being away from my family that needs me. That's my deterrence. I don't think nobody wants to come and be in this position. No matter what anybody says, I know that I'm truly sorry for it all."

An emotionally spent Combs lowered himself into his chair, staring straight ahead, as Subramanian took a brief recess to review the record. Upon the judge's return, he began by commending Combs on his life achievements, his inspiration to his community, and the program he developed for his fellow inmates at the Metropolitan Detention Center. "However," Subramanian added, "a history of good works can't wash away the record in this case. . . . The defendant will be sentenced to a term of fifty months of incarceration."

Combs sat stunned, unmoving, as he realized he'd be spending the next few years in prison. Based on a quick calculation, deducting the year he had already spent in detention and factoring in the potential to shave off time for good behavior, Combs was still looking at an early 2028 release date. As Subramanian continued, thanking the "brave survivors" who had come forward, Combs dropped his head into his hands, shaking it in disbelief and refusing to look up at Subramanian, who told him his violent acts were "not something, Mr. Combs, that you will ever be able to wash away." Subramanian added, "But there is a light at the end of the tunnel. You have the chance to not only recognize 'what went wrong, but what can be made right.' You will have a chance to show your children and the world what real accountability, change, and healing can look like. And I'm counting on you to make the most of your second chance."

Standing up, a visibly furious Combs took a deep breath and looked back at his family. "I'm sorry," he said, grabbing his belongings and walking away with the US Marshals. "I love you," he added before the door slammed shut.

# CHAPTER 11 | WHAT REMAINS

**SEAN JOHN COMBS, AS OF** this writing, is inmate number 37452-054 and counting down the days of his sentence at Fort Dix, a low-security federal prison in New Jersey. Combs spends his time working in the chapel library and participating in the prison's residential drug abuse program. His team managed to pull serious strings to bypass the lengthy waitlist and typical time requirements to secure him a spot in the intensive five-hundred-hour course that can last between nine and twelve months. In addition to treatment, the program is highly sought after for another reason: Upon completion, inmates can reduce their sentences by up to a year.

Combs' efforts to shorten his time behind bars have not been limited to prison programs. His appellate legal team has been aggressively searching for any and every legal avenue that would overturn the judge's sentence, nullify the jury's guilty verdict, or even discredit the very criminal law that Combs was prosecuted under. At the same time, some of his associates continued working behind the scenes to butter up well-connected figures in Washington, DC, hoping to earn the sympathies of Combs' former associate President Donald Trump. "I was very friendly with him. I got along with him great, and [he] seemed like a nice guy," Trump told Newsmax when asked about the possibility of a pardon for Combs. "I didn't know him well. But when I ran for office, he was very hostile." ("White men like Trump need to be banished," Combs said in 2020.) After failing to gain traction for clemency through unofficial channels, Combs personally appealed to Trump, making the case for his freedom in a letter. Perhaps recalling Combs' recent snubs, a thin-skinned and famously grudge-prone Trump said he wasn't considering his old friend's request.

Even within the confines of prison, however, Combs appears determined to manage his narrative. Within a month of his transfer to Fort Dix, he allegedly made a forbidden three-way phone call in which he instructed a female member of his team to contact a "digital person" regarding social media blog posts. During the same period, in what would have broken Combs' sobriety streak, officials reportedly caught Combs with a homemade concoction of fermenting apples, Fanta, and sugar. His team said the claims were false. "He's taking his time there seriously and working every day toward healing and coming home," said a spokesperson attempting to downplay reports of the prison taking disciplinary action against Combs over the phone call. "As with any high-profile individual in a new environment, there will be many rumors and exaggerated stories throughout his time there, most of them untrue," the spokesperson added. "We ask that people give him the benefit of the doubt, the privacy to focus on his personal growth." Yet, despite this broad and vague denial, the Bureau of Prisons pushed back Combs' release date by a few weeks.

To those who hoped justice would be served by the trial, the outcome offered little closure. Instead, many settled for the faint hope that his court-ordered isolation away from his wealth, family, and spotlight might force a measure of self-reflection. But Combs' continued efforts to shorten his sentence by any means possible and his alleged neglect of pledges of change when he believed no one was looking only hammered home what some knew about Combs all along: He believes he's done nothing wrong.

---

In February 2025, Voletta Wallace, the mother of The Notorious B.I.G., died of natural causes at the age of seventy-eight. Although Voletta could "do without the profanity" in her son's music, she recognized the "beautiful stories" he was able to tell and the profound impact of his artistry, and she had worked to carry the torch of his legacy cementing him as a hip-hop icon. She oversaw Wallace's estate alongside his widow, Faith Evans, and former co-manager Wayne Barrow, controlling his music catalog and rights to his likeness and approving tasteful biopics and projects about his life. Originally valued at $10 million at the time of Biggie's death, the estate had grown, with Voletta's help, to a valuation of $200 million. (Music publisher Primary Wave acquired a 50 percent interest in the estate shortly before Voletta died.) And the former schoolteacher shepherded the Christopher Wallace Memorial Foundation, using it to empower the local community through education and mentorship programs.

A funeral for Voletta was held the following month at the Frank E. Campbell Funeral Chapel on the Upper East Side in New York City, the same place where her son's service was held on March 18, 1997. It was a muted affair, unlike the spectacle that had preceded it some thirty years earlier. Community members and fans who wanted to pay their respects trickled into the public viewing where Voletta's casket sat nestled amid fragrant displays of dusty pink and white flowers, murmuring their surprise at the small turnout to send off a king's mother.

The day was a somber reunion for the early Bad Boy family. Evans, Lil' Kim, Mase, Wallace's former manager and RCA Records President Mark Pitts, former Bad Boy president Harve Pierre, Junior M.A.F.I.A.'s Lil' Cease, Wallace's close friends and Combs' bodyguards D-Roc and Rube, and even one of Combs' early chiefs of staff were in attendance, arriving at the service one by one. A majority of the group also paid a visit to 226 St. James Place, standing on the same steps where Wallace and his friends would shoot the shit and practice their early rhymes. There were notable absences—too many to linger on. Missing were Wallace's early champion, Andre Harrell, who died in 2020; and Wallace's idol Heavy D, who died suddenly in 2011. And of course, Combs, the early glue for their sometimes-dysfunctional family. The man who had made them kin.

Standing in as Combs' proxy was his look-alike son Christian, who hovered awkwardly around his father's peers as they posed for photos at Wallace's old doorstep. Aware of what the moment would signal to a wider audience, Christian's presence was Combs' clear message that he wouldn't let himself fall out of the picture. Until Combs was free to reclaim his place, his sons would serve as his representatives.

Though both Justin and Quincy continue to support their father, Christian has taken it upon himself to shoulder the effort to preserve Combs' legacy. Combs idolized his father, Melvin, wearing his portrait on a medallion around his neck; Christian treats his father with the same reverence. Their resemblance is uncanny; near carbon copies, some thirty years apart. As a toddler, Christian watched wide-eyed as Combs commanded crowds, throwing tyke-sized tantrums when he couldn't go up onstage alongside his dad. Growing older, Christian inherited his father's mannerisms and infectious energy and often wears a glittering Bad Boy chain around his neck, firmly tying himself to his father's shadow.

Striving to become an artist in his own right, he's released songs paying homage to Bad Boy and doubling down on his allegiance, with tunes like "Can't Stop, Won't Stop" and the more direct "Diddy Free," which he made with Ye, a.k.a Kanye West. "I'm this way because my whole life, my entire life, I studied my dad up and down," Christian told the judge at Combs' sentencing. "To me my dad is the greatest man in the world. He is my hero, always been my hero, and still is my superhero."

At a show by the recently reunited Total, they brought out their "nephew," Christian, for a surprise appearance. He shimmied his shoulders in the now-infamous "Diddy Bop," and tried to lead the crowd in a Bad Boy chant. The response was noticeably lukewarm, and Christian quickly dropped the effort. He was learning the hard way that inheritance easily passes down in terms of genetics and wealth, but not in fandom or cultural relevancy.

---

As efforts to hold Combs accountable began to plateau, the hope for a broader reckoning within the music industry similarly petered out. Even the few civil lawsuits that named Bad Boy employees or those linked to Combs have been stalled, amended, or quietly abandoned. In the days after Ventura filed her lawsuit, Uptown Records' Andre Harrell, who was a formative early mentor and friend to Combs, was named in a posthumous complaint brought by a Jane Doe. The corresponding court documents vanished from the online server, and the woman's attorney declined to provide any information about the woman's allegations. Two sexual assault cases against Harve Pierre—Combs' longtime friend from Howard University and former Bad Boy president—brought by Anna Kane and Pierre's former assistant have remained largely stalled since they were filed in 2023. (Pierre has denied the allegations.) Prosecutors had spoken of an alleged racketeering conspiracy ring that encompassed not only Combs but also staffers who were accused of helping funnel drugs to Combs and being complicit in their boss' abuse of women, yet Combs was the lone person who ended up facing criminal charges—ones that he largely was acquitted of. In the end, no one—not even Combs himself—was forced to fully account for what had taken place under his stewardship.

What remains of the chorus of accusations is now collecting dust at Combs' feet, as the public appears ready to move on. In the months after Combs' conviction, an undercurrent of commentary on social media—mostly male-dominated—began to tilt back in his favor, as people shared the hashtag #FreeDiddy and echoed arguments that his own camp had long advanced: He had been unfairly and selectively prosecuted. Being "freaky" was not a crime. Ventura was not truly a victim and deserved to face consequences alongside Combs. Accusers were exaggerating or lying outright in pursuit of a payday. As those narratives gained traction, the question inevitably lingered for those who had come forward against Combs: Was it worth it? Will they spend months—or years—wondering whether he might retaliate against them? Would the publicity cost them their current or future jobs? What regrets might surface in making their deeply personal trauma available for the world to pass judgment on?

Critics often chastise survivors who do not first pursue justice by going to law enforcement and seeing their claims through the criminal courts, but arrests and indictments can take years to materialize, and charges can be delayed or derailed by bureaucratic hurdles outside an accuser's control. Once a case enters the criminal justice system, control shifts almost entirely to state or federal officials, often leaving victims feeling sidelined.

Even when accusations do proceed through the legal system, victories can be rare and hard-fought. Civil litigation can drag on for years, frequently ending in settlements reached at the eleventh hour, just before a trial begins. Many of the civil cases filed against Combs between 2023 and 2025 have yet to see the inside of a courtroom. An overwhelming majority remain stalled as Combs' attorneys await a ruling on whether the revival window is preempted by state laws. Several plaintiffs who initially filed under Jane and John Doe pseudonyms were ordered by judges to reveal their identities, prompting some to withdraw their cases altogether.

Before truth has a chance to surface, it is often sealed behind NDAs that bury revealing depositions and silence the very people who brought the claims forward. Those who choose to speak publicly must brace themselves for sneers and accusations that they are money-driven opportunists.

The Southern District of New York's case against Combs illustrates these challenges. Building the criminal case itself was already a Herculean effort. Prosecutors assembled thousands of pages of text messages and emails, obtained bank and flight records, gathered corroborating witnesses, and collected video footage of freak-offs and the damning tape of Combs attacking Ventura. Yet even with that mountain of evidence, the outcome was convictions on lesser charges and a sentence much shorter than the government's recommended eleven years. Ventura's civil case, which raised the same accusations, had the opposite outcome. Within twenty-four hours, the matter was settled. Combs paid her $20 million, and both agreed to never publicly speak about the other. Had it ended there, they would have avoided any more of their most intimate and private moments being opened up for the world to dissect.

Ventura's case is a reminder of how rarely these stories reach a satisfying resolution. Even when allegations are taken seriously and evidence is assembled, justice often can arrive not through a courtroom verdict but through a quiet financial agreement. For many who come forward, that compromise may be the closest thing to accountability they will ever receive.

---

In the wake of Combs' fall from grace, there has been no widespread, industry-wide reckoning. When the allegations against the mogul first surfaced, some observers earnestly believed they might trigger a broader domino effect across the board, and that the long-awaited day of accountability would arrive for the record label heads, C-level executives, managers, producers, gatekeepers, and anyone who had enabled bad behavior to maintain the status quo. Some hoped that labels would confront the culture of misogyny in an ecosystem that critics have long said has gone unchecked and cast out predators among their ranks. A global 2024 report from MIDiA Research found that in a survey of more than four thousand women who worked as producers, songwriters, artists, and varying junior- to high-level roles within the music business, three in five said they had experienced sexual harassment. One in five said they had been sexually assaulted. Yet nearly three years after Ventura first filed her lawsuit against Combs, there has been no further fallout, no reinvigorated movement of any kind. Instead, Combs and what happened under Bad Boy's roof were treated like a self-contained anomaly.

Earlier cases brought against high-profile and powerful men in the music industry under the MeToo banner have had disparate results. As twenty women accused music mogul Russell Simmons, one of Combs' oldest friends, of sexual assault, he relocated to peaceful Bali, Indonesia. There, he practices yoga daily and plays host to his visiting celebrity friends. Shock rocker Marilyn Manson withstood claims of torture and sexual and psychological abuse from his ex-girlfriend actress Evan Rachel Wood and other women; far from facing meaningful consequences, he has walked in a Paris Fashion Week show and gone on a worldwide tour. Label head L.A. Reid, Backstreet Boys' Nick Carter, indie singer-songwriter Ryan Adams, feminist punk-rock singer Justin Sane (Justin Geever), as well as older rockers Tommy Lee and Axl Rose, have all faced varying degrees of scrutiny over sexual misconduct and abuse allegations. Yet most ultimately endured brief periods of public backlash before returning to normalcy—unlike in Hollywood, where accused men such as Harvey Weinstein and Danny Masterson are behind bars, while Kevin Spacey, Louis C.K., and Bill Cosby are among those being kept on the fringes of the television and film industries.

Apart from Combs, R&B legend R. Kelly is the only other high-profile musician sitting in prison for abuses exposed in the fallout of the MeToo era. Two juries in Chicago and New York City convicted Kelly of a series of heinous crimes involving minors and child pornography. Though Kelly's conviction has not fully erased the complicated relationship between accountability and celebrity in the music world. New jack swing pioneer Teddy Riley said in early 2026 that he would still consider working with Kelly from behind bars. "Everybody deserves a second chance," Riley told the *Los Angeles Times*. "Everyone deserves to repent, and everyone gets forgiven by God when you come to him. People miss his music." After public backlash, Riley walked back the comments. The support Kelly still has illustrates just how high the threshold for true accountability and justice really is. It took decades of allegations—at first overlooked—overwhelming evidence, federal investigations, and multiple criminal trials before the system finally produced a definitive consequence. And still, some aren't willing to disavow Kelly.

The absence of a broader reckoning following Combs' downfall becomes less surprising in light of this culture. Rather than triggering a sweeping, uncomfortable confrontation with the industry's culture of power and silence, the scandal instead reinforced a familiar pattern: The system absorbs the shock, isolates those who dared to speak up, and moves forward largely unchanged and mostly unchallenged. When a *Forbes* journalist asked Usher—an early Combs mentee who spent time at his "flavor camp" as a teen—the first word that came to mind when he heard Combs' name, Usher didn't second-guess himself. "Legacy," he answered. It was less than a year after Combs' criminal trial, in which the music mogul had admitted to rampant abuse in at least one relationship, and Usher said he didn't have anything negative to say about Combs. "I'm not saying that every man is perfect. I'm not saying that all of us don't have flaws," Usher explained. "But I can't with any sense of humanity not recognize the valuable contributions that this man made for us as Black entrepreneurs, for us as businessmen, for us as people who have transitioned culture and ideas into something that's tangible. So many people benefitted from what he created and I acknowledge that."

It was a sentiment that dozens in Combs' own circle had expressed to the judge ahead of his sentencing. Combs was a beacon of inspiration not just for the Black community, but for those who admired the classic American spirit of forging one's own destiny. They had reaped the benefits of the path he blazed, and although they knew that shouldn't absolve him of his misconduct, it was a factor they took into consideration as they lobbied for his freedom. Beyond being woefully unequipped—perhaps even reluctant—to tackle claims of sexual abuse against powerful figures, American society also has yet to confront its fawning relationship to celebrity and power, two forces that so often move hand in hand. It's a dangerous combination, one that too often shields the powerful from scrutiny, enabling the public to continue bestowing admiration, protection, and even leniency for their misdeeds. The figures we elevate to cultural royalty are frequently allowed to operate under a different set of expectations. Their looks, brilliance, charisma, or commercial success coalesce into an unseen force of social currency that can soften judgment or let them bypass accountability.

---

By the end of the 2020s, Combs will set foot back inside his palatial $48 million Miami waterfront home, warmly welcomed into the arms of those who have remained fiercely loyal to him. He'll still have significant wealth, although the constant drain of fighting off never-ending civil lawsuits will have taken a toll on his balance sheets. Eventually, normalcy will settle in, and Combs will take stock of the uncertain future before him and confront a question that has shadowed the latter years of his life: Where does he go from here?

Combs' temporary absence has allowed some of his former artists to experience a minor renaissance. People had originally flocked to Bad Boy out of admiration not for Combs but for the artists who defined the label. Danity Kane briefly regrouped as a trio—Aubrey O'Day, Aundrea Fimbres, and D. Woods—for a sold-out show in San Francisco. R&B group 112 launched a multicity tour with supporting acts in Total and Case. Day 26, of *Making the Band*, followed in their footsteps and hit the road in spring 2026. And Cassie's breakout song "Me & U" and follow-up single "Long Way 2 Go" began trending on TikTok, with some of her old performances going viral. "She really could've been a star," one person wrote.

Combs watched it all unfold from the sidelines. Never one to hold his tongue, Combs has been forced into a rare and uncomfortable silence for years. Through the country's most formidable lawyers, silver-tongued spokespeople, and stealthy intermediaries, paraphrases of his viewpoints and his messaging have been delivered to the public. Yet, Combs has always felt at his most powerful when he has the microphone in his hand. Controlling the narrative has long been central to his persona. Combs knows all too well how fickle the general public can be, and how swiftly sympathy can ping-pong from one side to the other. A moving comeback story overlaid with a rose-colored sheen of nostalgia is a tried-and-true tactic for a tale of redemption. The question is not whether he will speak, but what he will choose to say.

Through the criminal trial, memoirs, civil lawsuits, investigative reporting, and a slate of documentaries, the world already knows a great deal about who Sean Combs is. The December 2025 Netflix docuseries *Sean Combs: The Reckoning*, by Combs' industry rival 50 Cent and director Alexandria Stapleton, exposed a man with a dangerous streak who treated people like playthings; more than 22 million views were logged for the project in the first week. In many ways, people never had to look too hard to learn what they needed to about Combs; he's been telling on himself for decades, through his actions, words, and sometimes, in his own lyrics. His 2023 project *The Love Album: Off the Grid* is an open nod to the drug-fueled, days-long sexual escapades that had become a staple of his life. And the song "Homecoming" includes whispered ad-libs invoking Ventura's nickname "CC," even after she had moved on from Combs to build the stable, happy family life she had long desired.

Combs has both utilized and weaponized his fortune, industry status, and reputation to hide a volatile temper and disturbing behavior for decades. Dozens of people have accused Combs of playing games with their lives, sometimes for self-serving business reasons, other times for his own amusement. He's been described as a master manipulator and strategist able to play the long game to keep people—or a narrative—under his control. The word *no* is not a stopping point for Combs; it's the start of a negotiation he's determined to win. He's been accused of terrible deeds. Accusers have labeled him a narcissist, a monster, and a demon. And there may be other factors at play. There's an untamed rage that constantly boils underneath his surface. Drug use exacerbated his temper, but it wasn't the sole cause of it. Many have described him as deeply insecure, haunted by fears of abandonment that trace back to the earliest chapters of his life. But ultimately, only Combs himself can say what lies beneath the persona he has spent decades constructing.

Reducing Combs to a caricature of villainy alone would ignore the complexity that has long defined his influence. He has a family and friends who love him dearly. Some employees, artists, and ex-girlfriends compare gaining his praise and attention to basking in the warmth of the sun itself. He possesses a rare ability to make people feel seen, valued, and chosen. Combs is undeniably talented, with a natural knack for understanding his audience. He created music that defined eras and helped push hip-hop into the mainstream consciousness, expanding its appeal beyond inner cities. Is the whole of Combs, particularly his iconic contributions to music and what he represented to the Black community, greater than the sum of his darker parts?

Since the inception of Puffy, Combs has been the overpowering narrator of his own story, masterful at marketing himself as whatever shiny new version of himself he's decided to be. His intentions very well may be sincere and genuine. But trust isn't inherently earned, even with a good-faith apology. And meaningful accountability takes true atonement and time. A man capable of reinvention several times over, Combs will certainly have a narrative ready to sell to the world when he emerges from prison. The question now is not whether he will speak, but whether the public has learned enough about the real Sean Combs that they'll still be willing to listen.

# NOTES ON SOURCES AND METHODS

This book draws from hundreds of interviews with more than one hundred sources on and off the record. Over two and half years of reporting, initially for *Rolling Stone*, I spoke with numerous men and women who have entered the dizzying orbit of Sean Combs as employees of his various businesses, artists who signed to his record label Bad Boy, and industry associates whose careers overlapped with Combs' tremendous trajectory. Because of the sensitive nature of some of the allegations, many people voiced fear of professional retribution for speaking out publicly and requested that their true names be withheld or that they be described by the general positions they held while working alongside Combs.

Many people declined to speak at all, citing a variety of reasons. They felt it wasn't their place to comment on the accusations, they wanted to move past that time in their lives, or they said that what they witnessed didn't cause them any concern.

The book also pulls from thousands of pages of law enforcement records and court documents at the federal, state, and local levels, including police reports, investigative memos, civil lawsuits, and trial transcripts. Some records were obtained through Freedom of Information Act requests. At the time of this book's publishing, some civil lawsuits referred to in various chapters were still pending. Some of these civil cases might eventually be dismissed, whether through out-of-court settlements or due to a lack of evidence.

In a blanket statement, Combs has vehemently denied all accusations of sexual assault. "No matter how many lawsuits are filed, it won't change the fact that Mr. Combs has never sexually assaulted or sex trafficked anyone—man or woman, adult or minor," his lawyer said.

Over the course of Combs' three-decade-long illustrious career, he's been profiled, interviewed, and quoted countless times by newspapers, magazines, and filmmakers. There have been write-ups about his record label and his Bad Boy artists and real-time reports about his scandals and successes. I reference these interviews and clippings throughout the book, weaving in Combs' own words with his behind-the-scenes behavior. Together, these interviews, records, and archival resources help build out a fuller picture of Combs. In whole, the book draws from this mixture of sourcing material, primarily through interviews and court documents. A more detailed list can be found below.

**Chapter 1: Puffy**

Primary details from Combs' early childhood come from interviews with his childhood friend Tim Patterson, who lived below Janice Combs in Mount Vernon; Combs' schoolmates from Mount Saint Michael Academy; and several of his classmates from Howard University. The events surrounding his father Melvin's death are pulled from archival newspaper material from *The New York Amsterdam News*, the New York *Daily News*, and *The New York Times*, which chronicled the investigations of his murder and wider drug-trafficking accusation. Further anecdotes about Combs' childhood and teenage years come from property records, yearbook photos, music videos, archival news clippings, court submissions, and interviews Patterson and other associates gave in the 2025 documentaries *The Fall of Diddy* and *Diddy: The Making of a Bad Boy*. This chapter also incorporates numerous interviews of Combs and a few that his mother, Janice, gave to *The New York Times*, *Vibe*, and *Playboy*, and a short documentary from 2006 titled *Black and White: A Portrait of Sean Combs*. Janice previously denied any suggestion that she was an "abusive parent" to Combs. "I raised Sean with love and hard work, not abuse," she said.

### Chapter 2: Puff Daddy

Primary details from Combs' rise at Uptown Records, his reputation in the New York City nightlife, and the inception of Bad Boy Records come from interviews with Uptown employees, music industry and nightlife associates, and Bad Boy's Kirk Burrowes. Archival material from *Billboard*, *Vibe*, and other music trade publications, as well as Recording Industry Association of America (RIAA) certifications, are used to document the success and rise of Combs' earliest artists, Jodeci and Mary J. Blige.

Details about the alleged assault of Joi Dickerson-Neal in 1991 come from the November 2023 lawsuit she filed against Combs in New York and an interview she gave in the 2025 Netflix documentary *Sean Combs: The Reckoning*. As of this writing, her case is still pending. Through her attorney, Gloria Allred, Dickerson-Neal declined to speak for this book. Her former colleague Mike Nice Lewis corroborated that Dickerson-Neal alluded to the alleged assault in the 1990s. Details about the alleged assault of Liza Gardner in 1990 come from the November 2023 lawsuit that she filed against Combs in New York. In an amended complaint, Gardner named Jodeci's DeVante Swing as a co-defendant in her lawsuit but later voluntarily dropped him from her case. As of this writing, the case is still pending. Gardner also sued Aaron Hall, who has not responded to her complaint. Through her attorney, Tyrone Blackburn, Gardner declined to speak for this book.

The story of Sonya Williams getting ready before attending the fatal charity basketball event at City College of New York in 1991 is from the recollections of her sister-in-law Cynthia and older brother Sonny Williams. Archival reporting from the New York *Daily News* and *The New York Times* help tell the story of the tragedy and subsequent investigations and lawsuits.

### Chapter 3: Bad Boy

Memories of Combs' starting Bad Boy from his home in Scarsdale, New York, come from Kirk Burrowes, early members of Craig Mack's team, and producer Easy Mo Bee. A quote from former Bad Boy president Harve Pierre recalling working from Combs' basement is pulled from the 2017 documentary *Can't Stop, Won't Stop: A Bad Boy Story.* Letterhead paperwork and letters from Arista show initial correspondence between Combs' company and the powerhouse record label solidifying their early agreement. Details around the successful launch of Craig Mack and The Notorious B.I.G. come from interviews with early Bad Boy employees, archival reporting from *Billboard, Rolling Stone*, and *Vibe*, and interviews Combs and his artists gave at the time. Details about Corey "Buck" Jacobs' and Anthony "Wolf" Jones' friendship with Combs come from interviews with associates of Jacobs and Combs in the early to mid-1990s. Documents obtained through the National Archives and Records Administration track the FBI's drug-trafficking investigation into Jacobs, including extensive details on the illegal operation.

Accusations that Combs was violent at the Bad Boy offices and the Daddy's House studio in the mid-1990s come from first-person witness accounts. A county police report from March 1994 details Combs' altercation with Misa Hylton over their young son Justin. No charges were ever filed by Westchester County. Details of the alleged assault of April Lampros in the mid-1990s come from her May 2024 civil lawsuit against Combs in New York. As of this writing, the case is still pending. Through her attorney, Tyrone Blackburn, she declined to be interviewed for this book. Information regarding the East Coast versus West Coast hip-hop beef is pulled from a variety of sources, including unclassified FBI investigative reports into the deaths of Tupac Shakur and Christopher Wallace, a.k.a. Biggie Smalls. Further details regarding Duane "Keefe D" Davis and his accused involvement in Shakur's murder come from Las Vegas court documents, works published by retired Los Angeles Police Detective Greg Kading, and proffer agreement transcripts revealed in the 2025 Netflix documentary *Sean Combs: The Reckoning.*

### Chapter 4: The Impresario Becomes a Star

Details about Combs' transformation from label boss to artist were pulled from interviews with Kirk Burrowes and several Bad Boy employees. Details of Combs' relationship with Jennifer Lopez are pulled from memories of associates from around that time period, tabloid sightings of the pair, archival interviews Lopez has given to *Rolling Stone*, and her 2014 memoir, *True Love*, as well as Combs' and Kim Porter's recollections of the relationship that they gave to *Essence*. Faith Evans' feelings toward Combs insisting on her performing "I'll Be Missing You" at the MTV Music Video Awards in September 1997 are described in her memoir *Keep the Faith.* Details of the 1999 nightclub shooting are pulled from archival newspaper reporting, police reports, statements Combs gave, and records of the 2001 criminal trial, including testimony from Combs and his driver Wardel Fenderson, who spoke in *The Fall of Diddy.*

Police reports, obtained through record requests from departments in Cleveland, Ohio; Washington, DC; and New York City, helped trace accusations that Combs or members of his entourage traveled across the country with firearms. The incident at the Ritz-Carlton hotel in Ohio is described based on the recollections of the husband in the hotel room. Details about Combs' behavior on his *Forever* tour in 2001 came from interviews with artist Tierra Brown, who toured with him, and Austrian television personality Kathi Steininger, who alleged that Combs drugged and sexually assaulted her. She provided material, including a picture of herself with Combs and stationery from a hotel in Amsterdam, to corroborate her claim that she was taken on Combs' tour bus across country lines. The story about Combs sexually harassing a woman in 2001 after he was acquitted of the nightclub shooting came from interviews with the woman and one of her close friends.

**Chapter 5: P. Diddy**

This chapter pulls from interviews with Bad Boy artists and employees, Sean John staffers and models, and various assistants and interns who floated through Bad Boy's Manhattan offices, who detailed a toxic working environment and spoke about their interactions with and observations of Combs. At Combs' 2025 criminal trial in New York, several of his former personal assistants, including Capricorn Clark, David James, George Kaplan, and a woman identified by the pseudonym Mia, testified about what it was like working at Bad Boy, how drugs increasingly played a large role in his life, and about aspects of his sex life. Their accounts are used throughout the book. Though she didn't testify at the trial, private chef Jourdan Cha'Taun Atkinson submitted a lengthy survivor impact statement to the court detailing her experience, and she also spoke in the documentary *The Fall of Diddy*. It also contains interviews with contestants and production members on *Making the Band*. Details regarding Da Band's contracts come from a lawsuit Sara Stokes filed against Combs in 2025, alleging abusive working conditions and sexual harassment.

A judge dismissed a majority of the claims for being outside the statute of limitations. Danity Kane members Dawn Richard and Aubrey O'Day also alleged Combs sexually harassed them. Those accusations come from Richard's lawsuit, and statements and documents O'Day provided and made in *Sean Combs: The Reckoning.*

During Combs' criminal trial, Mia alleged Combs sexually assaulted her during her employment; her quotes are pulled from her testimony. Details regarding Thalia Graves', Anna Kane's, and Crystal McKinney's alleged sexual assaults in the early 2000s come from their lawsuits.

Insights regarding the turbulence surrounding Combs' relationship with Porter come from associates around the couple at the time, as well as a series of in-depth interviews the pair gave to *Essence* in the late 2000s. Their alleged relationship woes were frequently documented by tabloids and New York–based papers.

Police reports and archival reporting from the *New York Post*, *The New York Times*, and the New York *Daily News* detail Combs' brushes with law enforcement, including civil lawsuits that were later dismissed. Some details are pulled from court documents that were used as part of the 2025 federal investigation into Combs.

#### Chapter 6: Casandra Ventura

A majority of this chapter comes directly from the civil lawsuit Casandra "Cassie" Ventura filed against Combs in November 2023 and the four days of testimony she gave at Combs' federal criminal trial in 2025. References to texts, photos, and emails between Combs and Ventura come from evidence submitted in the criminal trial. (Combs settled Ventura's lawsuit while denying her accusations. He was acquitted of sex trafficking and racketeering conspiracy charges in 2025.)

Other details corroborating Combs' abuse of Ventura and their freak-offs comes from those in her orbit around this time period who testified at the criminal trial, including Dawn Richard, Deonte Nash, Bana Bongolan, Kid Cudi, Daniel Phillip, and Sharay Hayes, as well as Capricorn Clark, Mia, George Kaplan, David James, and Kerry Morgan. This chapter also pulls from interviews with songwriter Tiffany Red and other music industry associates who were present between 2008 and 2018.

Details regarding the physical violence and sexual harassment experienced by Nash and Bongolan were addressed in their testimonies and in their respective, active lawsuits against Combs. Jourdan Cha'Taun Atkinson alleged in a survivor impact statement submitted to a New York judge that Combs physically shoved her in 2008; a New Jersey police department report obtained through a Freedom of Information request shows Combs made a corresponding report against Atkinson.

### Chapter 7: The King

The opening text between Combs and his chief of staff Paul Offord discussing Gina Huynh comes from evidence discussed in Combs' 2025 criminal trial. Details regarding Huynh's relationship with Combs come from an interview she gave with blogger Tasha K in 2019.

Other details in this chapter regarding Combs and Ventura and the further breakdown in their relationship comes from the same sourcing and documentation used in the previous chapter. Other documents referred to, including texts between various parties and airline and hotel records, were submitted as evidence in Combs' criminal trial.

### Chapter 8: Brother Love

Details regarding Kim Porter's death and burial come from a report released by the Los Angeles County's medical examiner and various news reports. Evidence submitted in Combs' criminal trial shows he booked a hotel stay shortly before her funeral. Details surrounding Combs' arrest following the UCLA incident were obtained by records from the Los Angeles County district attorney's office. Details of other violent incidents are pulled from archival news sources.

Figures regarding Combs' charitable contributions between 2018 and 2024 were obtained through publicly available tax forms for the Combs Foundation. Descriptions of the state of Combs' businesses come from a variety of news reports and press releases detailing his many ventures, as well as interviews he gave to magazines and newspapers.

Anecdotes and observations about aspects of Combs' personal and romantic lives come from his heightened social media presence and those of the women he was linked to, as well as some civil lawsuits filed against him, including from Phil Pines, Rodney Jones, Chelsea Lovelace, and Seven Güzel, among others. As of this writing, their cases are all active. Pines also spoke at length about his experience in *The Fall of Diddy*. The scene regarding the music video for "Gotta Move On" was pulled from interviews with production members and dancers who were hired for the shoot. Three crew members who worked on board yachts chartered by Combs spoke about their experiences with him, and a lawsuit from stewardess Grace O'Marcaigh provides insight into a December 2022 charter.

The chapter also includes extensive details from the since-settled lawsuit Combs filed against British liquor giant Diageo over his partnership regarding DeLeón tequila and from subsequent court filings.

Information regarding the aftermath of Combs and Ventura's breakup, including text messages between the pair and her decision to sue Combs, comes from her lawsuit, and testimony and evidence given at Combs' 2025 criminal trial.

### Chapter 9: An Image Shattered

Details in this chapter come from pretrial documents submitted by Southern District of New York prosecutors detailing the scope of their investigation into Combs throughout 2024. Contemporaneous interviews, news reports, and court submissions color the scenes of the March 2024 raids on Combs' two homes. Civil lawsuits, as well as trial testimony and evidence from a woman identified as Jane Doe, help paint a picture of Combs in real time as the federal investigation unfolded.

The dozens of civil lawsuits that were filed against Combs in New York and California are referenced in this chapter and a small overview of their claims is given. Many of those cases are still active as of this writing. Footage aired in the Netflix documentary *Sean Combs: A Reckoning* captures a revealing look at Combs in the days before he was arrested in September 2024.

### Chapter 10: United States v. Sean Combs

This chapter pulls from trial testimony, court submissions, submitted evidence, source interviews, and my personal observations and reporting from attending every day of Combs' criminal sex trafficking and racketeering conspiracy trial in Manhattan and his subsequent sentencing in 2025. Combs was acquitted of the more serious charges and convicted on two counts of transportation to engage in prostitution. In October 2025, he was sentenced to fifty months in prison.

### Chapter 11: What Remains

This chapter offers my own observations regarding where Combs' legacy moves from here.

# ACKNOWLEDGMENTS

This book began as a reaction to untangling the narrative around an omnipresent celebrity figure who the world believed it knew. The side of Combs that was hidden away from the spotlight might have remained forever buried if not for the bravery and courage of the dozens of women and men who came forward to share their stories, beginning with Casandra Ventura.

I'm eternally grateful to those who entrusted with me their memories, perspectives, and wider thoughts for this book. In time, I hope they are empowered to share their own stories on their terms.

A deep thank-you to my editor Retha Powers and my agent Adam Eaglin for championing this book and for their wise guidance. Thank you to my colleagues Nancy Dillon and Jason Newman at *Rolling Stone*, who were instrumental to the early work that led to this book and to covering the 2025 criminal trial; to the Maxine Productions team who moved the needle in encouraging survivors to speak publicly in *The Fall of Diddy*; and to the work of all journalists and producers who have collectively contributed in keeping a paper record that ensures truth and history can't be rewritten. To the fact-checking and editing team who have sharpened and ensured accuracy of this work. To my husband, family, and friends, who have been a constant support throughout this process.

And also to the advocates and support networks who tirelessly show up for survivors when they don't know where to turn at first.

# INDEX

# ABOUT THE AUTHOR

**Cheyenne Roundtree** is an award-winning investigative journalist at *Rolling Stone*, known for her reporting on the entertainment industry and for pursuing stories that expose abuses of power. Her work has been recognized by the Newswomen's Club of New York and the Los Angeles Press Club. Originally from Dallas, Texas, she lives in Brooklyn, New York, with her husband. *Bad Boy for Life* is her first book.